the
beautiful
game

the beautiful game

SIXTEEN GIRLS AND THE SOCCER
SEASON THAT CHANGED EVERYTHING

JONATHAN LITTMAN

Perennial

An Imprint of HarperCollins*Publishers*

First Perennial edition published 2000.

Designed by Kellan Peck

Library of Congress Cataloging-in-Publication Data

Littman, Jonathan.
The beautiful game : sixteen girls and the soccer season that changed everything / by Jonathan Littman.
p.   cm.
IBSN 0-380-80860-9
1. Soccer for women—California—Santa Rosa   I. Title: Sixteen girls and the soccer season that changed everything. II. Title.
GV944.5.L58   2000
796.334'082'0979418—dc21   00-040717

00 01 02 03 04 RRD 10 9 8 7 6 5 4 3 2 1

For Katherine, Elizabeth and Sherry Lue

"That beautiful game I love so well, the game I live to play . . ."

—Pelé

CONTENTS

FOURTEEN   Beating the Ref   145

FIFTEEN   T Rex   153

SIXTEEN   El Niño   162

SEVENTEEN   Catherine's Commitment   170

EIGHTEEN   Bug Eyes   179

NINETEEN   Growing Pains   191

TWENTY   Round One   200

TWENTY-ONE   Cassie's Choice   214

TWENTY-TWO   Miracles   224

TWENTY-THREE   Last Rites   236

TWENTY-FOUR   The Second Stringer   247

TWENTY-FIVE   Overtime   257

                Epilogue   273

                Acknowledgments   283

the
beautiful
game

"**d**addy, where are the girl soccer players?"

There we were, sitting at what my curly-haired daughter calls the "Breakfast Place," awaiting the 7:30 A.M. start of a World Cup match.

I was at a loss. Though the promise of Minnie Mouse pancakes had helped persuade my three-and-a-half-year-old that watching a soccer game on television at the town diner would be fun, there wasn't much I could do about the conspicuous absence of women players. Thankfully, my daughter is a resourceful girl. She quickly discerned that one of the French midfielders, Petit, sported a ponytail, and we spent the rest of the game anticipating the moments when his gorgeous blond locks would briefly appear on the screen. "Petit, Petit!" she would cry.

Over the next few weeks my daughter enjoyed the Romanian team's neon-orange-dyed hair, and countless

other well-coifed players. But none of that could change
the simple fact that she knew the Men's World Cup was
a poor facsimile of the real thing. She'd already seen real
soccer players, and she knew that they had ponytails or
curls and were most definitely girls.

Months before my daughter and I trundled down to
the "Breakfast Place" to watch the Men's World Cup, my
daughter, her mother, and our eight-month-old baby girl
drove north an hour to Santa Rosa on a rare dry afternoon
in the midst of El Niño. We were going to watch a team
of fourteen-year-old girls play soccer. I had no idea what
to expect. Because the city's fields were flooded with the
rains, the girls were playing indoors in the school's basketball gym. My wife and children and I sat on the creaky
wooden bleachers, the lone spectators.

The girls began running laps around the gym, twenty
as I recall, the slapping sound of their sneakers echoing
off the walls. My eight-month-old began springing up and
down like a jack-in-the-box, clapping wildly. My three-
year-old couldn't take her eyes off the girls, who swept
by just inches from us, fanning us in their wake. As they
finished, they cheered each other on until one by one they
banged open the doors to the outside, cooling off in the
winter air, hoisting their jerseys to wipe the sweat off
their faces.

They were strong, fast, and disciplined. They were
every size and shape imaginable: tall, short, skinny, muscular. After a series of drills, they squared off in a scrimmage, and though the game was truncated by the gym,
they played with grace and fierceness. Passes were crisp,
and traps smooth and precise. Tackles were hard, even
with the threat of the hardwood floor. I had little doubt
that these girls would have trounced my eighth-grade
boys' team.

I had no idea if they were an average or an excellent

girls' team, but I couldn't think of a better place to take my two daughters on a Sunday afternoon. This was the game I'd played in college and continued to love, and for me there was joy in providing my daughters this early, gripping experience of how girls master the sport. Later that evening, on the ride home, my daughter couldn't stop talking about the noisy "stepping stools," and my wife and I were stumped. Stepping stools, stepping stools, what could she mean? The bleachers, of course! What an image for a three-year-old to hold in her mind. The thunderous clatter of girls sprinting up and down bleachers.

ONE

Tryouts

*e*lbows out and ready, the girl with the piercing eyes and apple cheeks figured she had an edge, maybe two. Jessica Marshall could play goalkeeper as well as field positions, and unlike the others, she actually knew the coach, and thus knew her elbows would count. But looking out at the sea of ponytails bobbing up and down on the vast grassy field, Jessica could also do the math. Out of the forty thirteen- and-fourteen-year-old talented girls at the tryouts, over half wouldn't last the week.

The air was crisp that April afternoon. Though a freeway bustled just a couple of hundred yards to the east, the only sound on the field was the swish of the grass underfoot, the lulling patter of the balls swinging between the players, and the symphony of breaths that rose like a tide. If this was a stadium, its walls reflected the community in which it stood. To the north loomed a destroyer-sized aluminum-sided warehouse, fronted by a fence bearing the names of local sponsors who had put up a few hundred bucks to plug their businesses: Downey Tire Center, Terchlund Law Offices, Round Table Pizza, and the local paper, the *Press Democrat*. Weeds choked the vast empty acreage beyond the fields, and to the west end, facing the freeway, towering eucalpytus trees promised some afternoon shade. The only amenities were a tiny blue wooden snack bar and a Porta Potti. Belluzzo Fields, they called it, the center of youth soccer in the Northern Californian city of Santa Rosa.

It was a city defined in great part by what it was not. Santa Rosa was not the prosperous and refined city of San Francisco, which lay more than fifty miles to the south. Nor was it the languorous wine country of Napa, just thirty miles to the east over the hills. Santa Rosa was an old town by western standards that was enjoying a little boom.

You could find the past in the Sonoma County Fairgrounds just a couple miles up the road from Belluzzo, where they still held Mexican dances and competitions for cows, horses, sheep, and goats. But the future was everywhere. High-tech companies had migrated north to Santa Rosa, and the town had largely shed its agricultural roots as it quickly mushroomed to nearly 150,000 people. Traffic often choked the two-lane freeway that linked Santa Rosa with the San Francisco Bay area to the south and Oregon to the north. Many parents zigzagged home from practice on side streets, fed up with the congestion. Developments were springing up all over. New homes were crowding the once rural Highway 12, which ran east to Sonoma and Napa, or west to the bucolic old town of Sebastopol, famous for its apples.

Coach Salzmann barely said hello, and certainly didn't smile. All they knew about Salzmann, they'd read in the brief letter alerting them to the tryouts for the Eclipse under-fourteen girls' team, one of over twenty squads sponsored by the Santa Rosa United Youth Soccer club. They'd been asked to bring the usual, "shin guards, cleats, water, a ball," but they hadn't quite known what Salzmann meant by "whatever else it takes for you to play your best." The letter had trumpeted the typical sports platitudes, goals Salzmann considered essential: "Dedication, Work Ethic, Discipline, Attitude, Competition, and Fun."

Jessica's deep-set eyes made the dishwater blond look as if she were squinting, questioning the world. A mouthful of braces made her self-conscious about smiling. *Fun* wasn't a word Jessica would use to describe the ordeal. The letter outlined how they would be put through skill work, testing their dribbling, passing, shooting, juggling, and fitness, and finally matching them up in scrimmages. This was a test, not only of their "technical performance," but also of their commitment. Salzmann made clear that effort would count plenty, suggesting they arrive fifteen minutes early to jog and warm up before practice started.

"I won't have any favorites," Coach Salzmann told the girls sitting on the grass on the first day of the three-day tryouts. "Just because someone was on last year's team doesn't mean they'll make it this year."

Lateness wouldn't be permitted. Interruptions were not taken lightly. Players engaged in giggling and chatting at their own risk. Coach Salzmann wasn't merely looking for the best players. Salzmann wanted the most coachable players, girls who, whether or not they realized it yet, were hungry for hard training.

None of this was any surprise to Jessica. She'd watched Salzmann crank three goals in a college game, get crumpled by a defender, and continue playing as if it were nothing more than a scratch. Jessica had played for Salzmann at a summer camp, and won a measure of respect by beating her share of boys. But Jessica also knew Salzmann's reputation for toughness was deserved. Talent wasn't enough in Salzmann's eyes.

Three months before, back in rainy January, Jessica had begun her own preparation. Her father, a pastor at Santa Rosa Christian Church, awakened her before dawn for the short drive to the local junior college. There, for an hour before the start of school, Jessica ran wind sprints and the stadium bleachers until her thighs burned. Behind the speed work was an old coach, an old dig. For Jessica had tried out for the elite Eclipse Class I team the previous year, and thought she'd shown well enough to make it again, just as she had two years running. Then she got the call. She was at home watching TV with her more gifted teammate and friend Shannon, a tall, chocolate-skinned girl with the olive-shaped eyes of a doe.

"I'm sorry, you didn't make the team," said the Eclipse coach, abruptly hanging up before Jessica could mumble a reply.

"What was that?" Shannon asked softly.

"I got cut."

Jessica collapsed in front of the TV and felt herself drift away, thinking how terrible she must be. Soon a formal letter arrived, adding what seemed to her a jab: *Work on your speed.*

Jessica cried through the night. Her parents couldn't comfort her. Shannon had no idea what to say. The blow was softened slighty when the Cavalieres, the parents of a girlfriend who attended the Marshalls' church, graciously sent flowers and a card saying they were sorry Jessica hadn't made the team. They understood. Their daughter, Naomi, had played a year for the unpopular Eclipse coach and decided not to return.

There was another under-fourteen girls' team in town, coached by a roly-poly Irishman with a blunt haircut that matched his square face, a man who'd never actually played the game in his life. Northwest Oaks Fury was a Class III team, a step down from the Class I team for which Jessica had played the last two years. (Few girls compete in Class II, an obscure category that allows mixed ages.) But despite that difference, when Naomi told her friend that she was trying out for Fury, it suddenly seemed the right place to play.

Fury wasn't any old Class III team. Oh, sure, its coach, Brian Halloran, had a daughter on his team, just like the Eclipse coach, but the comparison ended there. The Eclipse coach cursed during games and promised his girls trips to McDonald's or less running in practice if they won. But Brian Halloran earned the respect of his girls with his patience and philosophical bent. He'd taken several coaching courses and soaked up every possible game on the tube, the English Premiere league, the Mexican league, the Italian league, even the lowly U.S. Major Soccer league. Brian had a knack for motivating the girls, and he knew how to win.

Jessica's and Naomi's timing couldn't have been better. The year they joined Brian's Fury, Brian's third as a coach, the team won the Class III team equivalent of the Super Bowl, Northern California's Association Cup, amassing an improbable season record of 41-2-1. But while the mediocre Eclipse was summarily dispatched in the first round of the more prestigious State Cup, its players and coach didn't give the plucky Fury any respect, even when the teams tied in a practice match. And why should they? The best girls' youth soccer in the nation was widely believed to be played by year-round Class I teams, outfitted with the superbly trained daughters of suburban professionals. It was a stereotype, of course, but it wasn't without some truth. To see the class lines, all you had to do was watch the direction the soccer moms fanned out in their minivans after practice. Class I team girls headed more frequently to the eastern, affluent side of Santa Rosa, while the girls of Fury tended to live on the west side in ordinary middle-class homes.

More than a few Santa Rosa parents refused to sign their talented daughters up for Class I teams, put off by the widespread perception of snobbery, a perception that included the false idea that money could buy you a spot on the team. Months before, when word traveled that the unpopular Eclipse coach wouldn't be returning, Brian himself had been asked by several parents to submit his name as a candidate. But the board of Santa Rosa United had a new focus. The club wanted former college players to head its elite squads. A Class III parent coach—no matter how many games his girls won—didn't fit the bill.

Thirteen is the toughest age for girls in soccer, the stage at which girls begin an upward climb toward high school stardom and possible college play or falter and possibly quit the game entirely. At a time when parents expect their daughters to grow independent, gain confidence, and think for themselves, many girls do just the opposite. Their budding competence unravels. Their confidence falters. Girls may question their commitment to sport. Some experts say girls are torn between the stereotype of a "good woman" —selfless and feminine, sacrificing her own needs—and a society that reveres the more masculine goals of independence and freedom.

The facts are clear. Teen girls suffer a drop in self-esteem three times that of boys. Discouraged girls lose interest in trying challenging activities, and become less likely to trust their own abilities. But if they stick with it, sport, it seems, may be an antidote. Female athletes are more likely to graduate from high school and have more self-confidence. They're also less likely to have breast cancer or osteoporosis.

But Brian wasn't thinking about all these compelling reasons for a girl to play soccer. He looked upon his athletes as competitors. Without a challenge, he knew many of the girls' interest would wane. They'd reached the point where Class III team play, even an incredible Class III team like Fury, could hold them back.

And so Brian dedicated himself to making certain that his girls made the new Eclipse. A few weeks before try-outs he'd gathered up his daughter, Kim, Jessica, and whoever else needed the work and driven them out to the nearest fields for a little practice. Now all he could do was pace the sideline and hope they were ready. In his eyes, each of his former players had some fire. Beyond Jessica, who had polished her moves as well as her speed, there was Naomi, a quiet soul with a mane of curly, golden locks. The freckled girl with the confident, coun-try-sweet expression moved with the ease of a basketball guard. Naomi was a natural, quick and skilled at seem-ingly effortless dashes through traffic. Kim was Naomi's opposite in appearance and skill. Her turquoise eyes blazed as intently as the scowls she tossed around like darts. She was a blond goal-scoring machine, built low to the ground, adept at pouncing on loose balls and firing rockets with her powerful thighs.

Brian was pretty certain these girls and a couple other former Fury players would all make the team, though Jessica would need to make a good showing. It was Trin-ity, Angela, and Catherine he worried most about. Trinity was hard to get a lock on: One eye was nutty brown, the other blue-green. She had chiseled, Christie Brinkley good looks, and thick eyebrows that jumped or fell to forecast her mood. Trinity looked and played like a terrier; she was younger and shorter than most of the girls and hadn't played competitive soccer long. But Brian believed in her speed and her heart. Angela had played the previous year for Brian, and had made the mistake of switching over to Eclipse, where she got little training. Angela looked smart in a soccer uniform, boasting the finely chiseled legs of a track star and the balance gained through years of ballet. But Brian knew there was something missing. The porcelain-skinned brunette struggled at times to connect with her teammates, seldom anticipating play. Too often Angela was in the wrong place at the wrong time, her mind somewhere else.

And then there was Catherine. Oh, how Catherine had tested Brian over the years. She seemed older than her thirteen years, the broad shoulders inherited from her championship swimmer father announcing her strength. The rangy blond defender with a surfer's casual grin had always been blessed with equal measures of talent, popularity, and ambivalence. Kim the striker scored the goals and Catherine the defender saved the goals, and Brian couldn't begin to count the perilous balls Catherine had cleared off her goal line over the last years. Speedy, agile, and fiercely competitive, Catherine took enormous pride in her central role as sweeper, the last line of defense, a field marshal for the team. But practice seldom agreed with Catherine's busy social life. There were so many other school teams to play on and places to be. Brian pushed as much as he could, but after all was said and done, Fury was only a Class III team. If he pushed too hard, Catherine might just quit for good.

Of the forty girls on the field, none matched the grace and vision of Shannon. It wasn't only that she could bend a ball twenty-five yards to the foot of a sprinting teammate; Shannon could anticipate play, see lanes opening up where most saw only a blur. Her head balls were astonishing: She'd hang a foot above a defender and spike it like a volleyball player exactly where she pleased. When she dribbled, the ball seemed to lazily extend from her legs, tempting defenders. Would she slice a long pass to an onrushing teammate?

Coach Salzmann recognized Shannon's natural sense

of the game in the first tryout and interrupted a scrimmage to let her know how things would be. She was cruising. Heart and hard work, that was what Coach demanded. "You know I think you're a great player, and you've got good skill and I think you'd be very useful, but you haven't shown me anything about your heart."

The other girls could hear every word. "Whether you make this team will depend on whether you show me you have heart." But had the message gotten through? Shannon's face seemed a cross between a Buddha's serene gaze and a blank stare, the only acknowledgment that she'd heard, an abrupt, hushed "OK, OK."

Heart would have a lot to do with the battle for starting goalie. Three keepers were trying out, the Eclipse's returning goalie, a newcomer, and Jessica. After the Eclipse keeper outshone everyone, Salzmann wanted to give the newcomer more time in goal, so she asked the Eclipse girl to play on the field for a bit. The girl wasn't really interested, and told Salzmann so in front of several players.

One try, Salzmann thought. Sometimes that's all you get.

The newcomer got her chance. Salzmann offered instruction, and watched her alert brown eyes seem to soak up the words, her hands nervously twisting her goalie's gloves. A quiet, big-boned girl with the soft, warm face of a grown woman, her name was Cassie. Her parents had just divorced and the brunette was living with her dad in a new home in a new development. Heather was the other stranger, a girl who seemed as frail and fair as Cassie was solid and dark. At times Heather resembled an impish Gwyneth Paltrow. It wasn't just her classic features and slightly upturned nose. Heather's pointed elbows and impossibly thin legs sometimes gave her the appearance of a stick figure in motion. Her saving grace was her canonball shot and sharp moves, but Heather was an out-of-towner from nearby Rohnert Park, a modest city less than a quarter the size of Santa Rosa. The girl with the cornsilk hair wasn't counting on making the new Eclipse. Her mother shuttled her to three different practices, where she played for over five exhausting hours. Heather was trying out for two other teams in case she didn't catch Salzmann's eye.

Many of the girls from the old Eclipse had the opposite problem. The team had been their identity for so many years, they couldn't imagine life without it. Who the hell is this coach? wondered Arlene, a freckled girl with an unruly shock of Irish-Setter-colored bangs that boxed with her eyes. How could someone just come in and cut me from the team?

Arlene's best friend on Eclipse had phoned, telling her Salzmann had informed her she'd made the first cut. Everybody seemed to be getting the good news. Everybody, that is, except for Arlene.

"Don't worry, you'll get the call," Shannon insisted.

"Yeah," Arlene groaned.

All Arlene could think about was how unfriendly Salzmann seemed, all business with the clipboard and the three Sonoma State assistants. A slightly chunky girl who packed a wallop, Arlene wondered if her play hadn't been well received. Arlene was notorious for injuring players, and for years had been addressed by many opponents as "bitch." At tryouts, Arlene had watched the daughter of the old Eclipse coach crying and complaining of a stomachache. Arlene didn't have a lot of sympathy; she figured the girl was just facing the reality that she wasn't going to make the team. Now Arlene began to wonder whether she was headed in the same direction. Was it possible Salzmann just didn't see what her game was all about?

Finally, there were those for whom tryouts seemed jinxed, a magnet for injury or illness. Theresa glowed. Her forthright face, joyful smile, and engaging eyes announced that the bright girl was ready to take on the world. But the fawnlike brunette was also a gangly girl who seemed at times to be made of rubber, her body not quite up to her ambitions. Last year her older sister Mary, who rowed varsity crew at UC Davis, picked her up from the first day of Eclipse tryouts and noticed little red bumps on her face, a budding case of chicken pox. But Theresa was lucky. She had proved herself the previous year, and the coach took her back even though she couldn't participate in the rest of tryouts. This year she'd torn her quadriceps. Salzmann didn't know her from Eve. She'd have to gut it out.

Success was the standard in Catherine Sigler's family. Both parents had excelled as college athletes, mom a gymnast, and dad an all-American swimmer and now an executive for Fireman's Fund. All of the Sigler children were gifted athletes. Catherine, their second daughter, excelled at any sport she tried, swimming, basketball, volleyball, track, and, of course, soccer. But after playing the game for nearly a decade, Catherine was suddenly bored with soccer. Her friends groused that she never had time to hang out or to play school sports.

Partly out of a sense of duty to her old Fury teammates, Catherine attended the Eclipse tryout at Belluzzo, but that evening in the Sigler living room, the sea blue eyes that could be so icy clouded. Between the sobs, Leslie Sigler listened to her daughter's heartfelt fears about losing her free time. "I don't want to try anymore," she cried.

A tightly wound woman with close-cropped hair and searing blue eyes, she still had the lean, muscled frame of the great athlete she once was. She had never been a quitter and she couldn't see her daughter taking that road. They talked about high school, which was only a little more than a year off. Ursuline High School had the best girls' soccer team in the city, and its coach supposedly preferred girls who had played United soccer. But Catherine wasn't convinced. Many of her friends only played school sports. Why did she have to miss out?

"You'd be stupid if you didn't play," Brittany, Catherine's older sister, lectured, injecting herself into the family discussion. Her brother, CJ, said much the same, but the words rang softer. Catherine admired her brother. He was an excellent student as well as a top athlete, and she could always count on him to lend an ear when she just needed to talk.

"You're good enough to make the team," CJ encouraged his sister, finding a way to say what Catherine's older sister couldn't. "This will be a really good experience."

Two hours later Catherine nodded her head and smiled at the mother and brother who had heard her out. She wiped away her tears.

She'd give it a go.

The third and final day of tryouts, it rained. Another coach might have canceled. What could you learn about a girl slogging through the mud? Lightning flashed in the distance, and thunder rumbled. Jessica was having a hard time seeing with her contacts, and felt a chill coming on. Salzmann wouldn't let them wear rain slicks, just their regular shorts and jerseys. But Jessica reminded herself that Salzmann had phoned, telling her she'd made the first cut. Now all she had to do was beat Shannon and her long, nimble legs in one-on-ones.

Angela had a different dilemma. The former ballerina's battle was being fought in her mind, which danced between the watery field and the evening's activities. If practice didn't end soon, she'd be rushed for a relative's wedding rehearsal that night in distant Sacramento, the state capital. But then there was the stubborn fact that her future as a soccer player was likely to be decided in the next thirty minutes. One of the assistants from Sonoma State told her she was doing well, and encouraged her to keep it up. With the evaluator watching, Angela figured this was her chance. She eyed the girl she was facing one-on-one, and felt determination sweep over her. She would do whatever it took.

On the slippery field at Belluzzo, a sea change was taking place, and it wasn't only the mastery and dedication of the girls. Soccer had usually begun as something a dad taught them, a father of one of the other girls on the team, or sometimes, and often uncomfortably, their own father. Though mothers frequently coached early on, as the girls neared double digits, moms were considered obsolete nurturers, and dads usually grabbed the spotlight. Exactly why this was so was hard to pinpoint, other than the fact that the dad's services were free, and they generally took the task far too seriously. Dads generally knew little about soccer and too often coached the game as if it were some new cross between Little League and Pop Warner football. That's what made Coach Salzmann unique. Salzmann wasn't a mom or a dad. Salzmann was just old enough to drink, twenty-one. A college player. An all-American.

A woman.

TWO

Coach

Coach Salzmann began dialing. These were the easy calls, the seventeen winners. It was the losers she dreaded. In making the first cut, she'd already struggled through a few of them. The silence on the end of the line. The choked-back tears. The realization that just a few words could shatter a girl's world.

Emiria Salzmann agonized over these calls, and only later did she realize that many coaches cut players by letter, saving themselves the personal grief. But Emiria hadn't been through this before. Ever. Just months before she'd been in college, wondering what she was going to do with her life.

Emiria plopped down on the tattered old brown couch. This wasn't just any old couch. The lumpy castoff had been shaped by hundreds of female college soccer players over the years, and over her four-year career at Sonoma State University, Emiria herself had sunk into it countless times.

"What are you doing now?" asked the man with the shaved head, his skin creased and leathery from too much sun.

Emiria had a face that couldn't lie. At times her broad smile and full lips made her resemble a classic Russian doll. But in an instant the roundness could harden, her hazel eyes and dark brows scowling. Her team picture hung on the wall above her former coach, Luke Oberkirch. On her left was a plaque listing the "qualities that best exemplify our team: leadership, effort, attitude," and an old New York Cosmos banner. Before her was the mark she had left in Sonoma State women's soccer history. There, up among the dozen or so framed certificates, hung one in her name, Emiria Salzmann, all-American.

To Emiria this shoe-box office, shared with the men's soccer coach, was a sanctuary. More than once she'd poured out her feelings to Luke, and this day was no different. What was she doing? She really wasn't quite sure. It was her final semester as a philosophy major, and she would graduate in a few months, but after that her plans were fuzzy. Unlike some of her friends, she had no clear career path. She doubted she could ever sit in an office all day, patiently performing a desk job. And so she'd been working odd part-time jobs, even helping her father at his nursery.

Luke listened, letting her vent. It was part of what made him a good coach, the ability to observe, to dispassionately evaluate. And then, as he always eventually did, he calmly spoke his piece. "I really think you should get into coaching."

It wasn't the first time he'd made the suggestion. The summer before, Emiria had assisted Luke at his popular summer soccer camps. The kids tended to goof off with many of the other younger coaches. But Emiria demanded discipline and structure, and though the kids were sometimes intimidated, she got results. "You're really great with kids," he'd encouraged her. "You ought to think about coaching."

Emiria had never taken Luke's suggestion too seriously. After working the exhausting day-long camps, she couldn't imagine how anyone could commit to a season, let alone a year of coaching. And there was something else. As long as she could remember, her identity had revolved around being a soccer player and an athlete. That was how she was known and respected at the university and in her community. How could she leave that behind?

"I don't know if I'm ready, you know," she confessed to Luke. "I want to play."

But even as she spoke the words, Emiria knew that something had changed. She'd been taking a break from training, slowed by the back injury that had plagued her senior year. Just sitting for more than a few minutes pained her. One ankle was still bloodred, and her right thigh was knotted and shrunken from too many bruising tackles.

"I really think you should coach," Luke calmly repeated, his sunken eyes fixed on his old star. "It doesn't mean that you can't play."

One day earlier that fall as the season wound down, one of Emiria's professors commented on how rare it was to find an athlete who majored in philosophy. Emiria took the thought to heart and wrote a paper on the subject:

> What emerged in me was this dualistic existence . . . the . . . "thinking athlete." (I mean this phrase in its most literal sense.) This was simultaneously a curse and a blessing, for it brought with it a lot of misunderstanding (or

*actual non-understanding) of my intentions and what I was
trying to accomplish, and yet in the end it was just this
quality about myself that finally saw me achieve respect and
considerable success as an athlete. Many of my teammates
couldn't understand my intensity and my complete dedication to the sport; they couldn't understand why I worked
out 6 days a week for hours on end, why I gave up vacations
because I felt that time off was wasted time; they couldn't
understand why I trained even harder in the off-season than
the training we endured in the regular season. Becoming a
better athlete was a constant process, and I felt that if I
ever stopped to look at how far I had already come . . . I
would never really reach my potential . . .*

Success was anything but automatic for the "thinking
athlete." Emiria was overwhelmed when she first tried
out for Sonoma State's women's soccer team. Struggling
with asthma, she sat out her first season, saving a year of
college eligibility. She played as a sophomore but only
saw limited action. Emiria got her chance to start the third
game of the following season against Mercy Hurst of
Pennsylvania. She scored twice, the first of nine consecutive games in which she scored, and the launch of a phenomenal winning streak. The Sonoma State Cossacks won
an incredible seventeen straight—until they finally lost in
the semifinal of the NCAA play-offs.

But Emiria's senior year was a struggle. The team lost
seven starters to graduation, and Luke brought on nine
freshmen to fill the gap. Emiria's thighs became a prime
target for opponents' knees: One charley horse soon blossomed into three distinct bruises, her leg bloated down to
the ankle. She didn't dare see a doctor because a doctor
wouldn't have cleared her to play. Her pregame ritual
became legendary. Emiria had to arrive at the trainer three
hours early, get the knotted muscle massaged and then
zapped with ultrasound, drag herself onto a stationary

bike for a ride, walk for a bit and then jog a mile, then back on the bike, and finally, get wrapped like a half-dressed mummy, starting from her waist and then all the way down the bad leg to her ankle.

Then she tore ligaments in an ankle. She was out three games, but more pain lay ahead. Against Chico State, she was tripped, whipsawed between two opponents, simultaneously kicked in the back of the head and under the chin. She saw lights, and for a frightening moment couldn't move.

The pain was so severe that while warming up before a game, she began crying, not believing she could go on. Then came the emotional blows. Midway through the season, Luke called the girls together before a game. The team was struggling, and they were going to start over. Wipe the slate clean.

Emiria was in a daze. As cocaptain, she hadn't been entirely comfortable with Luke, feeling that the second-year coach was babying some of the women. Sure, there were players who resented her seriousness. But a new vote on captains?

When the tally came in, Emiria was out. Her leg wrapped like a massive package, she had to limp out early for the match and happened to be near the bench just as Luke gave the new captains a jubilant high five. "Way to go, guys!" Sobbing, Emiria thought about quitting, but that thought didn't last long. She played the entire game, and vowed not to say another word to Luke.

Despite the injuries, the loss of her captainship, and a team that lost as many games as it won, Emiria scored at least one goal in every remaining game. Before the season finale against Hayward State, Luke shut the locker room door and waited for the players to quiet down. He had something to say. Emiria felt as if she were in a dream. Luke was getting choked up, talking about the decisions he'd made throughout the season, thanking the seniors for their dedication. He looked straight in her eyes.

"I want to apologize to Emiria. Go into my office. Look at all the all-Americans on my wall. Not one of them has worked harder than Emiria."

Then he told the team what the game meant. If Emiria scored twice, she would become Sonoma State's all-time leading goal scorer. They hugged and shed more tears, and Luke said, "Let's get her the ball."

THREE

Catherine's Choice

"**N**o. I haven't gotten a call yet," Catherine snapped, fidgeting with her phone cord.

The defender was doing her best to remain patient, though it was getting increasingly difficult as, like clockwork, one after another of her old teammates phoned, barely able to suppress their joy. Trinity, Kim, Naomi, and Jessica had all gotten a call from Emiria, as well as plenty of Eclipse players: Shannon, Angela, even the hobbled Theresa. Heather and Cassie had made it too, and though Arlene had worried, Emiria had eventually called and told her she'd made the first, and then later, the last cut.

Catherine couldn't understand it. How could so many of her teammates have gotten the news and not her? During the final tryout, out in the pouring rain, she'd put out more effort. What could Emiria be thinking? Some of the girls who'd already been picked hadn't gotten nearly as much playing time as she had on Fury.

After hashing it out with her mom, Catherine finally decided to phone Emiria and find out for herself.

"I haven't made all the final decisions yet," Emiria said cagily to the thirteen-year-old seventh grader.

"Fine," Catherine said disinterestedly. "Whatever."

"I've kind of had a tough time deciding."

"Oh."

Emiria paused a beat. "Would you like a chance to play on my team?"

The Round Table pizza parlor was crowded with seventeen girls and over two dozen parents. On one side sat the numerous girls who'd made it from Brian's old Fury; on the other end huddled the survivors of the old Eclipse. The two newcomers sat in the uneasy middle, Cassie the goalkeeper wearing her usual generous smile, and the rail-thin Heather grinning nervously.

Phil Molling, the stocky team manager, ran the show. Emiria would be the coach and Luke would be the assistant coach, and Phil informed the crowd that he was volunteering his and Brian's services as parent coaches.

But privately Phil was worried about being a parent coach. He'd just wanted to share team manager duties. "We've got an assistant coach, we've got you. We should just stay out of it," he remembered telling Emiria before the meeting. A short, passionate man, Phil was surprised when Emiria "kind of insisted" that he and Brian shoulder the additional task. But that wasn't how Emiria saw the conversation. Parent coaches weren't her idea. Anybody who'd watched tryouts could see that she wanted to keep the parents' influence to a minimum. The truth was, Emiria knew practically nobody on the team, parents or players. Only when Phil suggested it might be helpful for him to share the assistant coaching duties with Brian did she reluctantly go along with his plan.

The plan was a surprise to Brian as well, who first heard about it when Phil called out his name. But Brian wasn't about to object. He figured Molling must be thinking that Emiria could use some help from a couple of experienced coaches. How could a twenty-one-year-old who'd never coached a team know what to do?

But these were backstage maneuvers. Out in the booths and tables of the Round Table pizza parlor that night, everything was harmony. The meeting proceeded smoothly. Luke formally introduced Sonoma State's all-time leading goal scorer to the crowd, telling of her impressive college career and asking that they give her time to grow. "You're not going to know what a good job she's doing until six months from now." Emiria seemed a bit young and a little nervous to a few of the parents, but she had no doubt about what she wanted to do. She listed the tournaments she wanted to play in, and addressed the question of the team name. Eclipse was out. Monsoon and even Fury were candidates, but Luke and Emiria had another name, and the majority agreed.

Thunder.

The second team meeting was held in what had once been a sanctuary of the Santa Rosa Christian Church, but now was a small basketball gym with stained-glass windows. Emiria was asking to be paid, a reasonable proposition except for that fact that most of the girls had been coached by volunteer dads all their young lives. The parents had all read her two-page proposal, outlining her experience and her goals of recognizing and honing each individual's unique creativity, fostering a "competitive spirit," and teaching what it means "to care for, and feel protective over, a teammate." But it was her fourth and final goal that stood out the most. Emiria promised to

be something the girls had never had. A tough coach not
about to take any guff: ". . . I want to develop great
attitudes on this team. I will not tolerate any attitudes that
I feel will hinder individual and team progress, or else
puts down other players and thus creates a separation
within the team. I realize that I won't be able to solve
every problem or clique that arises, but attitude problems
will be one of my top priorities at all times. It is my
opinion that a coach who does not deal with these sorts
of problems quickly and to the best of her ability is not
fulfilling her job as a coach."

Michelle Smith, the short and stubborn blue-eyed
mom of Shannon Peters, was doing her best to remain
calm. Emiria and the girls left the gym, and the parents
went over the proposed contract, Phil and Brian pushing
forward the agenda. To a single mom with two kids, a
thousand dollars a year or more for a fourteen-year-old
to play soccer wasn't chicken feed. Emiria wanted forty
dollars a month per girl, with a twelve-month commitment, with all expenses paid for travel and lodging at
tournaments. Close to ten thousand dollars.

Michelle had never heard of paying a coach before,
and she had some questions. "How young is she? What's
her coaching experience?" Questions that didn't get much
of an answer.

These early-season team meetings always unsettled
Michelle. She remembered how the old Eclipse coach
would always sign them up for countless tournaments,
saying how they couldn't live without them, paying the
fees himself, and then later the bill would come due. Before the night was out, Emiria would announce she
wanted to invite kids from other teams to Thunder practices. Only Michelle dared ask if the girls' parents would
have to pay. Later the topic shifted to the inevitable request and approval of spanking new bags, warm-ups, and
uniforms. Thunder's color was a striking royal blue.

Michelle was in the minority. Many parents had older siblings who'd already played Class I soccer. They knew the routine. They paid for music lessons; why not soccer? Uniforms, bags—those were just the incidentals. Carol Tuttle, Arlene's mother, consoled her friend. "Don't worry, Michelle, we'll just do more fund-raisers."

But Michelle couldn't hold her tongue. When Phil Molling reminded the parents how lucky they were to have Emiria, she let him have it. "You know, have you ever heard of someone having to prove herself first?"

FOUR

Pepto-Bismol

brian arrived early for the first Thunder practice at Slater Middle School, just in time for Emiria to walk by him without so much as a hello.

What the heck, Brian thought, shrugging, as he stood on the basketball blacktop beyond the low-slung buildings on the edge of the scruffy grass and dirt field.

Emiria got right down to business. She was ready for the personality players she'd heard so much about, the attitudes. She simply wasn't going to give them the air to breathe. Or the time to talk. Everything she wanted to do was neatly written on a three-by-five card. After a warm-up, she ran them through some simple drills: dribbling in a circle, quick traps, then simple one-on-one matchups.

Emiria knew she had to start slowly, so she began with basics, touch and feel. How to hit a simple push pass with the side of your foot. Not the front, not the laces. The side. Swinging your foot like a hammer, or a pendulum.

Lots of the girls would strike low on the ball, sending rough, bouncing passes that were tough to control. Emiria whistled practice to a stop. Showed them how to kick high on the ball, like a topspin forehand in tennis, making the ball hug the grass.

"Follow through!" she'd shout. "Don't stop short with your leg!"

"Look where your toe points!"

The trajectory of the ball roughly matched where your toe pointed. Jab at it, and the ball would usually slice right in the direction of the hesitant toe.

Brian hadn't moved from the blacktop, and Emiria hadn't said a word to him the entire two hours. But as the girls sprinted a final set of "doggies," quick five-yard dashes back and forth between cones, he had to admit, she'd been organized and set a hard work rate. The whole practice seemed to have a theme.

Touch.

"Hey, Emiria, what's going on, what are we doing today?" Phil Molling asked in a friendly tone.

Emiria didn't respond, her legs firmly rooted, her stern expression unchanged. There was something incongruous about the scene. Phil, the team manager, a respected geologist—the man who'd helped push through Emiria's contract—was being rudely ignored, just as Brian had been. The age-old rules were being turned on their head. Now it was the men who could only stand and watch.

Finally, after a few practices, Emiria begrudgingly asked Brian and Phil to move a few cones. Brian had decided to wait things out, to see if Emiria eventually warmed to their presence. But Phil was accustomed to playing a more active role. He'd been the Eclipse's assistant coach the last three years, played Division III soccer himself at Marietta College in Ohio, and had a coaching license. Phil was no Little League dad. Phil made perfectly reasonable suggestions. More direct play. A little less passing.

As the three of them stood on the sideline, Brian listened to Phil raise the ante.

"The girls aren't doing it right."

"No," Emiria insisted, not even glancing Phil's way. "They're doing it the way I want them to do it."

It didn't take more than a couple of practices for Emiria to break the girls of the fantasy that it would be fun to have a young woman coach. "Bitch," the girls would mutter, though never loud or close enough for her to hear.

After years of careful ballet training, Angela found Emiria's callousness distressing. She felt that she didn't know Emiria, that she was just some robot ordering them what to do. Everything seemed confusing and fast, and then Emiria was shouting instructions, and Angela hadn't understood, and her name was being called out once again. She laid these trips on them. Like getting there early. Naomi got tired just thinking about it. Practice started at four. Why did you have to get there early? Why run and stretch an extra twenty minutes on top of the exhausting two-hour practice? They'd never done that with Brian.

She wasn't nice. Freight train Kim mowed over Theresa, who unfortunately tried to break the fall with her hand. Theresa was crying, but as far as Emiria was concerned, Theresa was always crying, and she wondered if she should have taken a chance on one so injury-prone. Emiria suggested she finish the workout, and so Theresa cradled her arm and slogged through the final drills and sprints. She iced the wrist, but that night it swelled up. At school the next day the pain was unbearable: X rays revealed a fracture of her wrist. Emiria didn't seem to care. "Sorry" wasn't in her vocabulary.

The girls practically breathed "sorry." At times the phrase "Oh, sorry" was all you could hear on the field. They were sorry if they thought they'd made a bad pass; sorry if they missed a trap; sorry if they had a vague idea they might have done better. Sorry most frequently happened if the player they passed to had trouble controlling the ball or got tackled.

Emiria had watched girls and women say "sorry" all her life—on and off the field—frequently for things that weren't their fault. "Why are you apologizing?" she'd say, confronting a player. "She's not perfect. So why are you apologizing to her?"

Emiria noticed the girls sometimes apologized for another girl's failure, something boys never do. She'd whistle the play dead.

"Why are you apologizing! You just worked your ass off. You're holding the ball, you're getting clobbered. It's her fault you made a bad pass because she didn't get there in time for you to make a good pass. She should be apologizing to you."

Blame wasn't Emiria's objective. She wanted to break them of the habit of questioning themselves, show them that it wasn't always the most obvious player who was at fault. A lingering, self-defeating "sorrryyyy" only brought the rest of the team down. It was a team expression of weakness, an announcement of insufficient will. You could say "sorry" if it was quick, clipped, and positive, but soon the word was seldom heard. Thunder's motto became an upbeat and proactive "Let's fix it."

Nobody was very anxious to show up to practice. The team wasn't really together yet, the lines between the Fury and Eclipse players still drawn. Catherine and Kim did not like Arlene and Shannon, and the feeling was mutual.

Indeed many of the Fury and Eclipse players did not talk to one another. In Catherine's case, it was a matter of respect and stubborn old team loyalties. She'd long feared Shannon's strength, especially if she happened to be in firing range of one of her shots. Arlene? Well, Kim didn't like her, so Catherine didn't either. Arlene was pushy. Catherine prided herself on playing clean soccer, and Arlene played another game.

Those first few weeks it was hard to say who was more hated—Emiria or Arlene. Sooner or later you had to face the square-jawed Arlene one-on-one. Try to dribble Arlene and she'd likely take a good chunk of your ankle or shin, as well as the ball. Arlene couldn't care less if she hacked you, and she definitely never said "sorry."

Brian had seen Arlene play for years. He'd always admired the honesty of girls, the way, when the ball went out of bounds, they'd all stop and look at the referee to tell them whose throw it was. Arlene was the opposite. She'd just pick it up and throw it in. So what if it went off her foot.

The tackles? Brian assumed Emiria would eventually ask Arlene to hold back a little, at least on her own teammates. It didn't happen. Arlene shredded one of Kim's ankles in a dirty behind-the-back double-kick foul, and there were plenty of others who limped off after an Arlene attack.

Naomi thought Arlene the scariest person in the world. She considered herself small and not that tough, and didn't really like tackling much herself. She couldn't understand Arlene's fury. Why did she have to take people down so hard? Did she want to hurt them? How could Naomi possibly respect her when she played so cheap and ugly and didn't seem to care? Waiting in lines for the one-on-one drills, the girls would talk.

"What is she doing? She's like taking people out from behind. That's not soccer. It's football."

As the team gradually began scrimmaging, Arlene's physical style threw the girls off balance even more. Emiria would blow her whistle and stop play, and stare down Naomi or another beaten girl.

"How can you let Arlene continually dominate you! Every time you have the ball, she knocks you off it and gets by you.

"Doesn't it bother you?"

It was a feeling that began the moment they awoke. The dread, the fear. Today was a Thunder day. Fitness. Sonoma State. The track and, oh yes, those hills. A new twist on summer vacation. Moms got used to the silence in the car pools as they approached Sonoma State and wound through the campus. When they finally parked they didn't know what to say. The girls literally didn't want to get out.

The workouts began in the morning, but it was usually nearing ninety degrees by the time their mothers departed. The stadium resembled the ruins of an ancient coliseum, empty except for the lizards that slithered by the water fountain. At the far end stood the old scoreboard, its lingo—home, quarter, down, to go—a dated testimony to another age and another sport. The school's football program had been canceled, and the university had plans to renovate the facility into a soccer stadium to draw youth tournaments. But in the summer of 1997 those plans were only dreams. Beyond a few dozen aluminum bleachers and a decrepit scorer's box, the track was ringed by a sloped, misshapen wall of dirt, clumped high with weeds and wild grass.

Emiria liked the emptiness of the stadium at that hour. The girls would train alone, with only the sound of her commands and their heaving breaths. The track itself had recently been resurfaced, and it was smooth and fast. There would be no distractions. Fitness days were simple and brutal. They began with a half-mile cruise and then a mile and a quarter of brisk cycles around the quarter-mile oval, resting only briefly between. Then four half-lap sprints, capped off with six straightaway dashes.

The girls asked for water breaks, and Emiria told them they'd have to remind her because she herself had often trained so hard that she'd frequently skip drinking herself. It wasn't the best thing, but sometimes she'd just plain forget, and then their mouths would turn to cotton.

Routine was the enemy. She wanted their muscles and minds tough and flexible. Emiria would often send the girls on a cross-campus run to give them the challenge of hills and different surfaces, training their legs and reactions. They'd start in the stadium, chugging up a steep set of stairs that angled sharply up to the sky. Down and then out of the stadium, Emiria watching every step, as they crossed the road and trotted up a small, dusty knoll. The narrow path led them down to a vast column of eucalyptus trees, the acrid scent filling their nostrils as their feet slipped over the bed of leaves. They dreamed about running there for a few minutes, cool in the shade, but it was only seconds before they crossed to a hard, cracked asphalt path under the searing sun. Another few hundred meters and they turned at the Sonoma State sign, following the pine-ringed entrance back into the campus. The street was busy with cars and students walking to the university, and the girls felt a surge of excitement.

Shauna, a chestnut-haired girl of Italian descent, felt a certain pride. To Emiria she was a real-life girl-next-door Sandra Bullock. Shauna's parents both worked full-time, her mother as a nurse, her father as a sheriff's deputy. The former Eclipse star had just completed the seventh grade, and here she was running around the university like a college athlete.

The path wound under a few trees and then along a sidewalk blindingly white from the blazing sun. Off in the distance you could just make out the blue lettering on the outside of the stadium: SSU, HOME OF THE COSSACKS. But as they approached Emiria's unmoving profile, they knew they were only half finished. Up and down the stairs again and out for another loop, another mile and a quarter to go.

Not much could get you out of fitness. Jessica was right next to Cassie when she heard the goalkeeper make the strange sound. Bent over on the track, Cassie was retching. Jessica had never seen someone throwing up before, and certainly not during soccer practice.

The girls helped Cassie off to the side of the track, where she retched again. A couple of minutes later, an incredulous Jessica heard Emiria ask, "Cassie, are you OK?"

She mumbled something like yes, and Emiria told her to get back in and continue the workout. As a goalie, Cassie had never done much running, and certainly nothing like Emiria's grueling workouts. But there was no double standard on Thunder. Everyone had to run, and everyone feared that they'd soon be in Cassie's shoes. Shannon had flirted with a fantasy that more than a few girls briefly entertained. She wasn't ready to quit, she just thought maybe she'd like to play Class III soccer. Not run so much. Play a little easier. But the fantasy would pass, and as they ran there was only one thought on her mind.

What time is it? When's practice going to be over?

Never quite soon enough. One day after downing a milk shake, Shannon didn't feel quite right. She took a few swigs of Pepto-Bismol before practice, but it was too late to do much good, and sure enough, by the end of the workout, she, too, was bent over, spewing her recently ingested shake, burger, and fries. Luke happened to be coaching that day, and he gave her a high five when she came up for air, congratulating her on joining the Thunder barf club. The bottle of Pepto-Bismol became a ritual, a pink symbol of the challenge of Thunder soccer. Shannon brought it to practice every day in her warm-up bag, and the girls often asked for a slug.

But it was the hill that presented perhaps the greatest emotional and physical challenge. The hill was what you got after a track workout, and before the gut-wrenching, practice-ending several hundred sit-ups and push-ups. When Naomi first saw it she thought, Is she mad at us or something?

"More running?" more than one girl muttered. "What are you talking about? We already ran."

But Emiria marched to the top and turned and faced them. Fifteen times up. Fiteen times down. The workout wasn't finished.

"Come to me," Emiria ordered.

She stood at the top, motionless, staring down. How they hated her. Everything about her. Her high, imperious cheekbones, her frozen lips, the strength in her legs and her muscled arms, and most of all, the way she could inflict pain on them without changing expression, without seeming to care in the slightest.

They nicknamed the hill Grandpa, a steep climb next to the bleachers on the home side of the track. The weeds were long, sharp and prickly, and they sliced at the girls' legs as they fought upward.

"Come on, you guys!" Emiria shouted. "Move your legs!"

Gnats buzzed their ears, and under the grass and burs lurked ditches and rocks. The girls felt their ankles roll, and more than one tumbled. By the time they reached Grandpa, the sun was high, the temperature nearing one hundred degrees. The air was sickly sweet and dusty, nearly hot enough to burn their nostrils. Emiria wouldn't even let them rest on the descent. When they hit bottom they couldn't jog through and catch their breath.

"Power up!" she yelled.

"No walking! Run!"

To Catherine, the hill was huge, and represented the wall that Emiria was presenting, the unknown. The grass was up to her thighs, and it hurt, and she didn't fully understand what she was going through, and she didn't really care. She wondered why she'd let her brother talk her into this in the first place. Then Catherine's foot stuck in a pothole on the way down, and she twisted her ankle, and she couldn't walk anymore.

When they were done with the day's endless sprints and torturous climbs, Emiria looked down upon them and almost smiled. The girls collapsed against each other, crying, gasping for air, incredulous at what they'd done, joking about how they'd nearly fallen or tripped. Just to finish the workout was a kind of miracle.

The Fury and Eclipse girls still kept their distance, but there was something new afoot. No one had ever trained like this before. You couldn't help but be proud after surviving Grandpa. They hadn't played a game, but they had something in common. Parched throats and newly muscled legs. Stinging grass cuts they wore like a badge.

FIVE

The Player

*n*atalie's father, Jerry, had just gotten off work from the discount food retailer Trader Joe's, and begun the hour-and-a-half drive up Interstate 80 to the huge complex of fields just west of the state capital in Sacramento. The easygoing single dad with tousled hair and sandals figured he'd only be a little late if he was lucky. Thunder was playing its first weekend tournament in early July, the California Cup, and though he hoped to make the start of the game, he knew there would be plenty of other chances to see his daughter play in the months ahead.

The girl with the chipmunk grin was one of the many Thunder players ready for a new coach. She'd been born Natalie Muck, but when her older sister was mercilessly teased in school, her father had changed the family's Armenian name to Messina. Natalie had some Irish and Italian blood too, and her dark, exotic, diamond-shaped face was a puzzle. One minute, the short, strong-legged player seemed to be the youngest, most gleeful girl on the team. The next she was dishing out a drop-dead stare. You couldn't chalk it up to her parents' recent divorce. Natalie had always been the tough girl in the family.

Though she'd played for the Eclipse for four years, and thought her coach nice, as she grew older she began to notice things. Like the fact that he didn't seem to know a whole lot about the game. Or the way his daughter played even though some wondered whether she was as good as the other girls.

Natalie and a few of the other girls ruled over the coach. When he'd order them to run a lap, Natalie would grumble and suggest something even easier and she'd get her way. In an hour of practice Natalie probably played half an hour because she thought it so pointless.

Natalie knew she was missing out, that the repetitive practices and her own lackadaisical attitude were getting her nowhere. When she heard a woman coach was taking over, she was ecstatic. She never doubted she'd make the team. Indeed, of all the girls trying out for Thunder, Natalie appeared to have no challenge at all, other than perhaps getting in shape.

A couple of years earlier, during tryouts for Eclipse, her father noticed that every night when he put her to bed, Natalie's arm ached. The doctor prescribed ibuprofen, but when the pain persisted, Natalie had an MRI. Bone cancer was the diagnosis. They put the eleven-year-old through a battery of tests, drawing blood, sticking in an IV, getting a CAT scan. She'd need surgery, require chemotheraphy, and go bald. The doctor said she'd have a 75 percent chance of survival.

Natalie cried about losing her hair, but when the day of the surgery came, she was brave, picking the music she wanted to listen to before she went under. The surgeon sliced open Natalie's back and was surprised to find infection, and said it was a good sign. Two weeks passed, two weeks in which Nalatie's wound was left open so it could drain. Finally, the doctors had good news. Natalie had a rare case of cat scratch fever that had looked exactly like bone cancer. She was one of six individuals in the country in whom the infection had gone to the bone.

By the age of seven Natalie knew soccer would be her sport. She'd had the benefit of playing in the shadow of a talented sibling, like a number of other Thunder players, but that wasn't what drove her toward the game. Anna, two years her senior, was her role model, a fair-haired, graceful girl perhaps even more gifted at soccer, and a talented jazz dancer to boot. But Natalie's father saw the difference between the girls early on. Anna was a people pleaser, a girl who would smile even if she wasn't feeling well. Natalie made no such pretense. At times her father thought she bordered on rude, the way she'd speak her mind and couldn't care less about what adults thought. But Natalie's directness also meant that she did what she wanted, not what was expected of her. Though she played baseball as a young girl, Natalie tired of how much you stood around waiting for something to happen. She didn't mind basketball but found it repetitive. Soccer seemed to demand more skill. And for a change, it was a sport in which she could use her feet.

But after years of toying with the old Eclipse coach and dogging laps, Natalie was stunned by Emiria's rigorous training. Natalie cried at practice, and looked at Cassie throwing up and thought she was about to lose it too. Natalie's tanned legs were crisscrossed with grass cuts from running the hill. She thought seriously about asking to sit out, but this wasn't the old Eclipse. Everybody else was doing it and they were hurting too. She'd cry in the car pool after practice, and when she got home, she'd cry some more. To those who only knew Natalie's fearsome game face, this emotional side was a surprise. The girl who tackled and stared harder than anyone except Arlene could rival Jessica and Theresa in the crying department.

She heard the other girls say how much they hated Emiria, how she was putting them through hell. But Natalie noticed how Emiria would push them and then encourage them. They'd come off a run, and their recovery time would be better, and she'd congratulate them—and then make them do it all over again. Natalie believed this was a coach who could make soccer players out of them, who could teach them to trap, to pass, to see the field.

And for all of Emiria's hard exterior, Natalie sensed a softer side. One afternoon her dad was late to pick her up after practice, and after all the other girls' parents had come and taken them home, Emiria sat on the curb and talked to her, and Natalie decided for herself that the new coach was nice.

But Emiria was a coach, and like most coaches, she had to see her players on two planes, as individuals and as part of what she hoped would one day be a finely tuned team. She saw the naturals, girls like Shannon and Naomi who made it all seem effortless, and she hoped they would prove good models for the other girls of just how gracefully the game could be played. But she thought angry Kim had the most to teach her teammates. Kim was as opportunistic as she was haughty. She could fire a bullet from a bouncing pass, or loop the ball in to a galloping forward without looking. But the muscled thighs that generated her power also made her slow and vulnerable in the open field. Kim had to beat players with her strength, her anticipation, and her wits. She'd developed as a player not only by rigorous training, but by careful study. She'd watched hundreds of matches on TV and in person with her soccer-crazy dad, Brian. And that was why Emiria believed the girl who rarely smiled had so much to give.

Kim's skill was earned by study as well as sweat. Hopefully the girls would see: You didn't have to be a natural to play beautiful soccer.

Each of them had qualities they could build upon. There were the troopers, scrappy girls like Natalie and Trinity who did whatever Emiria demanded of them, and set an example of the value of hard work and determination. Jessica and Cassie both lacked quickness, but, like Kim, made up for it with drive and strength. Arlene was a category unto herself, a constant reminder that this was a contact sport, that physical presence and intimidation could set the tone for an entire game. Then there were the ones who, as Emiria put it, looked good in a soccer uniform. Kristin had the poise of a debutante, but she also had the sinewy legs of the competitive tennis player she'd been. Angela, of course, had those years of ballet training and track, but Shauna was a thoroughbred, from her dark, thick mane to her great soccer build. Her legs were stronger than most boys', and she had the balance and quickness to stay with any player on the field. Angela's close friend Erin, the fair daughter of Phil Molling, the assistant parent coach, also impressed Emiria. Nearly as strong as Kim, Erin boasted surprising quickness and old-fashioned hustle.

Emiria herself had been a power player, and could easily relate to players who resembled herself, believing that tall, slight players were by nature awkward and clumsy. But she made exceptions. At times the wispy, strawberry blond Jenny Drady looked as light and breakable as a kite on a blustery day, but despite her slenderness and lack of skill, she was also a nationally ranked distance runner who could run a quarter mile in a blazing sixty seconds. The gangly and injury-prone Theresa made the team because of her skill and smart team play. That Heather hadn't been dropped was something of a miracle. If she were any skinnier, Emiria thought Heather would have to go to the hospital. But after watching the frail blond beat the girls right and left with a simple cutback move, and fire low, accurate shots on goal, Emiria had been persuaded.

And finally, there was surfer-cool Catherine, the girl on the bubble. Several weeks into training, Emiria had no idea whether Catherine was her best or worst choice, the pivotal defender who would bring the rest of the team up to another level or send it spiraling down. One day she'd be on fire, the next she seemed distracted, her mind anywhere but on the game.

Emiria wanted to slow things down and remind the girls that soccer was a game that centered on the ball. Soccer shared much of the artistry of basketball, with the added dimension of striking the ball. As with tennis, golf, or baseball, the physics of striking the ball opened new dimensions to the deft player. Kick the ball on the inside of the laces and the ball would hook. Hit it with the outside of the foot and it would slice. Strike low and the ball would arch like a golf chip, or swing high and the topspin would make it hug the grass.

Emiria just wanted to teach comfort, being comfortable with the ball. So they dribbled through cones with one foot. Inside, out, inside, out, shifting their weight like a slalom skier making the gates. Dribbling a soccer ball can be prose or poetry. You can dribble with each side of your foot, roll the ball sideways by raking the top of the ball with your cleats, spin it around you with the side of your foot, and for the truly inspired, flip it over an opponent and juggle it forward on your thighs.

Trapping was a good place to start. If movement was the game, if spreading the defense by slinging the ball around like the Harlem Globetrotters was the objective, then just as important as the pass was the reception, the trap. Emiria watched it happen over and over again. A

bouncing pass, a girl waiting till the last second to reluctantly jump at it, banging it hard with her shin or her
knee, the ball bounding out of reach.

"If you're afraid, you tense up and your body becomes
hard," she explained at practice. "The ball might as well
be bouncing off a backboard."

It was a mind/body challenge. First you had to elimi-
nate the fear of being hit by the ball. To control the ball,
they had to welcome it. And so Emiria demonstrated the
Zen of the trap. She seemed to do nothing. Just let it hit
her and the ball dropped exactly where she wanted it.

"What's the difference between the way I trap and the
way you trap?" Emiria asked.

The girls could see it. "You're relaxed."

"I'm doing it so much easier," she agreed. "I'm not
trying so hard."

Her muscled body softened at the moment of impact,
her foot gave, her thigh absorbed the shock. She taught
them the dance too. Like so many sports, what mattered
was how quickly you anticipated the ball, how balanced
you were on your feet.

"Learn to be comfortable. If the ball's bouncing, move
to it and control it with your feet."

You could teach skills and tactics and fitness, but this
was another level. Comfort and joy. Like when the ball
touches your foot, it feels good.

But having been coached by men for most of their
years, many of the girls feared one particular trap. The
chest pass, the pass that people who don't know soccer
think proves women weren't meant to play the game.
Misjudge a chest pass and the ball would smack you in
the breast, and make you think twice about trying it
again. "This is the hardest trap for a girl to do," Emiria
told the team. "You've just got to find that comfortable
spot and hit it there every time."

And the first lesson was that the spot had nothing to

do with their breasts. It was just above on the sternum, under the chin.

They circled round and tossed the balls up. Arms dangling at their sides, the balls just hit them, bounding out of reach.

"Just relax," Emiria intoned. "Get your arms up so it becomes more circular."

Emiria demonstrated. Her arms rounded with the palms up like a woman in prayer. It was striking to watch. Change the mental focus, and the body and the physics changed. Leaning back slightly, they were catching the ball, actually seeming to pull it right down to their feet. The ball didn't have to hit them. Maybe it didn't even want to hit them.

"All right, you guys, we're playing four-on-four," Emiria announced. "Five passes equals a goal and you can pass back to the outside player."

Each team had a safety valve, a player behind the field they could pass back to if they were all marked and no one was open. Emiria didn't tell them why they were doing it. Just stood and watched. Ten minutes later, she stepped up.

"OK. So what is the purpose of this drill? What are we looking to do?"

A long silence and then the talkative Theresa tentatively replied, "Make a good pass?"

"No."

They were going to have to start from scratch. Fundamentals. The right answer was learning to check back to the ball. Like a basketball player breaking to the ball to create a passing lane. Checking back meant running toward the passer to receive the ball, cutting in front of the defender. It meant constantly moving to support your teammate, always anticipating where the pass might be headed.

Emiria didn't just quiz them on the purpose of the drill. She started showing them. Pushing the players around the field like chess pieces.

"Let's move her," she said, shoving the impassive Shannon back so two players were in a parallel line awaiting a pass.

"OK, what's wrong with this?"

A long pause.

"The defender can guard both of them?"

"So how do we fix it?"

Synchronized movement was the answer. One girl might check straight back, the other angle off to the sideline. Never be flat, never stop cycling. Free up an angle to beat the defenders. A forward might dash toward the corner flag, freeing her teammate to take her space and receive the next pass. Together, working in tandem.

And so, slowly but surely, Emiria began to teach the girls to break down the game. At first they seemed afraid to make a mistake, or perhaps they didn't want to be seen as the goody-goody. Kim or Arlene usually knew the answer, but neither girl was too keen on raising her hand in class. If they didn't talk in front of teachers or classmates, how was this any different? Arlene figured if she knew the answer, she knew it. Why tell anybody else? The players were bumping up against the classic feminine paradox. Every girl knows the punishment for speaking out is harsh. Girls who speak frankly are shunned.

The two captains the girls picked, Shauna and Naomi, the players with the enormous responsibility of helping their teammates mesh with one another on the field, were anything but talkative. It was no secret why the girls chose the girl next door, and the good-natured Naomi. Their work ethic matched their fresh demeanor. From the beginning they had performed perfectly together in scrimmages and drills, beating other players with quick give-and-goes, checking back to provide each other an outlet.

In years past they had played together, and it showed. They had commitment and drive, and there was a certain balance in that Naomi had played on Fury and Shauna on Eclipse. But out of all the girls on the team, they ranked among the quietest. How would they ever get the girls to communicate on the field?

To Thunder, the early July California Cup was simply the first test in a seemingly endless season. The dates seemed impossible. How could a season last more than a year? But it did. If you were as good as Thunder hoped to be, tryouts began in rainy March and the season culminated thirteen months later in the State Cup final in late April. The absurdly long season created another anomaly. At twelve months, smack in the midst of your team's frantic run for the State Cup, you had to pick next year's squad. One of the players the team was counting on for the State Cup might actually be cut from next year's squad.

Thunder had just finished stage one, two months or so of rigorous tryouts, fitness, and early skill work. Stage two was upon them, the summer tournaments, then the fall league, fall tournaments, a few weeks of Christmas break, winter training, winter tournaments, and the long, muddy trudge toward the spring State Cup. The thirteen-month season wasn't quite as bad as it sounded because you really only played about twelve months. Class I soccer was all about competition. High school soccer was considered a joke in comparison, with its two weeks of training and two-and-a-half-month season. You played high school soccer for fun, for school spirit. Class I soccer was about playing the best darn players out there. Which meant traveling. Which meant, if you were a parent with a couple of players, plenty of weekends spent on the road or by the playing fields, holing up nights in a crummy motel eating cold pizza with a bunch of kids.

The best clubs in the nation, teams from Los Angeles, Maryland, Texas, and Colorado, jetted to two or three out-of-state tournaments a year and sometimes even abroad to Europe or South America. Thunder was going to stick to a ninety-mile radius. Along with the California Cup, Emiria had signed Thunder up for a mid-August low-key affair ten miles down the freeway in Rohnert Park, followed the next weekend by the larger Santa Rosa Hall Memorial tournament, and finally the small Mill Valley/Tiburon Fall Kick Off, held fifty miles south at fields bordering San Francisco Bay.

Ordinary weekend tournaments like these were the lifeblood of Class I youth soccer, a traveling parade of family and competition that took place hundreds of times each year across America. The bigger ones were three-day extravaganzas, with a circuslike tent or two, vendors hawking the latest gear from Nike and Adidas, and rows of concessions selling souvenirs and hot food.

Girls made youth soccer enormously popular. They brought their numbers and their enthusiasm and their families, doubling the size of tournaments. Even the smallest competitions boasted five age divisions for girls, starting from ten and under to under fifteen. Add in the boys and count for the inevitable age groups that were often not represented, and that meant anywhere from six to eight championships. Mayors salivated over the math. Sixty-four teams of sixteen kids, one or more parents per player, plenty of siblings and relatives, and over a hundred coaches and referees. Two thousand out-of-towners paying tournament fees, staying in hotels, munching pizza, shopping, and going to movies.

Quick touches, smart give-and-goes, lots of combinations. Emiria couldn't believe her eyes. The first game of the season and the girls were well on the way to mastering classic, possession-style soccer. The victory was nice, but it was how the girls played that impressed her the most, the ease with which they shed their old habits. The second-round opponent would be a cakewalk.

But then there was the reality of the few hours' rest before the afternoon game. Sultry, hundred-degree heat sapped the girls' energy, and not everyone was at full strength. While clearing a ball out of the penalty box, Shauna felt that old ghostly hand clutch at her leg; once again she'd tweaked her hamstring.

"You guys aren't even trying!" Emiria groaned at half-time, clearly frustrated. "You look at me with these eyes like, take me out please! Pick it up!"

Emiria couldn't understand it. They were playing a long-ball team nowhere near their skill level. Why wouldn't the girls stick to their game? But in the chaos of the first few long, arching boots toward goal, the short passing style Thunder had mastered in the morning disappeared. Panic set in, and the girls started responding to what some Thunder parents were shouting on the sidelines. "Clear it! Get rid of it! Get it out!" They were lucky to escape with a scoreless tie.

The next morning, playing against the Placer Sharks, State Cup champions from two years before, Thunder was another team, building attacks out of the back, passing wide to players' feet, Ping-Ponging the ball up the field in short, diagonal combinations, working together on give-and-goes. The performance was even more impressive because the Sharks were a gifted team with a star forward who played a cross between a passing game and boom ball, a direct style that could be dangerous. But yesterday's impatience was replaced by utter calm. Slender Jenny miraculously punched a goal in close. And then, with Catherine off at another tournament that she'd committed to before joining Thunder, Naomi got her chance to prove she deserved the central defender position of sweeper. Emiria had already told her why she liked her play. Nobody guards the sweeper, and Naomi's catlike quickness and nifty dribbling might permit her to sneak by the defense. But even Emiria didn't expect her to take six people on and crack a left-footed shot at the top of the eighteen-yard line that hit the far post and ricocheted into the net for the game winner. It was beautiful, everything about it, even the way Shannon and others checked to Naomi, fooling defenders into thinking she'd dump it off as she ate up the open space toward goal.

But in the afternoon match against the Fairfield Eagles, a physical long ball team, once again Thunder lost its composure. The girls passed short for brief periods of time, but unable to head out many of the balls raining down, they began succumbing to the shouting on the side-lines, nervously kicking the ball out. Shauna's hamstring was cinching tighter, and the Eagles seemed a team full of Arlene clones, pushing, shoving, throwing Thunder off its game. Only the sturdy legs and tenacious play of Natalie Messina were keeping them in the game. Natalie was the kind of girl who would give anything to make a pass to a teammate. And despite taking a pummeling, somehow she kept winning balls and slowing down defenders.

Fifteen minutes of the game had elapsed when Jerry Messina finally arrived. The ground was so hot it felt like cement. He spotted Natalie playing defensive midfield, battling as always. Time seemed to compress. One moment his daughter was running right toward him, and the next she collapsed as if she'd been shot.

She'll get up, Jerry thought. Natalie had a history of going down hard.

This time she didn't.

Natalie's right leg and foot had twisted in opposite directions. The pain? Like someone smashing it with a hammer. They carried her off the field and put her in a golf cart, wrapping her foot in ice with an Ace bandage.

Emiria didn't know what to say after the loss, but her

closed stance shouted she was ready to abandon the girls. "Natalie's the only player that gave everything," she growled. "You should have lost five to nothing. If it wasn't for her, you would have gotten your butts kicked. You need to respect her."

The girls slowly walked over as a group and thanked Natalie for her effort. They didn't know it at the time, but they were saying good-bye. X-rays would show a break. Thunder had just lost its toughest midfielder for three months.

SIX

Angela's Score

*e*miria's three-by-five practice index card gave Angela's score.

On the agenda that day was the Sonoma State campus's hilly two-and-a-half-mile run. Twenty torturous climbs up the dusty stadium hill. A drill dividing the field into zones that forced the girls to pass the ball, as well as the usual hundreds of push-ups and sit-ups. On the back side of the card, Emiria marked the girls' times in the two-and-a-half-mile run. Angela was an impressive third in 21:03, just ten seconds behind the blazing Jenny Drady, and five minutes faster than the slowest girl.

The neatly groomed ballerina could have easily loped in somewhere in the middle, saved herself for the hills or the drills. But Angela had caught the fever. The training was a purge. Whatever they did—run, scrimmage, or a few dozen sit-ups—Angela gave more than she knew she had. She was cleansing herself, shaking out the memories of all the bad kids she'd been around the last year, the way her mom and dad had been upsetting her, the angst of a teenager.

Sure, Emiria was a bitch. The way she'd shout, "Angela, *pay attention!*" But something in Angela responded. In the old days, Angela would get to practice and fool around with her friends like everyone else. Emiria cut that all off with her stares and piercing words. And suddenly the discipline of practice became a sanctuary. Not just the physical exhaustion, but the fun, the exultation at finishing the hill climbs or making a great pass. For the first time in a long while, Angela felt really good about herself. Healthy. Confident. Sure, she'd continue to struggle with friendships, school, and family, but that didn't mean she couldn't take on her own challenges.

Angela wasn't by any means the only girl on Thunder struggling with adolescence. But she ranked among the most articulate and self-aware individuals on the team, one of the few who constantly questioned the meaning of things and events. It was a thoughtfulness that ran in the family. Perhaps better than any other Thunder parent, Joe Walsh understood what his daughter was facing.

What was the true landscape of a thirteen-year-old girl? Why did it make sense for some girls to pursue sport with an almost religious fervor? And if a girl decided to swim upstream in these harsh waters, what could parents really do? Motivation was never an easy question. If soccer truly was an exercise in building self-confidence, where did the sensitive, astute parent fit in? How could a parent support his or her daughter's journey? Know when to step in and when to gracefully step away?

Each school morning, Joe and Angela Walsh would squeeze into the family Diatsu and begin the twenty-minute drive to Herbert Slater Middle School from the home they rented on the west side. Though they'd transferred Angela to the school at the beginning of the seventh grade because it would make it easier for them to shuttle her to ballet classes, the move had an unintended, fortuitous consequence. The drive was an ideal time for Walsh to counsel and motivate his daughter.

And who better than Joe Walsh? Year after year, Walsh's girls' and boys' cross-country and track teams dominated city competitions. In the classroom and as a counselor, Walsh was a Slater Middle School legend. It didn't hurt that he bore more than a passing resemblance to the actor Joe Pesci. His Italian ancestry seemed to dominate: the big nose, the sparkling eyes, the way he'd tap your shoulder when he talked to you. But Walsh was Irish too, and beyond the casual drift of his thick, bushy black hair, he had a lyrical side, a love of great literature and the sense that life indeed was a drama.

The California League of Middle Schools selected Walsh as the Educator of the Year for the region from Sonoma County to the Oregon border. Walsh was ideally suited to talk about girl role models, and he did so with great enthusiasm nearly every morning, citing the latest achievements or outstanding attributes of the best Slater girls, a cast that varied from week to week, but invariably centered upon Sara Bei.

Walsh had taught Sara English and considered the slight Jewish girl with the wide smile a model student. The girl's parents had graduated from Stanford, and that only seemed to make her work harder. By the eighth grade, Sara's distance running already placed her among the nation's top runners. Her grades were perfect, and Walsh knew that she'd reach her lofty goals—Stanford and medical school. Nothing was out of her reach.

Walsh had watched Sara lift up countless girls in class and sport. There was a saying around Slater, "I Sara Beied it!" which meant, of course, that you'd tried harder than you imagined possible. Sara was the strong leader every school needs, a girl who proved it was OK to excel in schoolwork and be outrageously athletic.

Walsh knew that Sara was probably a one-in-ten-thousand girl, miles apart from what happened too often to girls when they reached the age of twelve or thirteen. Though Slater was one of Santa Rosa's better middle schools, drawing the vast majority of its student body from the prosperous east side, the district also included the Sonoma County Fairgrounds, home to some of the most crime- and drug-infested neighborhoods in the city. Walsh could write a book about the girls who had come to him from that part of town. They had mothers on heroin and jailed or abusive fathers, and they dressed scantily and defended themselves with foul mouths and fists. But they were still adolescent girls.

During the winter, Walsh noticed a thirteen-year-old girl he'd been counseling coming to school every day wearing the same T-shirt. He asked her if she needed a jacket and, if he got her one, would she wear it. She would. She was cold. Walsh dug up an old blue ski jacket at home, but when he offered it to the girl, she just shook her head. "Thanks, but . . ." Walsh should have known better. The jacket might have kept her warm, but it was hopelessly out of fashion.

It wasn't just the poor girls from the broken families. Something happened to girls when the teen years threatened. When Walsh visited local elementary schools at recess, he'd see dozens of girls happily playing basketball. But at Slater, girls just a couple of years older wouldn't touch a ball. By then it was all boys, grabbing balls and pushing and shoving and making obscene gestures at the girls clustered in their tight, talking circles, dabbing on makeup. Every day Walsh was surrounded by a depressing reality that had been codified by the media and quantified in national studies and statistics. Adolescent girls, Walsh knew from his students, seem to lose their impetus to speak up in class or raise their hands. School-work, especially math, suddenly becomes confusing and difficult for girls. Walsh even wrote a poem about it, "Makeup Over Math," the key stanza running:

While schoolyard bullies compare scars
and stare hard with marble eyes
at timid saints, familiar with failure
and the havoc in hallways
as children gaze into mirrors
choosing makeup over math.

Back in elementary school the same girls weren't nearly so self-conscious. If she'd been in the fifth grade, Walsh knew the Fairgrounds girl would have taken that coat and stayed warm. But a continent separated an eleven- and fourteen-year-old. Any day of the week, Walsh could see the girls of Slater making a beeline to the bath-room to touch up their lipstick and eyeliner. Makeup, clothes—this was serious business, business that drove girls to extraordinary measures. One day, driving home with his son, Walsh surprised a girl getting dressed be-hind his house, and watched her tear off down the street half dressed. Walsh sent his son after her with the shoe she'd left behind. Walsh knew exactly what the eighth grader was doing. She had to change back into the clothes her parents had seen her in when she left home.

As a coach, Walsh had always seen sport as a balm for girls against the vortex of adolescence. But sadly, he knew that for many lower-income girls, sports weren't an option, and not only because it would likely not be sup-ported by parents or peers. To play after-school sports, you'd have to have a physical, signed by a doctor, and you'd have to have insurance, and you'd have to have transportation after practice . . .

* * *

When Walsh heard one of his thirteen-year-old cross-country runners played on a traveling boys' hockey team, he figured she would be a perfect role model for his then seven-year-old daughter. But the night Walsh took Angela to watch a game, the girl didn't spend long on the ice. Time after time, she'd whack a boy against the boards and be whistled into the penalty box. She had a nickname, her first name followed by "animal," and her loyal following chanted it loudly.

But the girl didn't stick with hockey, and though she continued to run on Walsh's cross-country team, Walsh knew that she was frequently depressed and cried often. Perhaps it was her parents' divorce. Walsh wasn't sure, and he was her counselor. The girl who had so recently been a terror on the ice had been transformed. Up on Walsh's office wall, papered with photos and hand-scrawled notes and drawings from the girls and boys he'd counseled over the years, was a new photo of the former hockey tomboy with her cross-country teammates. Though just thirteen, she was one of just a couple of team members who wore elaborate makeup, and the only girl who seemed to be trying hard to look nineteen.

Boys, boys, boys. Walsh knew it was a knotty issue, and one that a man couldn't fully understand. Becoming a woman logically brought about a certain preoccupation with appearance. Girls were naturally becoming acutely aware of boys, and Walsh knew all too well that the boy factor was often a critical part of a girl's search for identity. These were not forces that parents could control. Lots of girls were not attracted to nice boys. Nice boys lived next door, had similar backgrounds, and spent a lot of time on schoolwork or sports. Nice boys were the boys your mother and father wanted you to go to the movies with, while bad boys had cars and alcohol and drugs and time on their hands. Dating a bad boy just might be your declaration of independence.

Walsh saw the damage all too often. That was why he loved sports. It wasn't just the self-confidence boost, the feeling of satisfaction that comes with physical ability and team play. Sports burned up time as readily as calories. Girls who played sports had less time for fashion, for makeup, for boys. Because the way Walsh saw it, if you're unsupervised and you're fourteen years old—boy or girl—you're at risk.

Walsh had counseled hundreds of girls over the years, and seen every imaginable problem, from rape to suicide attempts to the more subtle and common instances of plummeting self-esteem and depression. Walsh knew what most parents don't face, that even the most well-adjusted girl could suddenly find her childhood world transformed.

But Angela's days brimmed over with sport and school. Her afternoons were busy with ballet, soccer, track, and cross-country. An introspective girl, Angela adored books and kept a journal and loved to contemplate her experiences. What with sports and her honors classes, her life was filled with commitments and deadlines. There was always a report to be done or a practice to go to or a game to be played. But Joe Walsh also knew that his daughter was thirteen years old. Not every girl could be a Sara Bei.

SEVEN

Central Magic

Shannon's gazelle legs dragged as if she was ready to collapse. She waved to the sideline, motioned she desperately needed a rest.

"You can't be that tired!" shouted Emiria.

You promised! If I played my hardest, you promised to give me a break.

But after the game, serene Shannon learned that she hadn't played her hardest. How could Emiria know a thing like that? On and on Emiria drilled them in practice about giving it 110 percent. But does anybody really know what it's like to go 110 percent? Shannon felt she was giving it her all. How could another person really know how hard she was trying?

Some of the parents couldn't understand it either. The girl clearly was tired. Perhaps she simply didn't have the endurance to play in the midfield. The year before, after a summer camp with Luke, the Sonoma State women's coach had suggested Shannon play back, and the Eclipse coach had agreed and Shannon had played marking back the whole year. She liked it. The position was easy for her, and gave her plenty of time to rest.

Luke, for one, couldn't see what Emiria saw in Shannon. In his mind Shannon was just a steady, middle-of-the-road player. Sure, she looked like she was just going through the motions, but Luke knew that was deceptive. That was just Shannon's pace. She wasn't particularly quick, and he knew all too well that coaches often mistook gracefulness for lack of effort. Just because Shannon didn't grimace or reach awkwardly for balls didn't mean she wasn't trying.

After Luke's analysis the year before, Phil Molling's suggestion made perfect sense. Why not play Shannon at sweeper? But Emiria wasn't particularly receptive to suggestions. Not from Phil, not from Brian, not even from her old head coach, Luke. And she wasn't going to start explaining herself. Coaching wasn't democratic, and she feared if she started having to justify her every decision, she'd be inviting debate.

In Emiria's mind there were plenty of reasons for ignoring the seemingly helpful suggestion. Naomi could play sweeper, and if Catherine got her act together, she'd be dynamic. But Emiria didn't have anyone who could play midfield like Shannon. If she had two sweepers already, why would she want a third?

Emiria had another reason for not changing her mind. Sweeper was exactly the sort of position where Shannon could relax, the place her composure and skill would reign supreme. It was a defining position, a little like point guard or safety in football, with the poise of quarterback. The sweeper was expected to be the closing player on defense and the bridge to offense, a player who took in the whole field like a chess master seeing the immense possibilities on the board, anticipating play and weaving transitions out of the loose cloth of fifty-fifty balls. If the game were chess, the sweeper pushed several pieces at once. The sweeper's responsibilities required that she be composed and restrained. Stray too far, and the team would lose that glue. And really, that was part of why Emiria believed sweeper was wrong for Shannon. She wanted Shannon to strain, to fight for balls, to get caught out of position. She wanted that serene expression to break.

Why wouldn't she sub Shannon? If she rested Shannon, Emiria believed she would never learn the meaning of true exhaustion. Shannon seemed satisfied with being even-steven, 50-percent-effort Shannon, and Emiria just wasn't going to give in to that. She wasn't sure why Shannon was holding back. Maybe it was because she was so naturally gifted. Emiria wondered whether it had something to do with her not being close to her absent father. But whatever the cause, Emiria thought a lot of it had to do with fear. If you give all of yourself and it's not good enough, how bad a blow is that to your ego? How many people are willing to give everything they have and risk being rejected? This wasn't about athletics. It was about emotions and feeling accepted. Shannon was a popular girl without trying. Why should she take a chance?

Two leg hacks at the back of your heels aren't soccer, thought the scowling Kim. Football maybe. Wrestling perhaps. But soccer?

Kim could understand Arlene's tackling at tryouts. They were, after all, both trying out for forward, and she could be as competitive as the next girl. But now they were on the same team, weren't they?

Kim was accustomed to being a target for opposing players. The last year on Fury, she'd scored the vast majority of the team's goals. But those first few months on

Thunder, Kim was anything but overconfident. Coaches either respected her skills and power or wrote her off as too slow. And though Emiria had picked her, she knew she wasn't keen about her taking a week off from Thunder to meet a prior commitment she had as a guest player for the excellent Class I San Francisco Vikings team at the USA Cup in Minnesota.

But the pint-sized blond had a passion for soccer, and she wasn't about to miss the biggest soccer tournament in the country. She knew what she wanted and wasn't easily dissuaded. Her mother remembered one of the first times they went to watch her older brother, Brian Junior, play. The ball ran out of bounds toward them, and Kim focused and swung and smacked it a good ten yards back onto the field. "Look, Mommy." She beamed. "I helped Brian's team." She was three years old.

Kim wanted to play on a team right then and there, but you had to be four, so she had to wait a year. She didn't follow the herd. She'd run to the side, wait for the ball to burst free, take it on a straight line, and score. By the age of ten she made her first mental adjustment. Without speed, she needed moves. And so in the Halloran backyard, a living-room-sized patch of grass, she'd go one-on-one with her brother Brian, two and a half years her senior. He helped her with the mental concepts, breaking the game down. He'd teach her to tempt the defender with the ball like a huckster playing a shell game, cut one way, then back, shoving the defender back on her heels. It was all about strength and balance. If you were strong on the ball, if you could rock from side to side like a bumper car, who needed speed?

Brian was thirteen and getting serious about soccer himself, and so stubborn Kim, who had to do everything he did, got serious too. It wasn't just the challenge of playing against a quick and gifted older brother. Brian also happened to be a contemplative student of the game.

He taught her how to shoot, how to place her left foot parallel to the ball, the knee bent slightly, swinging easily like a golfer hitting the sweet spot.

The goals came naturally. Kim struck the ball with the force of a man, and learned to hit it on a volley from outside, loose in the box, whenever she had a fraction of a second. Coaches took notice, and she soon became a guest player for the highly regarded San Francisco Vikings. The year before Kim made team Thunder, she and Catherine had traveled with the Vikings to the USA Cup in Minnesota, the nation's largest soccer tournament. There were 800 teams from several nations. Pelé was there, and she traded jerseys with boys from Brazil and Mexico. The fifty-four fields were pristine, the tournament perfectly organized.

They'd gotten second the first year, and the following year once again reached the championship game. Down three to one, Kim charged the keeper and jabbed at the ball. The goalie and a defender sandwiched her, but they were too late to stop the ball from flying into the net. Pain shot up her knee, but she limped through the last five minutes. At the medical center they handed her a pair of crutches and told the thirteen-year-old she'd torn her anterior cruciate ligament or ACL. Frightening initials for a soccer player. Soccer is zigging and zagging. Tear your ACL and you might have to hang up your cleats.

Shannon was usually too tired to even shower. She'd collapse on the couch in her uniform, her voice a whisper. "No matter how hard I play, she won't take me out."

Another parent might have thought this punishment, some weird macho torture by an overzealous coach. But Michelle Smith had watched her daughter play for several years, and knew something her daughter didn't. This was Shannon's make-it-or-break-it year. She had been dominant for so long, so far above the competition, and then suddenly it was as if she were on a treadmill. Oh, sure, she was still growing, and she was as strong as any girl out there, but it was now clear that for all of Shannon's gracefulness, she wasn't the speediest of players. Her last year for Eclipse she'd tried out for the regional Olympic development team and made it, and then on Play Day, the day they pick the state team, she got upended, her whole weight landing on one arm. Her mother knew it was bad because she dragged herself off the field like a three-legged crab. Shannon hoped it was a bad dream. If there was no blood and no pain, maybe it wasn't so bad. But where her wrist had been hung a big dip like the handle in a ladling spoon.

The severely broken wrist ended Shannon's hope to play eighth-grade basketball, and her mother wouldn't let her play soccer for six weeks to make certain it had a chance to heal. But the truth was, they both needed a break. That season Michelle had watched with frustration as Luke and then the Eclipse coach had concluded that Shannon would be better in the back. Where did the men get these crazy ideas?

Had they accepted the face she was showing, a face some described as almost Eastern in its seeming tranquillity? There were those who thought Shannon was already playing her best, that Emiria was caught up in appearances, that Shannon was just a DiMaggio who would always look effortless even if inside she was giving it her all. But her mother didn't belong to that club. She knew her daughter and she believed Shannon was getting exactly what she needed. If a coach's job was to know her players, one-on-one, who they are and what makes them tick, then Emiria had Shannon's number. Emiria had figured her out from the start. She knew Shannon needed this hard work, because without it she'd never find her heart.

Michelle wasn't going to let Shannon waste the chances

she had never had. An early pregnancy had ended Michelle's dreams of college. After her mother died, she drove cross-country from Maryland with Shannon and her baby brother, out to Santa Rosa to start a new life. She lived with her sister in a small house in the troubled Fairgrounds until the gunfire and roaring cars drove them out. Gradually Michelle found work as a temp, and then made her mark at an electronics company where she worked for the president.

Her daughter was a natural athlete, the only girl on her basketball and Little League teams. Shannon was eight before she tried out for her first competitive soccer team, with three or four years less experience than the other kids. Though she'd never dribbled a soccer ball in her life, she seemed to pick it up instantly, and made the team easily.

Michelle had never had a chance to play sports. Though she'd made her high school's honor roll, there was no one to push her. Support and structured activities had been missing in her youth. But that wasn't going to happen with her daughter and her son.

And so, night after night, Michelle told Shannon she could handle it, that she needed to be thankful she wasn't "riding the pine," that other girls were begging for playing time just as hard as she was begging for rest. But Shannon wasn't thinking that way. She was beat, and though intimidated, she finally asked Emiria why she wasn't living up to her promise.

"Because I look to you as a leader," Emiria said plainly, her intense eyes giving Shannon nowhere to hide. "Because I expect and want more from you."

Responsibility wasn't a concept limited to Thunder's stars. Every player, from star to sub, had to care about her teammates. Take responsibility for every dribble and pass. Each time the girls stepped on a field, whether it was a practice or a game, Emiria wanted them to remember why they were there, the duty they had to themselves and their teammates to play with passion and be accountable for their actions.

Responsibility was a foreign concept for most of the girls. On the Eclipse, the coach didn't command the respect necessary to demand any sort of individual responsibility. Even Brian, though winning plenty of games, had found his grip slipping with the girls. Exactly why the men had lost contact wasn't clear. Brian was a tremendous encourager. He'd read *Training Champions*, by Anson Dorrance, coach of the great University of Northern Carolina women's squad. Anson was considered a national authority on coaching women. He'd laid it out in simple terms, discussed at length how women responded differently to coaching. Always assumed they were to blame. Shut down when you yelled. Needed more encouragement, more hand holding.

As a woman, Emiria didn't believe it was quite so black and white. She believed in encouragement—and confrontation. Didn't believe girls were so delicate they couldn't handle a little yelling. She knew it could work because at Sonoma State the coach she'd had before Luke had yelled at her during a game. She'd silently cursed her coach and briefly considered never playing soccer again. But in the second half, Emiria responded, finding an inner well she didn't know existed, proving to her coach and herself that she was the best player on the field.

Confrontation was an ugly, imperfect process. Some girls appeared to lack the self-confidence necessary to handle Emiria's lashings. A few parents thought Emiria was attacking their daughters, rather than trying to draw something new out of them. They weren't there every day, couldn't watch all of the practices. Didn't know that the same girl who'd been chastised might have been held up a day before for her effort.

Could only men draw strength in confrontation? Must young women be watered like flowers, never pushed too hard, never challenged? When did this supposed male sensitivity to the emotional differences between the sexes simply become the latest barrier to equality? The toughest, most aggressive girls on Thunder had older brothers or older sisters. They'd wrestled and played with boys from day one, emerging unscathed by all the battles. They were the most self-confident in the bunch. If they could handle snotty-nosed, foulmouthed neighborhood bullies at seven, why not a tough young woman coach at fourteen?

Soccer was confrontation. If a girl didn't have the guts to challenge an opponent for the ball, she wouldn't last a half. How could Emiria teach that tenacity without drumming in the principle of confrontation? Without encouraging courageous efforts and singling out halfhearted attempts? Without teaching the team that sport is character, that great athletes face their insecurities and failures head-on?

The girls had never experienced anything quite like it. Don't give your all in practice and a tongue lashing was just the start. Emiria just might sit you down. Publicly inform you you weren't being respectful to your teammates. Every girl was in tears at least once. But Emiria tried to balance it with encouragement, talk about how to work on a problem.

How the girls handled Emiria was often a reflection of how they'd viewed past coaches. Those who'd tired of being mentored by dads quickly accepted the new young woman's discipline. But if your coach had been your dad, how would you accept the replacement? Kim and Erin were the only two girls in that boat. Laid up with her bum knee, Kim was on the fence about the new team and its young coach. Erin Molling, too, was trying to sort out her feelings.

Her dad had been her coach as long as she could remember, and she thought him wise and knowledgeable about the game. Everyone knew that Phil's experience as a college player had given him great influence in tactics and personnel on the Eclipse. Erin couldn't separate the dad from the coach, and saw no need to. She thought him fun-loving and well liked by her teammates, a great encourager. So perhaps it wasn't surprising that Erin had difficulty accepting the passing of the paternal order. Erin missed her old team.

"Erin, you know what I like about you?" Emiria began, as the girls struggled to catch their breath, Kim and Arlene burning at the coach's praise.

"What?"

"You're always the first on the line. Ready for the next sprint."

The rest of the girls would walk back after sprinting, but Erin would turn right around, rest on the line, ready to go. Erin was focused and dedicated and responded to the challenge of Emiria's discipline. Her speed placed her up among the leaders at the Sonoma State workouts, and she impressed Emiria with her ability to win fifty-fifty balls. Erin played center midfield and forward and won lots of encouragement from Emiria, more than almost any other girl. The more Erin played, the more Emiria saw her as a possible impact player, without quite the skills of a Shannon or a Kim, but an all-round force who could score or fight for possession in the midfield.

Erin relished the encouragement and attention, but she didn't like her coach. Emiria seemed tomboyish and impolite, and though Erin recognized her swearing as typical of a woman college soccer player, she thought it inconsiderate of the team's younger girls. Emiria wanted to win too badly in her view, put too much pressure on them to motivate themselves, to have everything come from within. Erin was uncomfortable with all the competition, the pressure to beat out one another in practice. It seemed to bring a lot of tension and conflict to the team. Why couldn't they just get along, like they had on the Eclipse, when no one took it so seriously, and they all bonded and seemed to have so much more fun?

It all came to a head after a scrimmage against an older girls' team. Emiria was singling out some of the Thunder girls' mistakes and blamed a goal on her. Erin felt her teammates looking at her, the tears well up. That night she phoned her coach and told her she didn't need that kind of attention. She realized the goal was mostly her fault, but there were ten other Thunder players on the field. Why couldn't Emiria have just pulled her aside, away from her teammates?

"There's no reason for you to blame the goal on me and humiliate me in front of my team," Erin reprimanded Emiria, and then warned her. "I don't want you to take it personally, but I don't want it to happen to anyone else either because it's not a good thing to do."

Emiria wasn't exactly understanding. "You're going to have to deal with it," she coolly declared.

It wasn't the answer Erin had wanted to hear. Still her dad encouraged her to just hang in there, and sure enough, at practice and games, Erin bounced back. But in Emiria's eyes, performance was only half the equation. Commitment and dedication to the team were equally important. Emiria felt Erin was playing the prima donna, questioning her leadership and distancing herself from her teammates. And how was the coach to take Erin's glaring absence? That summer Erin and her family vacationed in Europe. Just when Thunder was struggling to come together as a team, Erin was touring the coast of France, Switzerland, and Germany for four weeks.

The timing couldn't have been worse. With Kim sidelined with her knee injury, Erin could have cemented a position in the midfield or on the forward line. But Erin returned from vacation badly out of shape. Though Emiria continued to encourage her, Erin began to doubt herself. She wasn't as quick as she'd been before the trip, and she found it hard to fit in. Her best friend from the old Eclipse had been cut by Emiria, as well as another close friend, the daughter of the Eclipse coach. Still another friend had recently decided to quit Thunder in favor of pursuing dance.

New teams could be a fresh start. But they could also be a harsh reminder of the fragility of friendship and family. In the space of a few months, Erin had seen her dad shunted aside, and her best friends judged inadequate. Kim and a couple other Fury girls seemed to actively resent Erin, and while she'd felt close to Shannon and Shauna, soon she found herself talking mainly to Angela. They had played soccer together for years and run together on the Santa Rosa Express club. At practice they started to keep to themselves, warming up together, sharing little pointed asides about Emiria. High school was only a few weeks off. Both Angela and Erin would have a chance to make varsity as freshmen.

High school soccer started to sound like an oasis.

Emiria felt she was showing the redhead respect. There were times when even she winced at Arlene's slide tackles, but she nearly always resisted the temptation to hold her back. It wasn't only that Emiria thought Arlene could teach the team an essential lesson about physical play, it was also about understanding Arlene. She was enormously skilled, perhaps the only player who could win a loose ball, turn, hold it in traffic, and drop off a sweet pass. Emiria wanted her to know that she was accepted, not only for her ability but also for her heart. The coach saw the girl's dilemma, her intense desire to be a star and yet go unnoticed. When Arlene played, her body revealed the paradox, the way her hands would some- times nearly stick to her sides, seemingly afraid to be seen.

And yet for all her understanding, Emiria thought Ar- lene absolutely hated her. She'd say something compli- mentary and Arlene would stiffen and turn away, as if the words stung. All the praise Emiria heaped on Arlene seemed to have no effect. She operated in her own world, isolated from virtually the entire team, talking to almost no one. And that made it even more confusing. Arlene, Thunder's Frankenstein, the girl who terrorized them and delivered their daily bruises, was best friends with one of the team's most popular girls.

On the surface they couldn't have been more opposite. Despite her harsh play, Arlene was a pleasant-looking redhead, a girl you might expect to find in any town in Ireland. But Shannon's chocolate skin, olive-shaped eyes, and regal cheekbones gave her an aura of mystery. Was she innocent or was that just the facade? Her features were neither African-American nor white. Arlene barely grunted to anyone the first several weeks, while Shannon was practically the team's social secretary, quick with a joke or a sarcastic crack. Arlene, of course, loved to rip off a brutal tackle and would shoot the ball from far out without apologies. Shannon, meanwhile, prided herself on her style, on never being out of form.

Those who didn't know them assumed that what brought them together was obvious. They both had single moms. A tall, hearty redhead who loved to laugh, Carol Tuttle had started life much like Michelle. She, too, had excelled in high school, and no one had ever suggested she go to college. Instead she worked on an assembly line spitting out silicon chip wafers for $2.25 an hour. Then after her first child's birth she opened a day-care service out of her small house in Santa Rosa, transforming the garage into a school, and the backyard into a playground.

The men in Carol's life were losers. Arlene's father hadn't stuck around long enough to meet his daughter.

After Arlene was born, Carol took control of her life. She faced up to the fact that she'd never had anything remotely like a strong woman role model. And as her daughter grew into a chubby, introspective little girl, Carol confronted family members about their alcoholism. But if Carol's personal struggle was highly particular, she was also part of a new American movement. Carol didn't simply nurture her daughter. Like countless mothers across America, Carol started coaching girls' soccer, eager to offer her daughter an opportunity she never had.

Arlene began playing at the tender age of three, and immediately gave an early glimpse of her character. As the other girls bounded after the ball like a herd of baby lambs, Arlene sat to the side, plucking strands of grass, apparently oblivious to all the commotion. Her mother wasn't worried. Arlene was an observer, getting the lay of the land, and sure enough, in due time, Arlene was in the thick of things. But Carol's days as a coach were numbered. When Arlene reached the age of eight, Carol got a call from the league, saying they wouldn't need her that year. The men were taking over.

Once Shannon and Arlene made the same under-ten team, there was no separating their families. Whenever Michelle was confused about a penalty or some development on the field, she'd ask Carol, and in the rare case Carol didn't know the answer, they'd wander down the sideline together and find someone who did. Arlene was distant at first, but little by little as the two single moms bonded, meeting often for meals or walks, Shannon and Arlene became fast friends.

It was true that their mothers made it easy for them to spend time together, but their friendship wasn't quite so simplistically explained. Girls don't stay friends till the age of fourteen just because their moms like one another's company or they both happen to lack dads.

Indeed, at first the girls couldn't stand each other. Arlene was jealous of Shannon's ability, and Shannon thought Arlene a ball hog. But together on an under-ten team, their talents clicked in the midfield and opposing coaches dubbed them "Central Magic." It seemed whatever sport they played, they were connected. In the fifth grade they played on the same softball team, and as fate would have it, Arlene was the catcher and Shannon the pitcher, and what faces they loved to make at one another. Arlene would invite Shannon to play baseball after school in her big yard, next to the toddlers at her mother's day-care center. But plenty of afternoons they'd while away the time playing board games, drawing pictures, or just listening to music and combing each other's hair.

Shannon gradually became more feminine, wearing skirts and designer shirts and blouses, while Arlene stuck to her soccer shorts and sweats and sneakers. Arlene had never worn a dress, and she had other quirks. The girl who prided herself on finishing the game with the dirtiest uniform washed her hands a dozen times a day.

They were an odd couple. Arlene would clean up Shannon's room for her when she'd come over. Like most of the Thunder girls' rooms, Shannon's was decorated with the standard Mia Hamm posters and could use a little cleaning. Arlene's room, meanwhile, was a paragon of order and obsession. On top of just about every Mia poster that existed and nearly sixty soccer pins, Arlene had patiently cut out and pinned up countless neatly trimmed magazine pictures of Hamm, other women stars, and little soccer balls. All of it ordered and organized, like the dozens of trophies in her case. There wasn't a piece of paper or a book or an item out of place. And unlike most of her teammates, Arlene actually had a poster of a male player, Eric Wynalda, a star on the U.S. men's national team.

Once they began playing on Thunder, with high school just months away, Shannon was bound to grow closer to social cliques and boys, just as Arlene was likely to stick to her world of sport. But that summer nothing had changed. They phoned each other every day, Shannon calling her by her nickname, R. They still loved to crack jokes, the more sarcastic the better, and they still loved to compete over just about anything. They each picked a big bowl of blackberries in Arlene's backyard and then baked a blackberry cobbler. Carol tasted each entrant and decreed Shannon's crust crunchier. Even Arlene, the ultimate competitor, the girl her teammates thought cared only about winning, believed that a truly dumb thing to say. Why couldn't she have said they were equal?

EIGHT

Keeper

*h*eather's house was the logical place to hold the July swim party get-together. Who better than a new player living in neutral territory, beyond the city borders in Rohnert Park, to bring the team together?

But after ten minutes of floating alone in the pool, the impish blond realized no one was going to join her. And that was when Emiria started talking. Perhaps it was the surroundings. Heather's family of five lived in a modest condominium, and they had actually been granted a partial scholarship to defray the cost of playing on Thunder. Or maybe it was just that Emiria felt it time to open up, to tell the girls a little bit about her childhood. Heather's mother, Stephanie, watched the girls go silent. What could you say? Only one pair of shoes to last the whole year?

But it was true. One of eight children of Dutch immigrants, Emiria had grown up dirt-poor. The family scraped by on welfare, aid to families with dependent children, and federal housing subsidies. Goodwill provided furniture and pots and pans, while clothes were usually hand-me-downs or whatever the Salvation Army had that day. A nun arrived every month to bring canned food, bread and eggs, and treats like boxes of cereal.

It wasn't only that they had barely enough to eat, and that each child had to make do with one all-purpose pair of shoes. Eight children was unusual those days in Santa Rosa, and Emiria stood out, what with the light maple color her Portuguese skin turned in the summer and the thick accents of her Dutch parents. She didn't quite fit in at school, and was forever hearing about the after-school activities her parents couldn't afford. Her parents scraped enough together to send Emiria and her sister for three months of ice-skating lessons, but while Emiria excelled at the sport, that only made it more painful when the money ran dry.

One day at school, a leaflet was passed out about a recreational soccer team. It was the sort of thing Emiria had learned not to show to her parents, but for some reason the seven-year-old asked if she could play, and this time her parents said yes. She was a natural, knocking in five goals in her first game as a forward. School, too, was a breeze. She skipped a grade, learned to read at an early age, and won writing and art contests. By the third grade Emiria could draw an accurate sketch of nearly any image. At first she rejected the typical rites of girlhood. Dolls and feminine things just weren't her cup of tea. She just didn't see the big difference between girls and boys.

At twelve she made her first traveling soccer team, an under-fourteen squad. She was rough, having played only five years, lacking the skills of the girls from affluent families who had begun as preschoolers. But she was aggressive and faster than most boys, running the hundred-yard dash in a brisk thirteen seconds flat when she was just thirteen. Her speed, her soccer skills, and her smile won her the attentions of her first boyfriend, a football and track star. Emiria was suddenly the object of appeal. She got her hair permed and began wearing makeup. Boys told her she should be a model.

Then the fourteen-year-old sophomore hit the wall. She couldn't hack her double-honors biology class and slogged through advanced algebra with trigonometry. She slid back to the normal honors class, but still struggled. The age difference between Emiria and her classmates struck her, and a sense of inadequacy crept in. Maybe I'm not as good as everyone thought I was, she found herself worrying. Maybe I've been fooling myself.

One day during a routine wind sprint she felt a tightness in her lungs. Emiria tried to hide it, but then it returned. The viselike pressure. The elusive air that couldn't be gasped, everything sinking into an echo, fading into the distance. Then in a game, just as an attack was coming on, she got slammed in the stomach. She couldn't get up, the breaths wouldn't come. I'm dying, she thought. I know I'm going to die.

It would be a year before she'd see a doctor, and she took the diagnosis of exercise-induced asthma as a death sentence. Who could understand a soccer player keeling over after a single sprint? And what possible comfort could she take in the doctor's casual suggestion that her asthma might have been triggered by some emotional trauma, perhaps something as primal as the fact that she'd been stuck in the birth canal?

The whirlwind of energy and zest that had fueled Emiria suddenly fizzled. Two or three asthma attacks would strike her in practice, taking her out of wind sprints or drills or scrimmages. The woman coaching the team thought she was dogging it, that it was all in her head. Emiria got the message; she just couldn't hack it. Nor did it help that her under-sixteen team had more than its share of upper-class kids whose parents drove BMWs and lived in big houses. Emiria didn't have the fancy clothes of the other girls, and her European mother was patently ignored by the other parents.

But Emiria was like her father, "Pops" as she fondly called him. She didn't know how to quit. When she was a third grader, her father had gone back to school to try to make something of his life, starting at the local junior college, and then graduating summa cum laude from Cal Poly with a degree in horticulture. A bear of a man with a shaggy head of salt-and-pepper hair, Muchtar Salzmann worked for the county, doing tests on apple trees, then saved enough to buy a run-down nursery, naming it Emerisa Gardens after his parents, Emerson and Merisa. By the early nineties, just as Emiria was finishing high school, Emerisa Gardens began to prosper.

Teachers would often ask Emiria why she always had to be better than someone else. Emiria knew why. Her father's motto was simple. Why do anything if you don't do it 100 percent?

And so Emiria worked her asthma into an asset. Hampered by her inability to run long distances, Emiria practiced her moves several hours a week. The ball was a steady partner, the field a green dance floor. She worked the maneuver again and again, the quick hip swivel to the outside and the burst inside, polishing the inside cut move that left defenders in her wake. Goals became Emiria's identity.

But the more she scored, the more her teammates resented her. They were generally older, and Emiria was yanking away the spotlight. Whether it was a practice or a routine game, Emiria knew only one way to play—all out. In her senior year, her high school played a team it had clobbered the year before. But this time they squandered opportunities and were locked in a desultory scoreless tie at the half. Angry, Emiria went out and pumped in five goals in the second half. Seconds after Emiria's last score, a teammate yelled that she was wide open, and she should have passed her the ball. "I can't believe how selfish you are!" the girl told her. "You already have four goals."

On the bus ride home, three girls picked on Emiria, calling her names. "All you want is your name in the paper! You're all about yourself!" Not knowing how to defend herself, Emiria cried. She had just scored five goals, and she was the most hated girl on the team.

Coaches were no better. No coach praised her scores or encouraged her in her quest to become a goal-scoring artist. None suggested the other girls should feed her the ball in pressure games. Some, like the woman who coached Emiria's under-sixteen team, seemed to actively resent her progress. When Emiria was recruited to play at Sonoma State, her ex-coach told her former star bitterly, "You'll never make it there."

Other than thick brown hair, Cassie appeared to have nothing in common with Emiria. The only child of divorced parents, she was a goalie, seemingly as distant in temperament from a striker as you could get. But of Thunder's sixteen players, it was hard to find a girl who took faster to Emiria's challenge.

Her real name was Cassandra, a name that seemed to match her perfectly shaped nose, warm eyes, peach cheeks, and classic femininity. But the girl they all knew as Cassie rivaled Arlene as Thunder's biggest tomboy, never wearing a skirt, never doing anything to her hair, belying the young woman she was fast becoming.

As a player, she had talent but little training. Oh, she'd been playing since she was five or six, but it was mostly recreational and Class III league. Her parents thought all the focus on winning a bad idea, that kids first had to get a chance to love the game before they got shoved into an ultracompetitive environment. Besides, Cassie's first love was baseball. As a seven-year-old she played Little League, and idolized Mark McGwire, and dreamed of being a ball player until she figured out it was a boys' game. At ten she decided she wanted to be a goalkeeper. The reasons were probably to be found in her neighborhood. The kids on Cassie's block were mainly boys, so Cassie got a steady diet of wrestling on the front lawn, climbing trees, and building tree forts. Cassie loved jumping, diving, getting muddy, and rolling around in the dirt. Goalkeeping in short.

Cassie's father was supportive when she told him she wanted to try out for Thunder, her first Class I team, but the truth was, he wasn't exactly thrilled. Cassie and her father had recently moved to a new house in a development west of town on Highway 12. Her mother had moved to Sacramento after the divorce, and worried Cassie was spending too much time playing soccer. Cassie's dad worked as a computer troubleshooter for Compaq, his schedule unpredictable, making it tough for him to pick up Cassie from practices.

Cassie never thought she'd make the team, and a part of her wasn't sure she wanted to. A dark-eyed brunette, she believed Class I team girls were all little blond Barbie dolls with a whole lot of money and attitude. At tryouts when the rain poured down, Cassie was the only girl without a waterproof bag, the only one to get everything soaked. When Emiria called to tell her she'd made the team, she didn't believe her at first. Then came the reality of competitive soccer.

"Well, I threw up today, Dad," Cassie told her father after one of the first workouts. He was shocked at first, but then it didn't surprise him at all. Back in Fort Jackson, South Carolina, where his parents lived, he'd seen plenty of soldiers in boot camp, laid out in the back of a truck puking out their guts. Cassie wasn't worried either. Practice after practice, bent over at the track, she kept one thought in the back of her mind.

What doesn't kill you makes you stronger.

On the eve of the mid-August Rohnert Park tournament, Emiria was scrambling to get everything together. It was only her second competition as a coach. There were the players' passes to get together, checking the roster, going over the possible lineups. When the phone rang late that night she hardly thought about it.

"Yeah. Sure. No problem."

The next morning at the field, Emiria paced. Where is she? How could she not be here? It's one thing to be missing a field player or a substitute. But your starting goalie?

"Jessica, get warmed up in the goal!" she barked.

Thunder was a first-year team with a first-year coach, and yes, mistakes did happen. Kim and most of the other girls knew exactly what had befallen Cassie, and didn't dare say a word. That late night call had been from the goalkeeper's dad, asking if Emiria would give Cassie a ride to the game. Emiria had just plain forgotten.

Depending on how you looked at it, the games that weekend were either a disaster or a faint ray of hope. Many of the parents saw more of what they'd seen in Sacramento. Lots of lost passes, indirect play, a general absence of defense. Luke summed it up during a halftime talk. It was nice that they felt confident enough to pass in front of the goal, but it wasn't going to win them any games. "Listen, we don't have the skill to pass the ball out of the six-yard box," Luke said calmly, and with a touch of humor. "Just clear the damn thing. Get it the hell out of there!"

Emiria had been pushing possession-style soccer so hard that the girls didn't seem to know when to draw the line. She would tell them not to pass near goal, but they still lacked a sense of the field.

Brian was especially frustrated, what with his defensive orientation. Once the old Fury had scored a goal, he'd shifted the fiesty Trinity, one of his top forwards, into the back and had her shadow the best striker on the other team. But Emiria didn't seem all that concerned about whether the girls were properly marking opposing forwards. Or for that matter, juggling tactics and players to win.

But watching Theresa back there, Brian wondered if they were on the verge of something. Tall, gangly Theresa was responding to the most threatening situations a defender could face—several onrushing forwards—by calmly dumping off a little three-yard dink pass to a teammate just yards from the goalmouth.

Theresa might as well have been trying to climb Mount Everest in sneakers. The thirteen-year-old who'd recently shed her wrist cast was trying to play college-level soccer. But Brian wondered. If Theresa wasn't afraid to calmly possess the ball, to pass it instead of nervously kick it out, what kind of positive message was she sending to the rest of the girls?

"Luke, here's the lineup," Brian said, stunning the Sonoma State women's soccer coach.

Luke had been looking forward to just kicking back in his wide-brimmed hat and shorts and watching the game. But Brian had news. Last night the team had chowed down at Kristin Young's house, and either the pasta or a bug had knocked Emiria for a loop. She'd spent the better part of the night throwing up. Concerned that Phil might try to coach the team, Emiria had anxiously called Brian and asked him to make certain Luke took the reins.

The timing couldn't have been worse. The Hall Memorial in late August was Thunder's home tournament, held at Sonoma State. Winning the Hall was a matter of some pride. Last year's Eclipse had brought back the trophy, so this year's squad, bolstered by the Fury players, was expected to repeat. And now that the big weekend had finally arrived, Emiria couldn't even drag herself out of bed.

But the girls adored Luke. They'd played in his soccer camps and watched him coach the Sonoma State women's team. Luke was a Santa Rosa coaching legend. He coached by instinct, responding to mismatches on the field with lots of substitutions and subtle tactical changes. After the first win, Phil Molling watched him make Babe Ruth–like predications. "Arlene, I want you to make this run," Luke instructed the girl, and then promised, "There will be a goal in a few minutes." Twice Molling watched it happen. He thought it unbelievable, uncanny, and shook his head in amazement. Brian, too, was amazed by how quickly Luke would sense weaknesses on the field with the precision of an engineer detecting a bad circuit, and then calmly tell the girls at halftime how they could pressure a particular fullback and score.

Three games, three jubilant victories, and then as Luke paced the girls through the warm-ups before the championship game, an ashen Emiria shuffled up like a ghost. She hadn't called and the team had assumed Luke would coach the final.

"What are you doing here?" a couple of the girls pointedly asked.

Whether Emiria heard it or not, the mood was catching. After Luke's second victory the girls had started joking about how they were winning without Emiria, how maybe she should just stay in bed.

This was a game Thunder simply had to win. It wasn't just that it was the first time they'd managed to reach a tournament final. There was the matter of principle. The

Eclipse girls had played this East Bay team before. They
had parents who yelled at opposing girls and banged
cowbells when their team scored. There had been incidents in the past, incidents that curiously always seemed
to involve Shannon, Thunder's lone girl of color. Once,
when she'd tried to make a clear against the East Bay
team, the ball glanced off Shannon's head and into her
own goal. "Pass it to the black girl," the parents had
yelled viciously. "She'll score for us again."

It wasn't the only time the all-white East Bay team's
parents had turned ugly. The girls' parents couldn't stomach a fair fight. In another match, Shannon used her pat-
ented hip check to win a few balls. This time she
happened to be near the opposing team's sideline when
the parents launched into a torrent of screams, demanding
the referee eject her. They got their wish. The ten-year-
old ran sobbing clear across the field and into the arms
of her mother.

Phil wedged himself between Brian and Emiria on the
sideline. Pushed out, Brian strained but couldn't quite
glimpse Emiria's expression.

"Luke had the girls in this formation," Phil began
boldly, informing Emiria that Luke had switched Trinity
to sweeper and juggled a couple of other players. Emiria
swayed slightly as the field swung in and out of focus.
She wondered if she was going to get sick.

Phil could see she wasn't keen on his comments, but
how could he resist? Emiria was doing an amateurish job.
Keeping a few girls off the field too long, not rotating the
way Luke had. What could you expect from a woman
who'd just turned twenty-two a couple weeks before? She
was in over her head.

"You know," Phil prodded, "Luke subbed Shannon."

Emiria steadied herself and glared. "I'm not going to
sub Shannon."

*   *   *

Thunder was ahead until the play.

Cassie went down for the save, paused a few seconds for the other team to clear out from her goulmouth, and then took a step to punt it out. It all seemed to happen at once. The referee blowing his whistle, waving his arms, the coach and players and parents on the other team yelling, "Five seconds! Five seconds!"

Cassie didn't know what was going on. The referee, responding to the shouting, had called an obscure infraction. Designed to stop a team from stalling, the five-second rule was almost never called. Goalies often hold the ball more than five seconds in a game, so calling the infraction when Cassie had just made a diving save was odd to say the least.

The worst Cassie could imagine was a penalty kick. But she wasn't so lucky. The referee placed the ball just a few yards from the goal, where Cassie had been standing. Thunder quickly lined up a wall of players to block the shot, but the East Bay team slipped it through, tying it up. The rest of the game was a panicked blur. In overtime, Cassie dove hard for a volley, reaching, reaching, reaching . . .

"Don't listen to that crap!" Luke exhorted a beaten Emiria. She'd heard the whispers. The inevitable comparisons to his earlier three wins.

"A final is different."

But that wasn't what some parents were saying. Losing brought the complaints to a head: Emiria doesn't communicate well with the girls. She's got them in the wrong positions. She's too young to be coaching. While the criticism was mainly limited to less than a handful of families, it was enough to make Emiria edgy. Luke tried to put her at ease. He'd already warned Brian that the results wouldn't be immediate, that they were trying to break old habits ingrained by years of poor coaching.

But Thunder didn't play well in the next tournament, and the tension on the sideline ratcheted up a notch. During a break before one of the games, Kristin's dad, Jeff, an insurance executive who still had the boyish face of the baseball player he'd once been, was sharing the shade of a tree with Angela's dad, Joe. The dads were ruminating about how their freshman daughters were trying out for varsity that fall at Montgomery High, but when they saw Emiria looking frustrated they waved her over. She'd never been so disheartened. Even she wondered when she was going to see some results. They'd play so well in practice and then falter in games. "I don't understand why the girls don't play as well for me as they do for Luke." She shook her head, looking as if she was about to cry.

"It's very easy," Jeff calmly explained. "They look at Luke as a god of soccer, and they play up to him and they want his respect. They don't see you that way yet, because you haven't earned it. You haven't been here long enough."

"Ignore all the negative talk," Joe and Jeff encouraged Emiria, the words visibly brightening her face. "Just coach. Do what you have to do. We'll support you as parents. We're going to stay with this till the end."

NINE

The Fabulous Five

Whether to play varsity; that was the question.

It was just the first of many high school dilemmas. Varsity soccer at San Rosa's high schools had become the premiere girl's sport: boy's football, baseball, and basketball wrapped into one. Make the team as a freshman and a girl won a confidence boost for the fall semester, if not all of high school. A nineties twist on the Big Man on Campus. The fourteen-year-old suddenly accepted into a revered group of sixteen- and seventeen-year-old girls, often after a few fraternity-like initiation rites. Then there was the fan factor. More people watched varsity soccer than club soccer. At big games there might be three hundred fans, including dozens of boys.

But the serious players had other factors to weigh. Some Thunder girls dreamed of college scholarships, of playing for a Division I traveling team and one day making the NCAA championships. They had no idea how few scholarships existed, how long a shot it was, but they did have some rough idea of the process. College scouts scoured the big club soccer tournaments, picking prospects from an already elite pool. High school soccer might be fun, but it probably wasn't going to help you win a college scholarship or, for that matter, even prepare you for college soccer.

Emiria, meanwhile, had a problem of team unity. Varsity teams demanded that girls practice or play games every school day. Eleven of the sixteen girls were eighth graders, and though many of them also wanted to play after-school sports, they weren't nearly as demanding as varsity soccer. How could Emiria have a double standard when over two thirds of the team would likely have no problem making most of the fall practices? If she didn't set a hard-and-fast rule, she risked not getting enough girls to make the trainings worthwhile. And so Emiria let the girls know in no uncertain terms. It was a question of authority and commitment, and the girls could tell from Emiria's words and steely expression how much it meant to her. Play varsity and miss Thunder practices and your playing time would suffer.

But Angela was going to take a chance. She relished the opportunity to make the varsity high school team as a freshman, to prove to herself that her dedication and commitment to soccer were reaping results. If that meant Emiria would give her less playing time, so be it. Things hadn't gone the way she'd hoped the last couple of years, and all summer long Angela had looked forward to high school as a fresh start. At first it had all sounded so simple and convenient. By transferring to Slater Middle School where her father taught, Angela could go straight from classes to her nearby ballet studio, then catch a ride home with her dad.

Years of study and rigorous training had put their stamp on her posture and face. Angela looked every bit the polished ballerina, and so perhaps it wasn't surprising that at Slater, when she ran cross-country, her teammates, including Sara Bei, dubbed her Princess Leia, after the pure, trustworthy, and decisive *Star Wars* archetype. It was more than her no-nonsense bobbed haircut and limpid blue eyes. Angela's emotions were as transparent as her fair Irish skin.

By the time Angela reached Slater as a seventh grader, she knew well enough to hide her love for ballet. The mocking had begun in elementary school, girls on her soccer team or kids at recess poking fun, flopping their hands about like a mock ballerina. What a joke, she thought. They just had no clue how difficult ballet was. You had to be constantly thinking about your steps, your timing, your style. By the seventh grade, Angela had been point for a year, suffering the calluses and aches that came with dancing on your toes. But Angela was also thirteen, and during her homework period at school she was so embarrassed she was a ballerina that she only told the other kids she was a "dancer."

Angela wanted to have friends who accepted her for who she was, but instead hid her love for ballet as if it were a contagious disease. By then she knew how most kids treated each other. Kids being nasty, cracking jokes about kids who were heavy or pimply, or just different. The meanness and immaturity depressed Angela. It was all so pointless and cold. She just wanted to protect herself.

Angela found a new identity: clunky, steel-toe tie-dyed boots, her dad's old blue running jacket, or occasionally fishnet stockings. She wasn't going to wear a brand, like the upscale Slater cliques that wore Tommy Hilfiger or Calvin Klein clothes as if they were school uniforms. Kids told her that her shoes were stupid, and her dad would sometimes just glare and say, "Oh well, you're trying to be like them." It wasn't long before Angela quit ballet, and though she sensed her parents were disappointed and her teachers told her she had so much more talent than she knew, the words didn't sink in. She had soccer to worry about, and making new friends.

At first it seemed Angela would have plenty of friends. "Oh, you're Mr. Walsh's daughter," the kids would chirp, asking her pointed questions about her celebrated teacher dad. They were kids who got better grades, and they had their own clique. Why not join in? Angela figured. One day after a class, Angela found herself following around a girl named Katie. Her father had talked about the girl often on the drive to school: Katie played sports and got good grades. But as Angela tagged behind Katie, the girl was joined by a circle of friends who began talking amongst themselves as if Angela didn't exist. She suddenly froze. Why was she trying to hang out with people who didn't accept her?

It didn't take long for Angela to find a new clique. They didn't play sports and they didn't like school much. But they definitely had a look.

Sometimes it was hard to tell the boys from the girls. "T" was renowned for wearing a dress to school one day, while another boy imitated Marilyn Manson, the satanic drag rocker, dying his long hair jet black and making up his face ash white. "V" was the perfect *Rocky Horror* movie groupie, wearing black lingerie and purple lipstick. Angela would meet the two or three dozen kids at break and lunch just outside the library, where the main subject of conversation invariably centered on the last screening of the *Rocky Horror Picture Show* or the weekend's parties. Drugs were also a popular topic. Pot, acid, whatever had been easy to get.

Though by the eighth grade Angela was a regular

member of Slater's so-called alternative crowd, she usually wasn't privy to those conversations. She chatted with her inner circle of a half dozen kids about everyday things. Sports or school were ignored, except for the teachers they hated. Angela understood. She was struggling with math. Her teacher wasn't very encouraging, and Angela had lost her focus. She'd learn something and the next day go blank.

Nothing was quite the same. Not Angela, not her friends, not her parents. Day after day, on the drive to and from school, her father would celebrate Sara Bei and the other Slater overachievers. But Angela wanted to be herself, not some Sara Bei knockoff, and definitely not "Mr. Walsh's daughter," a vehicle for some overachieving smarmy kids to get in tight with her father. Oh, sure, Angela might earn good grades (except for math) and run nearly as swiftly as Sara, but you'd never catch her hanging with such a squeaky clean crowd. Why couldn't her father see that she'd never be perfect?

The more she hung with the alternatives, the more her father's talks sounded like lectures, and the more charged the ride became. She knew he wanted to protect her, but why couldn't he also see that underneath all the makeup and posturing, some of these kids were really nice? Who else accepted her for who she was? Angela knew that they were lost, and she was trying her best to help them, and her parents just didn't seem to understand.

If only they knew how slippery it was, trying to find yourself as a teen. Angela felt she was caught in a whirlpool. Her quirky fashion and mixed-up friends were how she coped with smothering conformity. Her parents wanted her to be part of the Sara crowd, but it wasn't just the squeaky clean image, brand-name fashion, and perfect grades that turned off Angela. By the seventh grade, class lines stuck. Sara and many of the other girls her father idolized were far wealthier than Angela. Their dads didn't drive Diatsus, and those things made a difference.

And Angela knew better than most that everything changes for a girl in junior high, that appearances are deceiving. Seventh grade had been an empty, lonely year. She rarely talked to her parents and had only one good friend, who by the year's close was slipping away. The girl had quit playing sports, and ended up working at the Fairgrounds as a carny, a dead-end job if ever there was one. The last time Angela saw her, she was stoned. All Angela could think about was how weak her old friend had become, how she'd wasted her talents.

All around her, Angela saw girls in trouble. Like the trim girl who imagined she had the fattest stomach. Or the friend who was frighteningly skinny, and claimed she'd swallowed some kind of parasite that had eaten out her stomach. But why would she always nibble two bites of her lunch and announce she was full? Could she be anorexic or bulimic and have just put this story together as a cover? Though the girl was in honors classes, studied art, and played the guitar, all Angela could see was her overwhelming frailness and vulnerability.

Angela may have been part of the alternative crowd, but she was an observer who believed she had the strength to resist trouble. She never even asked her parents if she could go to a *Rocky Horror Picture Show* screening, and never went. She stood by the clouds of cigarette smoke and didn't inhale; she listened to the talk about drugs and didn't experiment. Day after day she heard of girls getting raped or pregnant. The sexually active girls amazed her. Thirteen- and fourteen-year-olds who didn't bother with boyfriends, who were passed around like leftovers and expressed amusement when they were called sluts.

Sex was a losing proposition. Angela's best friend in the alternative crowd, a boisterous, talented actress, got serious with her boyfriend, and was promptly deserted by her friends. Angela didn't feel that was right, and so she stood by her, becoming a close friend. At the close of eighth grade, they parted on good terms. But Angela's summer quickly glazed over into one endless Thunder workout, and she soon fell out of touch with her friend. Then one day she heard that the girl was spreading the word that she and Angela had fought, and that she hated Angela.

They hadn't fought, and Angela had no idea why she would concoct such a story. Maybe it was because she'd shared her intimate secrets, or maybe it was because Angela had grown so dedicated to soccer. Whatever the reason, Angela was heartbroken. She wanted to write about how people use you and throw you away. All she'd ever done was try to be considerate, and it had all been thrown back in her face.

As two of Thunder's strongest players, Arlene and Shannon could easily have made varsity. But after training for a few days with the Maria Carillo High School team, they decided to slog through a season of junior varsity and stay in good graces with Emiria. Were they missing out or making a grown-up choice? They weren't sure.

Phil's talented blond daughter, Erin, had no doubt about what she wanted to do. She made the Maria Carillo varsity, one of just two freshmen on the squad. "Freshy," the woman coach affectionately dubbed her. Erin adored her new team and coach, and didn't mind the initiation rituals one bit: being lashed to the goalposts one practice, and having to haul the water bottles and balls. Erin felt a tremendous security by being part of the team. She instantly had upperclasswomen as friends, even got a date to the homecoming dance. The coach was in her thirties and taught a leadership class. Gave them each a folder filled with inspirational quotes, and then asked them to write little assignments about their goals as a player and friend.

Erin didn't flinch when the coach made it clear that varsity players would have to attend every practice. She'd chosen high school over club soccer. Accepted that her playing time on Thunder would be drastically cut. The truth was, she was ready for a break from Emiria and her teammates.

High school was full of tough choices.

Arlene was excited about finally attending the same school as Shannon, but after following her friend around the school grounds the first day, Arlene faced up to the obvious. Close as the two girls were on Thunder, high school changed things. Shannon was extremely popular and hung out with a dozen very social girls. Arlene didn't know any of them, and wasn't sure she wanted to. The next day Arlene met up with Jenny the wispy runner, the other quiet girl on Thunder. Jenny's group was smaller, and welcomed Arlene in a way Shannon's crowd never would have. And Jenny could do something for her that her old friend couldn't. During the last couple of years, Arlene had taken to cussing and making sarcastic cracks around Shannon. But she found Jenny so genuinely nice and upbeat that when she was with her new friend, she'd clean up her act. Could Arlene, Thunder's foulmouthed slide tackler extraordinaire, really be tamed by the team's mouse?

Friendship and school weren't any easier to sort out for Thunder's younger stars. Kim feared the start of eighth grade almost more than Arlene's behind-the-back tackles. The moody girl had never been very confident in class, never been one to raise her hand or speak up. The teachers seemed so suspicious, always wondering if she was up to something, a feeling Kim could understand. Kim hadn't trusted people for a long time, hadn't believed it when she was praised on or off the field.

Kim had matured earlier than most of her classmates, and that fact left her out of sync with girlfriends just awakening to makeup and boys. And playing soccer all the time forced Kim to make hard choices about how she spent what little free time she enjoyed. Just that summer as she was training for Thunder, Kim had broken up with her best friend. How swiftly it could change. They'd shared a love of soccer for years, but the divorce of her friends' parents ended all of that. The girl started having trouble getting rides to practice and games, and soon quit sports altogether. Rising early to prepare her hair and makeup became her primary concerns. Kim grew bored with her boy talk and mean-spirited cracks, and finally phoned her up and told her they no longer had anything in common.

They were living opposite lives. Kim would go to practice, play games, do her homework. Her friend would go to the mall.

School was a piece of cake for Theresa, the often-injured player who acquired the nickname "First Aid." Confident and self-assured, Theresa excelled at whatever she put her mind to. Theresa won leading roles in drama, ran for school secretary the year before and won easily, all the while earning perfect grades. Theresa was the girl who just refused to stop raising her hand in class, the girl who corrected her teacher and got away with it, the girl who was smart without even trying. In school, Theresa was Thunder's Sara Bei, the girl you just knew was going places.

But Theresa's older sister Mary, seven years her senior, was wise enough to know how quickly all that could change. Theresa was, after all, just thirteen, beginning the eighth grade that fall at St. Eugene's, a highly regarded

Catholic school she'd attended since kindergarten. High school and its challenges were just around the corner.

The teen years weren't easy for Mary. Her parents simply didn't know that much about sports for girls. Mary's athletic experiences were nearly always individual endeavors, all too often pointing out her physical limitations. She was, for instance, too tall to be considered a serious ballerina. So when a saleslady said she'd be great at modeling, Mary decided to give it a try. They liked her height, her fine porcelain features; all she had to do was lose five pounds. She walked what seemed a ship's plank at the Santa Rosa mall, wearing slinky short skirts, creepy men at the runway's edge. Feeling she was missing out, Mary decided it would be fun to play volleyball, and asked her PE coach if she thought she'd be able to make the freshman team. The woman laughed. Suggested cheerleading. Mary did it for a couple of seasons, and as she had with modeling, began to wonder why.

College was a liberation. At the University of California at Davis, Mary broke with her past and went out for and made the crew team. She'd rise at 4:30 A.M., and row nearly three hours. No time to shower before class, sitting up in front in her spandex unitards and running shoes, her sweaty hair wrapped in a bandanna. Mary had so fully erased her cheerleading identity that threatened male professors assumed she was a dumb jock. But the rigor of rowing brought Mary close to a tight-knit group of hardworking young women, focused on sport and school. Mary and her tall, strong, and confident fellow rowers got nothing but respect from the men they met on campus. Though she rose long before dawn, Mary studied regularly till the wee hours of the morning. The hard physical work forced her to be disciplined. She wanted to be an attorney, like her father.

When Theresa's parents were debating whether they wanted her to play competitive soccer, it was Mary who pushed the decision forward, volunteering to drive her to practices and tournaments. To Mary it didn't matter that Theresa was perhaps the weakest athlete in a family of seven gifted kids, that her long-term prospects in soccer seemed slim. In soccer Mary saw the lifeboat of a strong group of friends who would be there for her sister when she needed them. Mary knew that Theresa's beauty would soon complicate her life: the attention from boys, the pressure to diet and date, the temptation of modeling.

She was going to do whatever she could to make sure Theresa didn't have to repeat her own mistakes.

The former tennis player sat and waited nervously on the field with the other girls. The coach was reading off the names. The list. The players who'd made varsity at Montgomery High.

Junior varsity will be fine, Kristin thought. I'll be happy with that.

She could think of no good reason to be confident. Kristin was not one of Thunder's top performers. Why, just a couple of years before, tennis had been her main sport.

One could easily argue that Kristin might not be as driven to make varsity as some girls. Her parents were well off, her father, Jeff, a partner in a prosperous insurance company, her elegant mother, Karen, free to raise her children and play tennis at a country club. Kristin seemed the epitome of the Barbie stereotype that had initially turned off Cassie from competitive soccer. Blond and extremely feminine, her hair never out of place, her clothes always fashionable, Kristin might have been a debutante. More than a few Thunder girls thought her house resembled a palace.

But Kristin was also shy, a girl who seldom got in the mix of things, a girl whose watery eyes were often cast down, occasionally bobbing up to seek approval. Her

mother noticed that even at Thunder get-togethers, Kristin
would often sit to the side and not participate. Whereas
Shannon might crack a sly joke and Angela might wear
one of her quirky thrift-store dresses, Kristin hugged routine. To her mother's mind, Kristin was talented, bright,
sensitive, and very much a follower. Could sport change
that, give her an edge?

"Angela Walsh . . . Kristin Young."

After a few seconds of shock, it began to sink in. She'd
made it! She and Angela had really done it!

Kristin quickly discovered that making varsity was a
big deal. Kids she barely knew would ask her if she'd
made the soccer team, assume she was on junior varsity,
and Kristin would proudly answer varsity. Her after-
school and social life became chock-full. On top of all the
practices and games, Kristin socialized with her teammates at big pregame pasta-feed get-togethers. Even the
initiation ritual was a kick. One day Kristin and Angela
had to wear their soccer shorts and shin guards to classes.

The Thunder mothers thought it remarkable that their
daughters were playing varsity as freshmen. Patty Walsh
was amazed at how dramatically the world of girls' sports
had changed in just one generation. Though she had been
the fastest kid in grade school, no one had ever encouraged her to play sports. Instead of going out for a varsity
sport in high school, Patty Walsh had become a
cheerleader.

Now her daughter was so athletic that she had to
make hard choices. Patty, like so many other parents, had
worried about the impending conflict between high school
varsity and team Thunder. By playing varsity, Angela was
certain to get less playing time on Thunder, and perhaps
anger Emiria. And there was a third possibility. What if
she made varsity and didn't play there either? What if
she ended up riding two benches?

Kristin's father was so concerned about that possibility

that he had a talk with his daughter. He had watched Kristin's confidence soar after making team Thunder and surviving a summer of gut-wrenching training sessions. Kristin seemed bubbly and shining, her mood almost always positive. But while Jeff Young was proud of Kristin making varsity, he told his daughter that he'd understand if it proved difficult. If things didn't work out, if she didn't get much playing time, they could talk to the coach and see if she could drop down to junior varsity.

But Emiria had trained them well. The girls of Thunder were making their own rules. Kristin, Angela, and three other freshmen started at Montgomery High, earning regular playing time, surprising themselves and their parents. And they, too, earned a nickname.

The Fabulous Five.

TEN

Soccer Dad

*i*t was painful for Brian to watch.

Three years of carefully placing the girls in defensive positions, and Emiria would just toss them out like spaghetti and see what stuck.

The first few times Brian dared speak, Emiria ignored him or muttered her disapproval. Brian knew by then what she was thinking. The girls just had to learn to play soccer. What difference did it make if the defense was disorganized if they were equally scattered on the rest of the field?

Emiria's technique was a purge. When you stay with what's comfortable, when you keep resorting to kick and run, individual limitations are masked. But trying to play intelligent soccer brought out each girl's weaknesses. Suddenly it was all too clear that lots of the girls had trouble passing the ball to feet, handling a trap, finding the open player.

But there came a time when even Brian, with all his patience, could hold back no longer. The opposing team was taking a free kick forty yards out, and a distracted Catherine looked as if she were taking a stroll at the beach, blocking Cassie's view instead of holding off the offense at the eighteen-yard line. A simple deflection and Cassie would be helpless. But as bad as it was, Brian didn't dare say anything at the time. He waited till after Emiria's grim halftime talk to speak to the coach.

"Emiria, is it OK to say something if I see something dangerous?" Brian carefully asked. "Like if they make a good pass, we're dead."

Emiria barely glanced his way, furrowing her brows. "Maybe if it's urgent," she spat. "Yeah, go ahead."

The begrudging reply was a breakthrough of sorts, the beginning of some dialogue between the old Fury coach and the new Thunder coach. Emiria slowly began asking Brian what the team needed to do defensively.

But the gradual building of trust between Brian and Emiria only highlighted the growing isolation of Thunder's other assistant parent coach. It was a struggle that Phil Molling could understand, the classic dilemma on every youth soccer team. Coaches see how awful the parents are, and parents see the tremendous power of the coach. And Phil was one of the few who had been on both sides of that tug-of-war. Just last season, Phil had been the Eclipse's assistant coach. On that team the head coach knew little of the game and often yielded to Phil's helpful suggestions. Phil had been considered Eclipse's technical genius, his input desired, his opinions respected.

But on Thunder, Phil was just a dad who had played soccer a quarter century ago at a small Ohio college. Phil knew the situation was radically different, that he was offering suggestions when they clearly weren't wanted. But still he plowed ahead, making recommendations on positions, on playing time, on tactics. He felt it was obvious what was wrong with Thunder. Emiria had a black-and-white view of the game. She was, after all, a forward, a goal scorer. That was what she knew, and Phil simply didn't believe forwards could coach. Goalies, sweepers, and midfielders understand soccer because they see the whole game unfold before them. But to Phil, a former defender himself, forwards don't understand what it takes for the ten people behind them to get the ball.

The summer tournaments had weighed on Emiria, the criticism, the pressure. She was physically and emotionally drained, struggling to be patient but wondering how much longer the parents would give her that liberty, wondering if the sheer weight of the losses would drown her efforts. Maybe her expectations were too high. The girls still seemed intimidated by opponents, easily rattled out of their game. Perhaps it was too much to expect fourteen-year-old girls to learn to play soccer in a few months.

Perhaps it was the fact that Thunder was about to play its first league game against a good team in Marin County, the team entering a new stage in its long season. Whatever the reason, just before the game Emiria decided it was time to show her other face. She'd been so tough and distant for so long, feeling that she had to set a disciplined tone with a new team and a questioning group of parents. She took her job seriously, perhaps too seriously. It wasn't easy, but that day she made a conscious choice to let go of some of her determination, to let the girls see her as a whole person.

At the pregame talk Emiria felt more lighthearted. League is going to be a new start for us, she encouraged the girls. Let's just go out and enjoy ourselves. Play simple. Talk to each other. Have fun. And she told the girls something new.

You are a great team.

The fear disappeared and a calm confidence spread.

The girls went out and played their best game ever: creative, possession soccer, talking to each other, moving, anticipating spaces. The control and speed amazed Emiria. She thought it beautiful, a beautiful game to watch. Arlene punched in a volley to make it 1–0, but Thunder could have easily netted several more, and not surprisingly, the goals began to come in bunches. Thunder began winning games, showing hints of its promise. The next three matches, the team notched thirteen goals and gave up none.

Minutes after the Marin game, a spectator ambled over as the girls pulled off their cleats. He told Emiria he'd been watching the game and was impressed with how she talked with the girls. "They obviously have a lot of respect for you, and they're a great team."

How fitting, thought Emiria. After all the losses and grumbling on the sidelines, a perfect stranger apparently thought they were doing something right. The man asked for a copy of Thunder's schedule so he could see the girls play again. Emiria was touched.

Somebody actually believed.

Brian stood next to the goalpost with Emiria, watching the scene unfold. If you could distill the challenge before the team into one series of plays, this might be it. Was Emiria nuts or a genius? Was she pushing them to new heights or risking everything to prove a point?

It's practice where a team first shapes its character, and Emiria was frustrated that afternoon at the lack of intensity. They were playing four-on-fours, in which the winner stays on and one team serves it to the other. Arlene served the ball to Kim, and the sturdy forward held it for a couple of seconds before Arlene promptly crumpled her from behind. Brian grimaced. Though Kim's knee injury in Minnesota had fortunately turned out to be only a slight tear, she was far from being totally healed.

Kim got up slowly and shook it off, firing a nasty glance at the redhead. She'd been pissed at Arlene for some time. Now that they were both forwards, they actually had to work together, and Arlene had been dribbling or favoring other players—anything but passing to Kim. A couple of minutes later, Kim got the ball again, and it was instant replay. Slide-tackled straight from behind. This time Kim was wincing, but sure enough, like a tagged boxer, she swayed to her feet. They could have been doing slapstick. As if on cue, the third time she got the ball, old red bowled her over.

Kim tried to get up and flopped back. She wasn't going to make the ten count. She rolled over onto her knees and slowly crawled off the field, the scrimmage continuing as if she weren't there. Arlene had knocked Kim out. She was done, unable to play.

Was this madness? Why didn't Emiria order Arlene to cool it? Wasn't this red-haired wolf simply going to hospitalize the whole team, slice them down one by one until she was the only one standing? But that day Kim and the team got the message. Arlene was a wilderness experience. Earn her respect, learn to defend yourself, hit her before she hits you, or suffer the consequences of the wild.

And so Kim learned to protect herself. Like so many of the girls, she'd been standing flat with Arlene straight behind her. Gradually she learned to turn a little sideways, holding the ball out slightly, her arms and elbows working like a running back smashing a forearm to the helmet, making it hard for Arlene to land a direct hit, and easier to scoot by if she swung and missed. And Kim did something else for team Thunder. She laid out some vicious tackles on Arlene herself. So did the normally gentle Naomi, who'd regularly been getting bumped off the ball. Catherine, too, lowered the boom of her broad shoulders. No longer would the team easily be surprised by bigger or more physical opponents. The moment of hesitation, the element of doubt that clouds so many girls' teams, was being wiped away. Gone were the days when the girls would hold up momentarily and cry, "Foul!" Arlene was teaching them that the only foul is when the referee blows his whistle.

Up top around goal, Arlene started to pass to Kim, and Kim returned the favor by holding the ball well, by passing it back or firing on goal. One by one the girls earned Arlene's respect. It was as if she had welcomed them into her club. And Emiria began shouting something else at Thunder practices.

"Way to hit Arlene!"

In drills or small side scrimmages, they kept tabs on goals or successful sequences of passes. Emiria divided them up into teams. Practice was competition.

Even the classic one-on-one against a defender and goalie became a team event, building camaraderie. The girls divided into two squads, cheering on their respective teammates. The defender would serve the ball from the goal line, striking it thirty-five yards to the sprinting forward.

The objectives were simple. Defenders needed to quickly close down the angle on the forward without over committing. Forwards had to make a clean trap and attack with speed.

But some defenders would come out too fast and skid by, beaten by an easy dribble. It was a question of balance, of sprinting, and easing down as the forward neared. Naomi and Shauna were naturals, blessed with speed and fast feet and the patience to wait for the forward to commit. The margin of error was slim. Kim taught them that hesitating didn't work. Give her too much space and a good angle and she'd crank a shot from outside.

Forwards learned the first trap was critical. Tentativeness in trapping or dribbling didn't fly. The drill taught initiative. Too many girls would slow as the defender neared, turn their back, shield the ball.

"Don't lose your momentum!" Emiria shouted. "Attack with speed!"

Emiria loved to focus drills in the penalty area for the simple reason that everything counted. Increase the intensity by introducing scoring. Four-on-four in the penalty area was a favorite. The other girls standing on the perimeter, ready to serve the ball in if it went out. Time not stopping for anything. No one on offense or defense. Win the ball and you can go for goal.

The drill taught so much. Passes had to be accurate, touches quick. Each team learning to transition quickly from offense to defense. And if ever there was a drill that taught the significance of winning a fifty-fifty ball, this was it. Lose a dribble or make a sloppy pass to a teammate going to goal, and the defender might score. The girls served the balls in on the perimeter, itching for their chance to play the winner. And all the while, the clock ticked and Emiria kept score.

Phil Molling considered it his duty as team manager to be the sounding board for the Thunder parents. It was a duty that he believed had nothing to do with his daughter or the fact that she, along with the other varsity girls, had been getting less playing time. Phil considered himself a man of principle, a liberal in a family of liberals. His mother had walked with Martin Luther King, and Phil prided himself on taking unpopular positions. At the very same time he was Thunder's team manager, Phil was under attack for the coaching of his younger daughter's recreational team. Phil knew he was driving the parents and some of the kids nuts. He'd insisted on taking eighteen players, the maximum allowable, wanting to give more kids a chance to participate. Parents and kids rose up in protest. But the opposition only made Phil stick even more stubbornly to his position at a team meeting. He didn't care if half the team hated him. "We each have our own agendas. Here's my agenda," he said bluntly, explaining his crusade. "That's just the way it is. It's not going to change."

On Thunder, Phil was in the opposite position. Here he saw himself as trying to bring people together, to help the parents and Emiria reach some understanding. He'd seen what had happened on Eclipse, parents talking behind the coach's back, creating opposing groups and splintering whatever unity there might have been. That was why he wanted to be fair. He only wrote down a complaint he heard twice, and if his daughter told him something, it didn't count. But even with that higher standard, he soon had a laundry list—complaints about unfair playing time, harsh language, and the supposed denigrating of the kids. Phil had to do something before it was too late.

"What's wrong with this team?"

It was Luke Oberkirch on the phone to Kristin's dad, Jeff Young, wanting to know what all the controversy was about. By now the grumbling on the Thunder sidelines had spread like a virus. But while it seemed mysterious to Luke, Jeff had a pretty good idea how the incubation process had begun. Twice Phil had come up to Jeff and tried to get him to gripe about the team.

"I think he's got it in for Emiria."

"Thanks," Luke said. "What are you hearing?"

Jeff told him about the parents who had begun to openly say that the girls don't play well for Emiria. Phil's wife, Lou Ann, was complaining to the other mothers that her daughter didn't get to play, that it wasn't fair. "It's

ruining the whole program," Jeff warned. "You really
need to talk to Phil, Luke. You're the only one he'll listen to."

A meeting was already in the works. "That's why I
wanted to talk to you," Luke explained. "He's been bad-
gering Emiria, saying the parents are fed up."

"That's not true," Jeff insisted. "If he's saying he has
a majority, that's not true."

Phil walked into the meeting at Luke's cramped Sonoma State office. Brian had staked out the sagging old
couch, Luke leaned back at his desk, and Emiria sat in the
middle. Phil grabbed the seat near the door, and suddenly
wondered if he'd been set up.

"What's the point of this meeting, Phil?" Luke asked.

Phil hauled out his handwritten list of nine or ten
issues. The first was that Emiria was being too hard
on the girls, getting too personal, denigrating the kids.
In Phil's mind this was the least offensive of all the
complaints, the least likely to anger Emiria. He wanted
to see how the wind was blowing before he got too
deep.

"Who said that?" Luke demanded to know.

"They don't want to be named."

"Phil, don't play this game with me," Luke said angrily. Emiria had seen this transformation before. The
coach with the cool of a lifeguard could sting. "When you
come here and say something as serious as that, you better have names."

Phil reluctantly named two Thunder mothers and then
realized he'd grossly miscalculated, stumbled into a land
mine of loyalty. Luke was going to be loyal to Emiria,
because without it, Phil didn't see how she could function.
Phil hadn't thought about that before he called the meeting. If he had, he wouldn't have said a word.

"So basically," Luke said, undercutting Phil, "three

sets of parents out of sixteen are wondering what's going on, and the rest of them are fine."

Brian swung forward on the sagging couch, incredulous. He thought this was all about antsy parents obsessed with the win column and not the girls' best interests. "This is a long-term project we're working on," he explained to Phil. "We're not going to get results in two months. They haven't even been taught basic skills. I think they're making remarkable progress."

Emiria was blunt. She hadn't appreciated Phil trying to coach her team in front of the players. She wasn't that kind of person. She didn't agree with Phil's ideas on training, motivation, substitution, or anything else for that matter, and she wasn't about to be lectured now.

"Phil, you're asking me questions about things that have nothing to do with you whatsoever," she said, her face red with anger. "These are my decisions. My call. The reason why I've taken charge is because that's what this team needs. One person to look to. Not two or three. One person that will set everything for them. Anytime there's a problem, the girls come to me."

The leathery-skinned college coach called time. "What's going on here, Phil, is you don't agree with Emiria," interrupted Luke, fixing his eyes on the man by the door. "That's the whole deal."

Luke felt in an awkward position. He was friends with Phil and had run clinics for his under-twelve teams in the past. Phil did know more about the game than most parents. But so did Brian, and somewhere along the way Brian had found the faith to turn his daughter over to Emiria. That obviously hadn't happened with Phil. He had disagreed with Emiria's view of the game and tried to change her, and now it had erupted into a full-blown personality clash.

Luke stopped Phil before he could reach the second complaint on his list. "Phil, we've got a situation here where we've got three assistant coaches: me, Brian, and you. You've got too many roles on this team. You're a parent first, a team manager second, and a parent assistant coach third. That's way too much input. I think you've got to get rid of one or two of them."

ELEVEN

Trust

*L*ose to Sebastopol?

Thunder stuck to its usual script in the late September tournament. Exciting, possession soccer in the early games, lots of good talk between the girls, then panic in the later rounds. But this was a new low. How could they tank a 0–4 game to Sebastopol?

There were lots of reasons why it was embarrassing to get trounced by the Sebastopol Strikers. First was the fact that the old Eclipse coach had taken his daughter to the team, along with a grudge. He wasn't the coach of the Strikers, but you couldn't miss him on the sidelines. And the success of his new team seemed to prove a point.

The Strikers played classic long ball. They were big and fast and aggressive. Thunder looked scared. Defenders just couldn't handle the booming crosses. Naomi, Kristin, and Theresa seemed unsure of when to pass or clear, and Cassie couldn't reach a couple of high shots that flew into the net.

October didn't get any better for Thunder. Sebastopol trounced them again 2–0 at Belluzzo in a league game. Then Thunder fell by a goal to the Marin team they had mastered a month before. It was worse than being inconsistent. Thunder seemed to be going in reverse.

Phil Molling was out of the country on business for a few weeks. But before he'd gone, he'd questioned whether Emiria's tactics would work. "I guess you've resigned yourself to a mediocre season."

Maybe he was right.

Kim had been hoping for a new coach for a long time.

Some coaching dads would have favored their kids, but Kim thought her dad was just the opposite. On the Fury, he didn't start her for several games, even though she was clearly a star. Never praised her in practice or games. Went extra hard on her. Finally she'd blow up. What did he expect?

Brian had a standard reply. "You have to treat me like a coach and not your dad."

Kim had her own stock answer. "Then treat me like a player and not your daughter!"

Brian hadn't known what to do about his daughter. When he coached Kim on Fury, she'd get so worked up for a tournament that she could take days to calm down. The smallest comment could set her off. "What business is it of yours!" she'd yell. "I'm doing the damn homework!" The Halloran family had a name for the looks Kim dished like knives: *The death stare.*

To Brian, Kim approached games like a soldier about to hit the beach. And if things didn't go well, she was likely to implode. Players on other teams often saw she could be easily antagonized, and keyed on her. Kim's composure would crack, her mind stuck in the personal fight. She'd dribble when she should pass, or just uncharacteristically kick the ball wildly. Everyone knew when she was getting down on herself. She'd literally hang her head, not a great idea for the shortest player on the field.

But Kim saw her predicament differently. Her father's incessant twenty-four-hour home coaching routine drove her crazy. Italian league, Mexican league, whatever soccer was on cable, the Halloran family watched. When nothing was on, there were tapes to study. No one else on the team has to go through this, Kim fumed. Why me?

Maybe Brian couldn't see the pressure building. Couldn't see that Catherine stopped all the goals and Kim had to score all the goals. That if his daughter didn't have a great game, they'd lose. That if she cracked a shot and rattled the bar, that might be the only chance they had to win.

"You really should run today."

Kim didn't want to hear it anymore. She knew she should be running. She knew she was slow. But she wasn't stupid. How was running going to make her any faster? She was born slow—and short. It was fate.

All of her father's talk about soccer, constantly praising some talented local player or someone they watched on TV, it all seemed a comparison to Kim, an impossible comparison. The more enthusiastic her dad became, the more Kim fumed. Even her choice of idol reflected her struggle and her self-image. The phenomenal Mia Hamm was too speedy and perfect for Kim's taste. She preferred a less glamorous U.S. National Team member: Tiffany Milbert, a short, pugnacious blond. Kim admired how Milbert didn't get a lot of publicity, yet played her heart out.

But once Kim started playing for Emiria, things began to change. She was happy that people would no longer think she was being favored by her dad. Happy to finally be able to prove her ability to a new coach. And she decided that her tussles with her dad couldn't go on anymore. She was ready to move on. She was thirteen. Older, wiser. When he'd cajole her to watch a game on cable, she'd say no or just calmly go to her room and shut the door.

Dad wasn't her coach anymore.

"You're going to have to trust me," Emiria calmly told the girls at Belluzzo, the sun dropping behind the eucalyptus trees, darkness near. She knew the losing was taking its toll, that some of the girls were beginning to wonder if all this passing made sense.

Even the girls who usually fidgeted sat still. "When I tell you something, it's because I know what I'm talking about. I've been there," Emiria said, not sure what she was going to say next, yet confident the time was right. "I've been through what you're going through. If you're having doubts, having pains, having fears, it's all normal, and I understand it. You have to believe that I'm here to help you. You have to believe in the system and believe in me. And if I say something, it's what needs to be done. You're going to have to learn to trust me and have faith in me.

"I will take you to the next level."

Until that day, Kim hadn't been sure about Emiria. Wondered why she kept letting Arlene hack her. Worried about the losing. But for some reason she and several other girls totally believed Emiria. They'd heard the grousing of the parents and even some of their fellow players. But something in Emiria's self-assured expression convinced them. They were going to give her a chance.

Emiria halted the scrimmage. The mistakes weren't new. Plays like this had been losing them games. A weak back pass to the sweeper begging to be intercepted; dumping the ball off to a teammate with two or three girls on; clearing the ball up the clogged middle when the wings were open.

"What's the better option here?"

Theresa, Shannon, or Kim volunteered answers, and then the team played the familiar game of human chess. But the game had gotten more advanced. Now they'd study not just the first pass but the second or third.

"Shannon, what a great idea!"

So what if Shannon's pass had been intercepted or run out of bounds? Sometimes the lesson was about the pass they didn't anticipate. Shannon wasn't the problem. She'd imagined the space; knifed it between two defenders; lobbed a deft one-touch through ball over the top; or sensed it was time to switch play out of a congested area, and slipped it back to a fullback who punched it up the opposite flank. Too often, though, her teammates were caught flat-footed. Hadn't anticipated the same possibility. And that half-second delay squandered a great opportunity.

Emiria was unrelenting in exposing their weaknesses. Except for Shannon, the team was still consistently getting beaten in the air. Against boom-ball teams this meant certain defeat. So they practiced head balls until their foreheads were sore. Catherine and Naomi learned to target Shannon on goal kicks, so she could flick the ball on to a teammate.

Corner kicks were another disaster. A corner kick is a gift. A free kick taken from the corner flag, a set piece won when the defense is the last to touch the ball before it goes over its goal line. But often Thunder's kicks sailed harmlessly out of bounds behind the goal. Fell far short of the near post. Or lofted easily into the goalie's arms.

Emiria framed the goal with players. Someone in the keeper's face and on the far post. A couple of girls making runs to the near post to flick the ball on. And finally, a few players near and outside the box, ready to pick up a loose ball. The practice paid off. In one game, three of Thunder's four goals came on corner kicks.

Behind every practice and every game was Emiria's stubborn belief. She wasn't teaching them anything magical or new. These were all basic principles of soccer: quick touches, move the ball, create space. What was different was Emiria's will. She wouldn't permit anything to get between simple soccer and the girls.

Opponents, for instance. Emiria seldom even mentioned them. If an opposing team had a speedy forward or was strong in the air, she generally kept it to herself. This stubborn refusal to adapt to another team's skills drove some parents nuts. Unlike Luke, Emiria resisted making adjustments on the field. She knew it might hurt them in the short term, that a fast player might exploit a mismatch. But this was a larger test of wills. She had to force other teams to conform to their style, and that could only happen if the girls believed. And why should the girls believe if the coach didn't trust they could survive on their own?

Make the other team adjust. Possess the ball and make them realize that boom ball just won't work. Dominate the first few minutes of a game, and a kind of mass psychology would take hold. Deft passing had a mesmerizing quality. The weaker team would inevitably try to imitate the stronger team. And the stronger team, playing the game it understood, would often win. Thunder knew it worked. Every time they won, Emiria would gather them in, look up from her diagram-filled marker board, and ask the same question.

"What worked well?"

"We played our game."

But standing between Thunder and its game lay a few obstacles. Like the normal life and pressures of thirteen-

and fourteen-year-old girls. School, for example. Or getting more than eight girls to make practice regularly.

Most of the girls were starting the eighth grade. But Jessica faced another challenge. Last year the metal-mouthed blond had done home schooling, and she was anxious about being in a classroom again. But it didn't take her long to discover she loved going to Rincon Valley Christian. At the small, close-knit school, she warmed to being around people, to suddenly being involved socially. The girls were like sisters. And while most of her friends played basketball and volleyball, her obsession was accepted. Her history teacher called her the soccer queen. Her friends, soccer chick.

Class was fine. Jessica loved to raise her hand, excelled in math. Later she'd get a physical, and the nurse would ask, "Do you ever get depressed? Do you have friends who smoke? Would you ever get in a car with a friend who had been drinking?"

Jessica popped off a series of no's to the warning-sign questions. The nurse was impressed, especially when Jessica told her about all the good things that seemed to be going on in her life: her passion for her studies and sport, her new love of the social side of school. "It looks like you're pretty confident," the nurse told her. "It's good that you're playing sports."

But if Jessica seemed to be sailing along, it wasn't just because she had the benefit of a close-knit school. The gap between eighth and ninth grade could be huge. Naomi attended the same school, and just like Jessica, had gotten straight A's. But this year was different.

The even-tempered Naomi enjoyed many of the same advantages Jessica did. Starting on the school's varsity soccer team won Naomi a certain respect. Juniors and seniors on the boys' team talked to Naomi, admiring her play. And she valued the friends she made on the school team. But as the season progressed, Naomi was torn.

She'd juggle her school team games and Thunder practices. Straggle home at 6:30 P.M. each school night, sometimes later if the car pool dropped her off last. Take a shower, get some dinner, and then start her homework about 8:00 P.M. Her vibrant smile, even her great posture, began to slump.

Naomi was a straight-A student, but she wasn't the fastest reader. Twice a week she'd study till midnight, and she rarely was in bed before eleven. Often she got less than seven hours of sleep. Weekends weren't much better. There were nearly always games and practices for Thunder. Two weeks straight without a single day off was pretty common. The grind began to wear on Naomi. She'd make one of her dazzling runs in a game and wouldn't quite recover, feel her legs turn to jelly. Forwards would outsprint her, knock her off the ball. Everyone could see she was beat.

Naomi's mother, Sandy, a disarmingly gentle woman with understated strength, wasn't the least bit surprised when Emiria phoned. She knew her daughter's schedule was grueling and didn't like it one bit. But she was trapped. Her daughter wanted to be on two soccer teams and earn good grades. She'd already given up on social time, friends. What else could go?

"I'm just concerned because I don't think this is normal," Emiria worried. "A girl Naomi's age should have endless energy, and I'm just concerned that there's more to it than she's just tired."

Then at a Thunder potluck dinner, Brian and Emiria cornered Naomi's dad. "You need to take Naomi to the doctor. She's not her normal self."

By now Naomi was worried. Maybe she had mononucleosis.

The doctor put Naomi through a battery of tests. Took blood and urine samples. Tested her thyroid, checked her for mono. "There's absolutely nothing wrong with you."

The doctor shook his head before a relieved Naomi and Sandy. "Your coach just needs to give you a break."

Sandy could have given that diagnosis in her sleep. She didn't agree that a girl of thirteen or fourteen should have boundless energy. She was a woman; she could remember. And to refresh her memory, just a couple of years before, her older daughter had dragged through the same phase. For her it had been the seventh grade. Naomi was becoming a young woman at the same time she was training like a marine and burning the midnight oil studying. Was it any surprise she was exhausted?

The tall and popular Catherine had a different dilemma. That spring when she'd tried out for Thunder, she'd been pissed about having to skip a lot of school track and basketball practice for the team. In the summer she'd lodged a silent protest. She was the only girl to take a two-week break from the team, staying with relatives in Minnesota after competing in the USA Cup with Kim. Catherine missed going to the mall, seeing movies, having parties. Hey, soccer wasn't her life.

Little Trinity knew all about Catherine's soccer fatigue, because she and Catherine were great friends and suffered the same affliction. Back when they played on the Fury, two months of the season they didn't even listen to Brian. Constantly bad-mouthed him. Sometimes the rest of the team caught the bug. Just fooled around, stopped doing drills. Brian would steam. Yell. Walk away. "You've got to pick it up on your own!"

The attitude didn't change with Thunder. That fall Catherine seldom made Thunder practice, and Trinity heard every excuse. "I've got volleyball . . . basketball . . . I don't have a ride . . . my Mom's gotta . . ."

When Catherine did make practice, Trinity sensed she lacked a certain commitment. Her head was somewhere

else. "Oh my gosh, did you see that guy at the mall? . . .
I'm going out with this guy, he's so fine."

Not that the mischievous and giggly Trinity was im-
mune to boy talk. "Catherine, Trinity!" Emiria yelled. "Do
you want to be here right now?"

But there was something else going on besides boys
and school sports. Catherine was angry. "Why is Naomi
playing sweeper?" she'd ask Trinity. "I can do it. I've
played it way longer than her."

Why did Catherine covet the sweeper spot? It wasn't
just that she knew her speed and strength gave her an
advantage. Catherine wanted something on Thunder that
Brian had handed to her on a silver platter. She confided
in Trinity that she liked the other girls depending on her,
liked being the last girl who could get her foot on the ball.

The one they could trust.

TWELVE

Sidelines

*i*t happened one day at Belluzzo.

Emiria gathered the girls in at midfield for her halftime talk. "I expect you to be a leader out there, Shannon," she said, slicing her hand toward the girl, a mannerism she'd acquired from Luke. "You have vision. Thunder needs you to control the midfield. I need you to step up."

But Brian could only see fear in Shannon's blank face, her doe eyes wide enough to catch the looks of her curious teammates. There was nothing new about what Emiria was telling Shannon. She'd been saying as much to her for several weeks. The difference was that Emiria was telling Shannon what she expected from her in front of her teammates. In the middle of a league game.

It was a big thing, an honor really for Emiria to single out a player in front of the girls. But Shannon had her doubts. Sure, she wanted to be a leader, but what if she fell short and disappointed Emiria? Or let her team-mates down?

Emiria wanted perfection, and Shannon knew she couldn't deliver it. So she hatched her own secret method of handling the spotlight. Created a personal safety net. She'd hold back a little, dump off a back pass when she might have tried a riskier through ball. What else could she do? She didn't want her coach mad.

Shannon had reached the point as a player where she feared failure. Everything seemed to be riding on her performance. The team, her identity, her future. Soccer was the most important thing in Shannon's life. The more she thought about it (and she thought about it a lot lately), she'd dropped everything for soccer. Basketball, volleyball, softball, time with her friends, her family. She missed every one of them.

Shannon admired Emiria's work ethic, the way she pushed her to become a better player. Liked everything about her except for the yelling. The "Don'ts." The Don't do a back pass. The Don't dribble. But even on the hardest days, the days the yelling reverberated in her ears, Shannon knew Emiria was offering her something no coach had ever given her before. The challenge to be the best player on the field, the chance to rise above her friends. And as the second half began, the girls called out her name, cheering her tackles and passes.

Shannon was one of the few girls who dared dream of playing on the U.S. Women's National Team or the premiere University of North Carolina squad. Thunder was her stepping-stone. Her chance to prove what she was made out of.

But while Shannon was struggling with Emiria's pressure to be the best, unsure of whether she wanted to be the brightest star, other girls on Thunder just wanted a chance to be a part of the team. To contribute. Many of them had excelled in individual sports. Parents and friends sometimes wondered whether they might have been better off sticking to their solitary pursuits. Three girls in particular reflected the pull of team play, a force that at times seemed as elemental as the tides. They weren't stars. Their parents' concerns were perfectly natural. Couldn't standing on the sideline cancel out whatever positive effect they might gain from the team? What would all that self-doubt do to a girl's self-confidence?

Jenny Drady didn't look like a soccer player. Paper-thin with perfect posture and long, lean legs, she looked exactly like what she was, a gifted runner. Muscle, she lacked, but she moved with an ease that spoke of grace and speed. By the sixth grade it was clear the shy, fine-haired girl was born to run. She competed in the national cross-country championships that year, and by the seventh grade started thinking about college track. Jenny had tremendous endurance and cruised faster than most girls could sprint.

She enjoyed many team sports, but by junior high her world had narrowed to soccer and running. The two began to conflict. Her parents wanted to support her, but at times they were frustrated. Jenny had a gift, and they couldn't help but wonder whether she was wasting it. Their daughter was ranked in the top two hundred distance runners in the nation. If she'd quit soccer and focus on running, she might easily win a track scholarship to a Division I university.

But by the eighth grade, Jenny had discovered how totally different the two sports were. She still enjoyed running, but soccer offered her something she hadn't found in the solitary joys of long-distance running. After Jenny made team Thunder, her passion for the team grew. She loved how they shared everything, how they were one heart. It didn't matter to Jenny so much that they won or lost. What counted was how they shared the experience.

That fall Jenny diligently attended all the Thunder practices, rarely making cross-country practices or weekly meets. Still, her raw talent wouldn't be denied. Though she only trained three weeks for the nationals in Oregon, amazingly, Jenny finished thirty-second in the country.

Yet her continuing success as a runner didn't sway her. She loved soccer. Emiria was the first coach she'd ever had who seemed to know what she was talking about, how to teach them and make them better players. The losing didn't matter to Jenny. She could see the team growing in every practice. Jenny reveled in the intensity of the drills, the way they'd always be moving, always be calling out each other's names.

But Jenny couldn't change the facts of nature. Her speed was better suited to a track. Only when she broke loose on the wing, taking the ball to the corner, could Jenny stretch out her legs. All too often, though, she got tangled up in her limbs. Jenny had trouble mastering trapping and passing. The ball seemed unfriendly when it came her way, bouncing awkwardly. Taking the ball from Jenny wasn't hard. The girl who ran with the wind sometimes seemed to have the same mass as a summer breeze.

Add these facts to Emiria's view of soccer and Jenny was in a pickle. If possession soccer was the game, where did a girl fit in whose main talent was dashing down the line? Could Jenny help her teammates? Or was she destined to be a sideline soul mate whose confidence would surely wind down with her playing time? Had she thrown away a chance to be one of the nation's best distance runners only to be a substitute on an average soccer team?

Thunder's princess was eight when she started playing soccer. It wasn't love at first sight for Kristin Young. The first year wasn't bad, but the next season she started grouching. Karen and Jeff Young shook their heads at one another, wondered if they were doing the right thing, and signed up their reluctant daughter anyway. If she didn't want to play, they'd only be out thirty-five dollars. And sure enough, once Kristin saw her friends, she changed her mind. She liked being part of the team.

But tennis was Kristin's first love. Three times a week she rose at about 5:30 A.M. for lessons from the pro at her family's club. Tennis ran in the family. Kristin's mother and her younger sister Ashley were both fine players. It wasn't long before the family began ferrying Kristin to weekend tournaments, driving her as far as Sacramento for competitions.

But by the age of twelve, the predawn routine was growing old. Kristin and other girls complained about the pro. He'd buy them doughnuts and make them hot chocolate and then tease them that they were too fat to eat the treats. And there was something else going on in the Young family. Ashley was the more gifted tennis player. She didn't like to lose. Had the killer instinct that Kristin lacked. Two years separated the girls, but the gap between them on the court quickly narrowed. The younger sister started beating her older sister regularly.

The Youngs worried. How could they stop the sibling rivalry from turning into a disaster? What would this do to Kristin's confidence? But before they could give much thought to intervening, Kristin solved her own problem. Told her parents that tennis was getting old. That she'd soured on the individuality of the game. That she'd rather get a chance to make friends with some girls. Know them socially apart from sport. In short, she wanted to play more soccer.

Some parents might have been furious after spending thousands of dollars on private tennis lessons. But after mulling it over, the Youngs thought it the right move. They'd never seen sport as an end. Kristin had decided to graduate out of tennis on her own. That in itself was proof that all the lessons hadn't been for naught.

There was one little problem. Kristin's ambitions aside, she had played mostly recreational and Class III soccer, and even at that level, she'd had her share of failure. Nerves and a flu right at tryouts had helped get her cut from a team when she was just eleven. Kristin was devastated, heartbroken about not being able to play anymore with her friends. But she soon pulled herself together, confiding in her dad that soccer meant the world to her. He signed her up for Luke's summer camps, and she worked diligently on her skills and conditioning.

Kristin would sometimes joke to her mother that her dad should have been a coach. But Jeff Young recognized he didn't know enough about soccer to help his daughter with the technical aspects of the game. He saw himself as a motivator. He'd reassure Kristin about how strong a player she'd become in the last few years. Try to focus her before a game. Inspire her to play as hard as she could, have fun, and do her best.

Jeff Young might seem the last dad you'd expect to encourage his daughter in sports. Jeff played his generation's manly sports—blew out his knee on the gridiron, and then limped along in baseball. In high school, Jeff had watched guys kicking a ball behind the gym and thought it a stupid game. Girls couldn't play soccer at his school, but Jeff didn't think much of the ones who hit a softball or spiked a volleyball. Jeff preferred cheerleaders. They were the girls you invited to the dance.

But now, nearing his forties, Jeff Young looked forward to his daughter's soccer games. In twenty years he'd witnessed a revolution. A macho child of the seventies, he was watching his daughter play the football of the nineties, and loving every bit of it. Kristin warmed to playing a team sport, and the truth was, her father couldn't imagine a better place for his daughter to spend her afternoons. The discipline of soccer had focused her on school. Her grades were excellent. And the once shy girl seemed to be slowly coming out of her shell. One night Jeff listened while Kristin and a friend practiced an oral report they had to deliver before the class in Spanish. In the past, Kristin would have fretted about the prospect. But she wasn't nervous anymore.

Kristin Young had made the varsity as a freshman. She was friends with a baseball player who admired her athletic prowess. Twenty years ago Jeff Young had been that baseball player. But now his daughter had a choice. She didn't have to squander her talents or time on doing what boys expected. The cheerleaders her father had once admired were the past. Kristin could be a kick-ass soccer player, feminine and smart. Boys didn't have any choice in the matter, and the smart ones stood on the sidelines and cheered.

Angela, too, had left behind individual pursuits to dedicate herself to soccer. But there were times when she wondered if she'd made the right choice. How far might she have gone in ballet? What about track? Though Angela wasn't a Jenny Drady or a Sara Bei, she was a gifted runner, blessed with speed and endurance. She wondered how good she'd be today if only she'd kept training. There were times when Angela mourned the simpler days, when she was ten or eleven and dance and sport were simply fun.

But Angela was enormously proud of playing varsity at Montgomery as a freshman. And though she struggled with Emiria's harshness, she knew that she'd never have made the team without her coach's strict training and deep understanding of the game. Making varsity had its pluses. Angela was one of the Fabulous Five freshmen, and most of the upperclasswomen on the team would say hi to her at school. But soccer wasn't a miracle cure for the trials of adolescence. The social side of school wasn't easy for Angela. Kristin invited her to parties, but Angela never felt comfortable enough to go. Kristin's friends came from upper-class families and seemed to talk around Angela rather than to her. Not quite accepting of her non-brand-name approach to fashion. Or the quirky crowd she hung out with at school.

Then there was the reality of competitive high school athletics, the Darwinian nature of sport. On the field, the more Angela and Kristin played, the less time some of the seniors got. Parents bitched. Sometimes during games. Seniors too. Lots of people wanted the Fabulous Five to Flub.

That was the other side of playing on a team.

A team was like a family or a town. Part of the joy and pain of the team was that the smallest break in faith could nudge the clan from harmony to conflict. Throw sixteen teenage girls into the mix, add nearly thirty well-meaning parents, and you had nearly fifty reasons to pull apart. Mutinies were common on youth teams. The reasons might be as varied as the game. Every parent and child had unique expectations. And if the team was losing, the coach was vulnerable.

All it took was one family to start the chain of events. An evening phone call to a friend.

Michelle Smith was a good place to start. She had become friendly with the Mollings. They had all grown up on the East Coast. Sat together at church. Shannon and Erin were friends, veterans of the old Eclipse.

One night Lou Ann Molling broached the $64 million question. How did Michelle and Shannon feel about Emiria? It was a difficult call, and they spoke for nearly an hour. Michelle sympathized with the Mollings, and knew it must be hard for them to watch their daughter's playing time dwindle. But the steady brunette wasn't going to

change her mind. Michelle told Lou Ann she stood behind
Emiria, felt she had read Shannon well and knew what it
would take to motivate her. But the next day at school,
Shannon got the impression from Erin that their mothers
felt the same way about Emiria. After school, Michelle
told her daughter that the Mollings were mistaken.

"Shannon, that's a misunderstanding. Lou Ann has
some problems with Emiria. I don't have those problems."

But while Michelle held her ground, the trouncing by
Sebastopol had opened a wound. They were losing, after
all, and over the past several weeks, Natalie's dad, Jerry,
had found himself on the sideline in his sandals, listening
to Phil. And why not? Phil had played college soccer and
seemed to know a lot about the game. Maybe Phil had a
point; maybe he was right about Emiria wasting some of
the faster players. Now that he mentioned it, it did seem
kind of odd that Kim played the whole game. Erin was
a talented, strong player, quicker than Kim. Why wasn't
she getting more time? Jerry listened as his friend recounted the helpful suggestions he'd offered to Emiria
and the testy rebukes he'd gotten: "I'm the coach." And
Phil was right that Brian appeared to have concluded that
the only way to get along with Emiria was to agree. The
way Jerry saw it, Emiria wasn't going to listen to
anybody.

Finally one day, Phil gave Jerry a call at home. He
talked about all the money they were spending on the
team, the embarrassing losses, even the big, toothy grin
the old coach of the Eclipse had worn when they'd been
trounced by Sebastopol. When he asked Jerry if he was
frustrated, Jerry had to admit that he was. After the call,
Jerry had a chat with Jessica's dad, Steve, who also knew
a lot about soccer, having coached and refereed for years.
The Marshalls had their own concerns. Jessica hadn't been
accustomed to Emiria's swearing, and her mom and Naomi's mom had a talk with Emiria about toning it down.

The Marshalls, like many of the Fury families, still felt a certain loyalty to Brian, and not only because of his success. Brian had been a great motivator, a wonderful father figure for their daughters.

But Steve helped put things in perspective for his friend. He agreed that Thunder's ups and downs had been frustrating, and Emiria seemed to be experimenting a little bit, perhaps too much. But he added that despite the harshness of the new regime, the girls appeared to love the new coach, a fact that Jerry hadn't missed.

"Let me talk to Natalie," Jerry finally told Phil. His logic was simple. It didn't matter what he saw or felt. During the summer, Natalie had been stuck in a cast for two months waiting for her broken foot to mend, sweating out another month to build back the muscle on her withered leg. Back with a vengeance, she was one of the few players Emiria could count on to fire up her teammates and battle in the midfield.

What right did Jerry have to decide what was right for his daughter? And so one evening while they were talking, Jerry asked Natalie what she thought of Emiria as a coach. She flashed one of her trademark chipmunk smiles. "She's great, she's really good, and she's helping us."

That did it for Jerry. I'm not going to try to get her out of here, he thought. My daughter likes Emiria, so I like her.

Lou Ann Molling meanwhile was just struggling to help her daughter. Erin was her oldest child, the first to hit the treacherous teen years, and every day was an emotional whirlwind.

Erin loved her high school team, and as the weeks went by that fall, it was clear that she wasn't going to bother making a single Thunder practice. The consequences were severe. No practices meant no starting on Thunder.

Standing on the sidelines was a troublesome place for a girl like Erin. She refereed games when she had the time, and so she believed coaches and players should respect the ref. Whiling away the minutes as a Thunder substitute, she got plenty of time to scrutinize her coaches during games. Emiria had ordered the girls to be silent. No talking to the refs or opposing players. Wasn't this hypocritical? Emiria, and Brian especially, clearly talked back to the refs. Erin just couldn't let this violation go. When Emiria would blast the ref, Erin would come to the ref's defense. "He's doing the best he can."

Same with the ban on talking to opponents. Erin didn't care that Emiria had strictly forbidden chitchat with other teams before games. When they played the younger Santa Rosa girls' team, as her teammates were pulling their cleats on, Erin strode over to the other side of the field and said hello to her friends, openly defying her coach and teammates.

Erin couldn't help but be a lot like her father. When your dad openly questions your coach from day one, who are you supposed to support? And the truth was that Phil respected what he saw as his daughter's independence. Erin's mother, too, supported her daughter's small protests against her coach. Emiria didn't seem to grasp that friendship and fairness mattered to a fourteen-year-old girl.

Everything seemed backward to Lou Ann Molling, a slender woman whose soft features often betrayed her strong feelings. Take the issue of Erin not getting lots of playing time. If Erin had a problem with her situation, she was supposed to come to Emiria, instead of Emiria being the adult and approaching Erin. Wasn't that too much to expect of a fourteen-year-old girl? Finally, Lou Ann reached the point where she couldn't hold back her feelings any longer. She phoned Emiria and asked if they could talk.

Emiria had been expecting the call. "OK. When?"

"How about after practice tomorrow," Lou Ann calmly replied.

But the next afternoon when the cars of the soccer moms and dads circled through the parking lot, Lou Ann was nowhere to be found. Emiria waited and waited, and then got in her old beater car to drive home. Just then she spotted Lou Ann, several cars away. As Emiria walked over she noticed the woman reviewing what appeared to be notes.

Emiria believed your body mirrored your soul. To her, the pretty woman before her seemed thin and weary. Emiria confidently took the passenger seat, and the mother told the coach what she'd learned. Her daughter just thrived on words of encouragement. As parents, they'd learned it the hard way.

"Phil and I took a parenting class, and we realized that's what Erin really needs. Words of encouragement," Lou Ann told Emiria. "She'll try hard. She'll work for you. She'll do almost anything you ask as long as she has words of encouragement."

Emiria could see her frustration. Lou Ann seemed near tears. "You know, it hurts as a parent when you see your daughter hurt."

Lou Ann handed Emiria some of Phil's soccer newsletters. One talked about high school girls, and how coaches are frequently befuddled by their wildly oscillating moods. How what seems a trivial incident at school—say, a cryptic comment by a girlfriend—can totally distract a girl during a game. Lou Ann wondered if Emiria was being too demanding by insisting the girls give 110 percent. "You know, at this age level," Lou Ann said, "I guess you have to be more lenient and try to understand where these girls are coming from."

But Lou Ann had another, more particular objective. She had a list of handwritten questions that she wanted Emiria to answer. She wanted to know why certain girls were getting more playing time than her daughter.

"Which girls?" pressed Emiria.

"I'm just using examples," Lou Ann hedged. "I'm not going to name anybody you know."

The conversation grew edgy. Lou Ann felt Emiria was trying to drag things out of her. Emiria struggled to be respectful, but the list of questions tried her patience. Other mothers might have concerns, but they didn't quiz her with written questions after practice. Or question why she played certain girls.

And a parenting class? Please! Emiria had survived seven siblings and poverty, pulled herself up by her own cleats, earned a college degree and all-American honors, all with parents who didn't have the money or leisure for parenting classes. What did Lou Ann want, some kind of baby-sitting service for underprivileged suburban girls? Emiria had never had a coach—man or woman—who worried for a second that she'd had a bum day at school. Did she really think that was her job? To be a parent, to gauge all the girls' moods on a minute-by-minute basis, to go easy if they had a rough time in Mr. Smith's algebra class?

The women couldn't understand one another. Lou Ann couldn't fathom why Emiria wasn't more sensitive to the girls, why she couldn't explain to her daughter more clearly why she wasn't playing. Emiria, meanwhile, wondered when the Mollings would let her be. Phil wasn't Thunder's coach. Neither was Lou Ann. They believed in leniency and she believed in discipline. They bowed to encouragement and she upheld personal responsibility.

Emiria didn't debate whether you could coach both ways, but she knew that she wasn't going to let parents sway her. Indeed, one of the newsletters Lou Ann gave her stated that the dilemma for parents is that they "inherently take a subjective angle of their child's situation, whereas the coach must hold onto an objective viewpoint of the team's development, more accurately the good of the team."

What was the good of team Thunder?

Angela, meanwhile, couldn't win for trying. Unlike Erin, she'd managed to make some Thunder practices while playing varsity soccer, struggled to maintain contact with the girls and the coach. But still, coming back was hard. She'd heard grumblings about the playing time she was already getting over some of the girls who'd been to more practices. After the high school season she hardly felt welcomed back by the team. The girls seemed to come at her harder in practice. And she couldn't help but notice the obvious. The girls who'd attended all the practices had naturally become better friends.

Angela wasn't sure how the feud began. Was it Erin's anger at not getting lots of playing time after high school? Or Emiria's cool distance? Angela wondered if Emiria was a threat to Erin's father. On Eclipse, if Phil had a problem with Erin not playing, he could bend the coach's ear. Emiria, on the other hand, believed you had to earn your playing time. Parents couldn't win their children favors.

Faced with that immutable fact, Angela had opted to grin and bear it. She was not going to make it obvious that she was unhappy with her coach. She'd give her best effort, no matter what. Absorb everything she could from the experience, and survive what she didn't like. But it wasn't easy when she practiced with Erin, when her main experience of the team was colored through her close friend's eyes.

One night Angela confided in her mother that Phil and Erin were making her uncomfortable. Patty Walsh hadn't been to many of the games. Hadn't even known what Phil was talking about when he told her one day, "What is it with Emiria and your parents?" But as her daughter started to tell her about her predicament, Patty Walsh grew concerned.

Phil and Lou Ann and Erin were putting Emiria down in front of Angela. Patty Walsh didn't think that was appropriate for adults. Here her daughter had dedicated herself to winning a spot back on the team, and they seemed to be trying to influence her. It was one thing to express an opinion, but what right did another girl's parents have to try to pull their daughter down?

Patty and Joe decided to talk to Angela. They weren't going to get in an argument with the Mollings. This was about their daughter. Making choices. They suggested that if the Mollings continued to try to influence her, she should suggest they switch their tactics. Try to communicate with the coach. Work to a solution instead of a fight. But the more Patty and Joe talked to their daughter, the less they worried. Angela seemed to realize that it was up to her to decide what she wanted to do. Not a friend and teammate. Certainly not her parents.

"Hey, it's too bad what's happening to Erin," Angela told them one night. "But I can make up my own mind."

THIRTEEN

Arizona or Bust

brian shook his head.

"Did you get this from Luke?"

"No," Emiria replied. She'd just thought it over, made it up.

Thunder was having trouble switching the ball, so Emiria had devised a drill to teach the tactic. She marked off ten-yard borders on each side of the field. The idea was simple: Heighten the advantage of switching the ball, swinging it wide to the wings. In the middle of the field the girls were handicapped—only allowed to trap and pass, no more than two touches permitted. But switch the ball wide to the free zones and a girl could dribble and take as many touches as she wished. The drill forced the girls to pass to the outside, or Ping-Pong it quickly inside and then bounce it wide. The drill made the girls think.

By now the girls who had been coming to practice all

fall had a huge advantage over those who'd been playing high school varsity or juggling eighth-grade teams. It wasn't just the constant running and sprinting, the phenomenal fitness Emiria demanded. The once fuzzy concepts of switching play and checking back to the ball were fast becoming second nature. Emiria was teaching the girls college soccer, and they were eagerly soaking up the tactics and new skills. Her challenges, her demands that they think about what they were doing—that they solve their problems—were gradually taking hold. Now when Emiria would stop play and ask what was wrong, the answers were analytical.

Gone were the long, awkward silences that had punctuated the early practices. Theresa, Jessica, Shannon, nearly every girl would speak up. Nobody had to raise her hand in this grassy classroom. And nobody felt bad about pointing out mistakes, even if your best friend had goofed.

They were all on the same team.

Nobody could quite understand it. The rejections.

Thunder wasn't getting accepted into the better tournaments, and the girls were naturally taking it personally. It was bad enough that they were failing. Now they couldn't seem to even get an invitation to play. The likely reason was not one parents wanted to face. Everybody knew that the top-flight competitions chose teams partly on their record. Maybe the losses were keeping them out.

But there was one big winter tournament Thunder still might be able to get into. During the long President's Day weekend in February, some of the best youth teams in the country would flock to Phoenix, Arizona, for the President's Day Tournament. Emiria and Luke had mentioned the tournament in the very first team meeting, and despite Thunder's rocky season, Emiria hadn't changed her mind. Santa Rosa usually got socked with Pacific storms in the

winter, and there would be no top competitions in the
area that time of year, let alone a dry field. The timing
would be perfect. State Cup was set for the following
month, late March. Arizona could be just what Thunder
needed. Something to train for and look forward to. A
tune-up and a treat for the team. Thunder had never traveled by airplane, and Emiria thought the trip might pull
them together.

"Why do we need to fly to Arizona when we can't
win here?" complained a dad at a team meeting that fall.
The girls had been asked to leave the room for the obvious reasons. Talking about money and losing could get
ugly.

But the question made sense. Thunder hadn't won a
single tournament within ninety miles of Santa Rosa. The
competition in Arizona would be far stronger. What
would that do to their daughters' self-confidence? And
there was the money. Arizona would mean plane tickets,
rental cars, hotel rooms—on top of tournament fees. A
big step for a floundering youth team. To date, the most
expensive Thunder tournaments hadn't knocked parents
back more than a shared motel room and pizza bills.

Lots of Thunder parents didn't have the cash to
blithely spend several hundred dollars on a desert outing.
The idea of a tune-up for State Cup seemed a bit fanciful.
Did anybody really think they'd get past the first round?

Phil Molling called a parent meeting at his offices for
the evening of November 5. The timing was auspicious.
In three days Thunder would play Sebastopol for the
league title. With seven active children, Theresa's mother,
a deeply religious woman with mahogany eyes, had fretted through her share of parent meetings. Kathy Piasta
didn't think Emiria a perfect coach, but she also knew
nothing was easy with thirteen- or fourteen-year-olds, let
alone trying to bring them together on a team. Her worst

fear was simple. That the parents would turn hostile and confront Emiria. That the young coach would be disheartened and quit. She'd seen it before.

Kathy Piasta wasn't alone in her fears. Brian, the man closest to Emiria, was dreading the meeting. He felt shut out, unable to get a pulse on where the parents were headed. He couldn't begin to guess who still backed Emiria, and who might have lined up with Phil. On the drive over he anxiously told his wife, "This might be the end."

They met at 7:00 P.M. in a boardroom in Phil's offices, sitting in a semicircle. Phil considered himself the facilitator. His job was to get the group together, to give them a chance to air the problems he believed were holding them all back. Kathy wasn't the only parent who prayed that night for open communication, for a positive discussion. The team had been together for such a short time. If the girls were just getting to know each other on the field, the parents were even further apart.

Joe Piasta could see the tension in the room, the clear division between the Fury and Eclipse parents. More than a couple of conspiracy stories had been circulating. Some wondered if Phil was not secretly maneuvering to get Emiria fired or reprimanded by the Santa Rosa United board. Others speculated upon a more Machiavellian scheme. Might Brian be cozying up to the coach so that when Emiria became discouraged he could take over the reins?

The meeting began haltingly. Phil felt it wasn't his place to set the agenda, but some in the audience wondered. Kristin's mother, Karen, believed Phil was bringing up issues to see if other families would come around to his way of thinking. And sure enough, soon the meeting turned negative. As they groused about the losing, the frustration gradually bubbled up. Parents wondering out loud whether Emiria wasn't demanding too much from fourteen-year-olds. Where was the encouragement, the understanding many of them believed their daughters couldn't live without? To the Mollings and a few others, the mentoring they'd been promised from Luke or another senior coach hadn't happened. Emiria's maturity was an issue. Was a twenty-two-year-old ready for the responsibility of coaching? What about the swearing?

Arlene's single mom, Carol, tried to put it all in perspective, reminding them that this wasn't finishing school. Emiria's occasional swearing, for instance. Kids heard far worse at school or at the mall than they ever heard from Emiria. "You know, you have to balance that out," the redhead said flatly. "That's your job as a parent."

The debate moved to money. Parents were upset over having to pay Emiria's salary when she couldn't deliver. Angry that she stubbornly insisted on dragging the team to more tournaments. When the discussion reached Arizona it seemed to stall. One mother dramatically announced she wouldn't send her daughter unless she could bring her whole family along, an expense she couldn't possibly afford. But most of the parents had already recognized that neither they nor the rest of their families could accompany their daughters to every tournament. Carol thought they were circling around the problem, that money was an easy excuse, a way to skirt the real sore spot. There was an elephant in the room, and Carol decided to point it out. She knew what everyone wanted to talk about, why they'd come that night.

"Let's talk about playing time," she said, pausing. Nobody dared, so Carol kept at it. She knew why a few parents were uncertain about Arizona. They didn't want to spend hundreds of dollars to watch their daughters sit on the sidelines.

"I think it affects the whole team," Carol volunteered, speaking for those too cautious to let their views be known. "It's not just the girls who aren't playing. The girls on the field don't feel good about the girls on the bench."

As the father of one of those girls on the bench, Rich Drady, Jenny's dad, spoke up. "I'm not going to go to Arizona and spend all that money to watch my daughter sit on the sidelines."

Michelle knew what the Dradys must be feeling. "Shannon plays so much," she confessed, admitting to a little parental guilt. "Sometimes I wonder why she doesn't come out of games."

But Brian knew that playing time depended on a lot of things, not the least of which being what the team might need in the future. He'd been to all the practices. Playing time was more than just a question of talent. "We've just got to trust that what Emiria's doing is in the best interest of the girls," he declared. The best players didn't always get the most time. "The strongest girls are the ones who play. It's the players who are putting out in practice."

As the discussion slowly worked round the room, Theresa's dad, Joe, mulled it over. The straight-faced, balding attorney had seen enough teams over the years to know that playing time was rarely fair in the eyes of adults. There would always be moms and dads who worried, thinking their kid might be on the outs with the coach. But that wasn't why he thought they had gathered there that night. In his mind this was an elaborate dance, a roundabout debate on whether they still believed in the experiment. What with his weekend army reserve duty and seven other kids, Joe had only seen the team in snapshots. Sure, the kids were struggling, but they were improving. Joe Piasta respected Phil Molling, thought he'd given his heart to the old Eclipse, considered him a friend. But this was a new team, a new coach.

Joe spoke his piece. "Wait a minute! I don't care how many games the team wins or loses. We've got a young coach teaching these kids good soccer. Something moms and dads can't do. That's why she was brought in." The parents, the girls, the coach, it all seemed familiar to Joe. "You know, this whole situation reminds me of the movie *Hoosiers*," he told them. "The kids are ready to play it right. Let's give them a chance!"

Brian thought Joe had found the perfect analogy in the film about a small-town basketball coach and a hard-luck team. Hadn't the coach told the dads to butt out, and then rebuilt the team from the ground up? Made the kids take five passes before a shot?

Wasn't that what Emiria was doing? Wasn't that why she and Phil Molling had locked horns? A young woman asserting her will upon sixteen girls and thirty parents. Forcing fundamentals down them like gruel, teaching discipline, cutting out the parents, losing games. Joe Piasta wasn't the only parent in the room thinking their daughters weren't ballerinas for a reason. This was about a team with all its trials and tribulations. Wasn't this something girls could survive?

Brian had been trying to hold back. He knew that he was seen as an Emiria supporter. But Joe Piasta's eloquent defense seemed to turn the tide. The Piastas were viewed as one of the most impartial families. Theresa wasn't a star, and even spent some time on the bench. If the Piastas were willing to ride it out, perhaps other parents with average girls might have open minds.

"We've got to have a little faith," Brian began softly, nodding his head. "These are the best sixteen girls in our entire area. We need to let them develop. The girls are getting first-rate, college-level training."

Brian had watched every practice and game, and was in awe of what he was witnessing. His defense of Emiria fully dispelled any wild ideas that he might be angling for her job. Brian was the most successful coach in the room, and he was openly acknowledging that he—or any other dad for that matter—couldn't approach what Emiria was offering their daughters.

*   *   *

Lou Ann Molling spoke as much as anyone that night, complaining about Emiria's harshness and the encouragement she felt was sorely lacking. Though Carol had known Lou Ann for years from the Eclipse, and sometimes shared a pew with her at Steve Marshall's church, she couldn't disagree more with what she was saying. These weren't problems that parents could resolve. This was about each girl's commitment and responsibility. Arlene and Shannon had decided to commit to the team and not play varsity soccer as freshmen. They, too, had had trouble figuring out Emiria at the beginning of the season, but they had stuck it out, gaining skill and toughness and a different sort of encouragement.

Was this only about kicking around a ball? If Thunder was a life lesson, a preview of the competitive, cutthroat world of college and business, why should parents control the team's destiny? Were their daughters so delicate that a coach, however tough, would scar them for life? And there was something else. Jerry Messina had seen it for himself by asking Natalie what she thought of Emiria, and hearing firsthand that she admired her coach.

To girls who had been trained by dads most of their lives, what message would it send for parents to decide that a woman coach was not made of the right stuff? Many believed Emiria a powerful, if imperfect, female role model for their daughters. What would they be saying if they declared a woman too hard, too distant, too emotional to be trusted?

But there was something else that happened that night. Brian listened to the pride the parents had in their daughters. Jessica's mother, Maggie, a petite woman who'd beaten her athletic husband in a marathon before giving birth to a handful of children, made it clear that winning or losing wasn't her concern. What she and so many other parents seemed to care about was whether the team was going in the right direction for the girls.

Phil Molling thought it just proved group dynamics, that people rarely wanted to rock the boat. But Brian felt it proved hope was stronger than fear. He listened to Phil diplomatically bring up what might be negative issues, and watched the parents turn them into a positive. What many had feared might be a mutiny nearly turned into a pep rally. Kathy Piasta felt her prayer had been answered. The parents got a chance to air their concerns, and settled on patience. Agreed it could take a year, maybe two, for the team to gel.

Phil Molling and Joe Piasta drew up a list of issues that Angela's dad, Joe, was designated to talk to Emiria about. The vote on tournaments was nearly unanimous. Arizona was in.

The timing was uncanny. While the Arizona trip was more than a couple of months off, the girls had a big game that weekend. In three days they'd play for the league championship.

FOURTEEN

Beating the Ref

*t*he girls lined up for their sprints.

"Think of Sebastopol!" Emiria shouted. "You have to want it. No one works as hard as you do."

It had come down to one game against the team that had defined Thunder's season. Since the ugly losses against Sebastopol, Thunder had won two and tied one, the latest victory an 8–0 runaway. The winner of the season's final game would take the league championship.

Not surprisingly, Sebastopol had become a source of motivation. Every drill had Sebastopol stamped on it. They went one-on-one against Sebastopol players. Scrimmaged against Sebastopol. Cleared headers against Sebastopol.

There was nothing nice about what the girls did, though it was the sort of thing that parents would have thought nothing of had it been done by boys. But to the girls of Thunder it made perfect sense. Many of them still held strong feelings about the old coach of the Eclipse. Some were still angry about how he'd seemed to favor his daughter. And so the dad and daughter became motivational figures. Targets of lighthearted jokes. Thunder wasn't just squaring off against an arch-rival, it was playing the old daddy-daughter routine. Playing a game about fairness.

"Take a walk along the field," Emiria told the girls. "Check out the wet spots. The mud."

The girls fanned out, looking over the sections of the field they'd most likely play. Though it was clear and cold that November morning, the rain had been steady the last couple of weeks. The mounded belly of the field resembled a pig trough. The penalty boxes weren't much better, and the rest of the field was dotted with potholes. Even the grassy sections were iffy. Pools of water where the ball would stick.

Cow manure, Naomi was thinking as she walked her turf. That's what it smells like. Rotten apples, thought Cassie, catching a strong whiff by the goal. Theresa had the most sensitive nose. The field smelled to her like rotten eggs and spoiled milk. It wasn't as crazy an idea as it sounded. Sebastopol was farming land, with plenty of cows and chickens nearby.

On one end stood an aging football scoreboard, the other end open, distant mountains just visible through the mist. This was Analy High School, home field of the Sebastopol Strikers. Goals were set up in front of the Analy Tigers' bright yellow football goalposts, and that morning the old blue and aluminum bleachers looked especially barren. But the girls were used to being the first to arrive at deserted fields. Being early was a Thunder tradition.

The girls noticed something different about Emiria.

Her mood seemed lighter and she actually cracked a couple of jokes. Arlene had never seen Emiria so excited and funny before a game.

Theresa felt little of the pressure Emiria had put on them in earlier games. She listened as her coach told them that they were still learning and they had to believe they would get there. Had to have faith in the system. She wanted them to win not because it was for the league championship but because they were the better team. "Just go out there and be your best." She smiled. "If you go out and have fun, you'll win."

As Emiria looked out at the girls, she knew she didn't need to say much. They weren't afraid anymore. All the energy that had been flowering in practice was just waiting to be released.

Out of the heap of blue Thunder sports bags and balls, the ritual began: slipping on the game socks and cleats, taping socks or ankles, the girls joking but purposeful. Emiria didn't have to say a word to get them started. The captains led the team in warm-ups, pacing them around the soggy field in an easy jog to get the blood flowing.

After a stretch and some sprints, they broke off into pairs, easing into the game. Two touches back and forth, Emiria walking the perimeter. On other days she'd pause before a couple of girls and urge them to pick it up. Sharpen the pass. Make the trap clean so you could step right into the pass. But she didn't have to say much this morning. The energy was there.

"One touch!" the captains cried out, the patter of the balls sounding a tribal beat, the breaths gradually rising. And then the circle. The heart of the warm-up. Sixteen girls darting around like bees in a hive. Girls dashing into space, crying out for a pass. Naomi! Theresa! Catherine! Voices rising in a chorus. You could feel the whole team in that music, sense the closeness of the girls calling out one another's names. The soccer seemed to follow the voices. The checking back, the looping around to the side, the diagonal bursts. The circle was the sport distilled. The game's essence.

Sebastopol was just wandering in as the girls were breaking a sweat. This, too, was a Thunder tradition. Informing opponents they were outmatched before they'd even flipped the coin. Thunder's pace accelerated. The girls relished this moment. The other team spotting them in their gray practice jerseys, breathing hard. So often the opposing girls responded with a lackadaisical disdain, as if to say, "Why work up a sweat before you have to? This isn't the game." But the Thunder girls were racehorses. Six months of grueling training had cranked up their thermometer settings. Half an hour of hard work warmed them to just below a rolling boil. Exactly where they wanted to be.

As the game drew near, they moved to goal and loaded up. One by one the players fed one another for shots. Emiria stood by the post and watched the screaming, low bullets slap the back of the net. Rattle the post. Glance off Cassie's glove.

Arlene, Shannon, Kim, Naomi, Angela. Everybody was firing cannons today, and even Emiria smiled as the shots hammered a new rhythm and energy. She looked at the pregame shots as a team statement of purpose and readiness, and this morning there was no doubt. Only when the ref waved them off would they stop. Emiria left no time for idleness, no empty minutes of waiting. Sixty seconds before game time the girls sprinted to the sideline, tearing off their sweaty practice jerseys. Standing there in their sports bras as they reached for their freshly laundered dark blue uniforms, they cut quite the picture. Arlene had shed fifteen pounds since making the team, and several of the girls boasted rippled, barrel stomachs. Six-packs, Emiria liked to call them.

Thunder was ready to play.

*   *   *

How it happened was a bit of a puzzle. The referee hadn't shown up, so someone suggested that the old coach of the Eclipse, and Brian ref the game together. But Brian had another commitment that morning, and couldn't guarantee he'd be there the whole game. Several Thunder parents had the experience to take over the job. Jessica's dad, Steve, Heather's mother, Stephanie, and Phil Molling all occasionally refereed and were more than able. But they all had the good sense to stay out of it.

Finally a seventeen-year-old kid who was supposed to be a linesman was elected to be the center ref. Though Emiria couldn't believe her eyes when the old Eclipse coach took the linesman's flag on the sideline, there was something wonderfully appropriate about the irony. All week long they'd taken the old coach and his daughter's names in vain, using them as a source of inspiration. Now they'd get a chance to literally defeat both of them in one sweep.

Thunder came out hard from the opening minute, passing well despite the muddy field. But the narrow pitch worked against the girls, giving them little room to possess the ball. Quickly Sebastopol fired a few long balls to McKenzie Blechel. She was a state Olympic development program player, fast and strong, and Naomi struggled to keep pace. This was the part of sweeper that haunted Naomi the most. She couldn't imagine how Cassie could handle the pressure of playing goalie. For her, sweeper was bad enough. One slip on the slick field and McKenzie would be one-on-one with the keeper.

But soon it became abundantly clear that Thunder would have to overcome more than the formidable McKenzie Blechel and her teammates. The old Eclipse coach started raising his flag as if he had a twitch. Calling fouls on the girls he'd coached since childhood. His old team. Offsides, rough play. You name it, he called it, and almost always against Thunder. If the ball went out, it didn't seem to matter who touched it. The flag nearly always pointed in Sebastopol's direction.

"Come on!" Karen Young cried.

Nearly sixty parents, siblings, and friends lined the sidelines, and half of them started booing. Thunder parents couldn't believe it when the calls continued. They paced the sidelines and shook their heads in disbelief. Could this really be the man who for years they had trusted with their daughters?

Naomi's mom, Sandy, was embarrassed for the man, and she hardly even knew him. He obviously couldn't be objective.

"I can't believe he's going to make us lose this game!" Thunder parents grumbled angrily. "If we lose this game because of him, it's going to be pathetic!"

Sandy agonized. Had their daughters trained half a year for this man to ruin everything?

Kim went down from a tough foul, and Arlene fretted as she went off limping. Every time Arlene went upfield, her old coach flagged her offsides. Three times in a row. But when Kim came back on the field, Arlene stopped worrying. He couldn't call everything a foul. Eventually they'd get a chance.

Erin Molling fired a ball to the right nearly twenty yards out. It bounced, and Kim struck it on the volley. Surely it would slip wide, but the sailing ball curled in the air toward the near post.

When Kim abruptly turned and trotted back, her head hunched between her shoulders, everybody assumed the worst. But then a couple of Thunder girls started jumping all over one another. The young ref finally put his arms out and pointed toward the center line. Kim, the nonchalant, had put them ahead.

One beautiful goal wasn't likely to be the difference

over Sebastopol. The Strikers equalized. The game see-sawed. The questionable calls continued. Sandy watched a few Thunder parents boil over at the prospect of losing the biggest game of the season because of one dad. And then Sandy decided she had to let it go. If that's where the game ends up, that's where it ends up, she thought. After all, that's what it was: a game.

Before halftime, Thunder's redhead made her state-ment. Dribbled three girls in the penalty box with her legs and elbows, and poked it by the outstretched keeper. Classic Arlene. All strength and drive. Arlene watched her old coach raise his flag and get into it with the kid ref. She couldn't believe it. He was trying to call some-thing again. But finally she heard the kid say, "It's a goal!"

The game really wasn't in doubt from that point on. Naomi knocked in a cross in the second half to make it 3–1. After a while the seventeen-year-old ref started wav-ing off the middle-aged dad's calls. He still managed to call a penalty kick to pull the Strikers within a goal, but even that didn't matter on this day.

As the final minutes ticked off, Thunder stood firm against the booming long balls. Clearing out the headers, calming down the ball, playing its game. The girls weren't perfect. At times they still lost their cool and struggled with the Strikers' physical style.

But this was a team that only weeks ago had blown them out. They'd beaten their old coach, proved that pa-tience could beat brawn. One game can mean an awful lot in a season. That morning on the muddy, stinky field, all the losses, all the questions about style and defense, seemed to disappear.

Out on the field the girls felt so good they didn't stop at the final whistle. They ran to the trough in the middle of the field and started sliding belly and feet first in the

mud, everyone, that is, except for Arlene, who was happy
to watch.

Over on the sideline, the unimaginable happened. Phil
Molling walked up to Emiria and gave her a big hug.

FIFTEEN

T Rex

Confidence was a slippery thing on a team of sixteen girls. To Arlene the big win over Sebastopol proved how far they'd come, that if they wanted something badly enough, they could overcome any obstacle. But over the course of a season, a practice, or a game, confidence came in waves. Some girls had it, some didn't.

Gangly Theresa was one of those girls who seemed at first like she'd never have it. Theresa cut corners when they ran laps. Ran a foot short of the line when they were doing wind sprints.

"Theresa, if you're last one more time, the whole team is doing ten more laps!" Emiria shouted.

Theresa was one of three or four girls who cried when the workouts were grueling. The cheerful face that so often beamed her joy also reflected her sensitivity. Theresa leaned on a teammate's shoulder, breaking into sobs.

"You want to become a better player?" Emiria challenged her.

"Yeah."

"Why does everything hurt?"

"Well—"

Emiria cut her off. "You're just excusing yourself because you don't want to work harder."

But Theresa did work harder. Though her natural gifts were few, she was a wonderful team player, and intuitively understood the importance of a quick trap and pass. Her game was selfless without being passive. Switching, stepping back to offer a teammate a safe angle for a back pass, Theresa mastered the basic tactics as easily as she did algebra.

As Theresa gradually began to receive her share of compliments from Emiria, she returned the good sentiments with her own faith in the coach. She knew it couldn't be easy for a rookie coach to turn them into a team. To her way of thinking, some of the girls hadn't been very understanding when Emiria had returned from her sickbed to lose the championship game at the Hall Memorial. But lately it was getting hard to remain objective. She noticed the Mollings appeared frequently at practice, not so much to watch their daughter as to keep an eye on the young coach. On one drive home that fall, Emiria seemed to be all Erin and her mother talked about. Theresa felt uncomfortable with the conversation, and decided it was time to switch car pools. She wanted to make up her own mind about her coach. On her own terms.

But it wasn't going to be easy. That fall before a scrimmage against a local team, Emiria talked about each player and what they needed to do. Everybody, that is, except for Theresa. Same thing at halftime. Totally ignored her. Theresa was furious. She didn't feel like she was playing well to begin with, and now her coach was acting as if she didn't exist. The field was slick and she slipped and fell a couple of times, and Emiria called for her to come off. When Angela sprinted on and slapped her hand to take her place, she whispered, "I have to tell you something after the game."

As Theresa took her place on the sideline, she noticed Emiria and the girls were laughing. Later she learned why. Emiria had told Angela to replace Theresa because "she's so slow."

The slight couldn't have come at a worse time. Theresa had been struggling with Emiria's exhausting fitness drills, her will slipping. It seemed that all Theresa had to do was make one bad pass, and Emiria would yell. Theresa felt clumsy, and her heart and mind just weren't in it anymore. At school, all she could think about was soccer. She'd talk to her friends about it, and they didn't seem to understand. Thought she was making too big a deal out of a silly game. "Gosh, why are you so into it?"

One night she told her dad what she wanted to do.

"If you quit now, you're going to regret it," he warned her. Theresa loved her dad, loved how encouraging he could be. But he was a trial lawyer, a lieutenant colonel in the army reserve, and sometimes he encouraged a little too much. Theresa couldn't stand lecturing. She knew what she was facing with Emiria. Theresa thrived on encouragement and realized she wasn't likely to find much on Thunder. But the eighth grader knew she had a choice. Fit the coach's expectations and get what she wanted. Or decide it was only a game.

Seven children, all of them athletes in one shape or form, had taught Kathy Piasta the importance of taking stock of a situation. Letting it go a few days instead of overreacting. She'd been through similar traumas before. She wasn't happy about what had happened, but she felt it important that her daughter communicate. That she decide what she wanted.

"OK, Theresa, this was a tough practice." Kathy

seemed to agree with her distraught daughter. "It could have been said differently, but get beyond that. What is your goal here? What is it that you're trying to accomplish with soccer and your life?"

Theresa had always reminded her father of his side of the family, the Polish side. That's where he thought she got her humor and dramatic flair. But the athletes came from the Croats and Swiss on his wife's side, and along with her dad's blue eyes, Theresa appeared to have inherited his clumsiness. Of the seven Piastas, Theresa was arguably the least likely to succeed in sports. When she started playing recreational soccer at eight, her father never took it too seriously. Basketball and baseball were the bigger sports in the Piasta clan.

Joe Piasta was surprised when Phil Molling and the Eclipse coach wanted Theresa on their team. They nicknamed her "T," though Joe Walsh dubbed her "T Rex," a name that captured her feistiness and herky-jerky adolescence. Theresa ran with a local track club to try to get faster and build up her endurance. But even with all the effort and Phil's generous support, she struggled. Joe and Kathy constantly worried they were making a mistake, that their daughter's love of the game was setting her up for an emotional catastrophe. What would happen if one year she didn't make the team? Maybe she needed another sport. But while Theresa played a little basketball and volleyball, she was ambivalent about other sports. As the years went on, Joe proudly watched his daughter become part of a soccer community, a tribe of girls and parents. Most of his other children were gifted, natural athletes; his son was considered one of the best soccer players in the city. But Theresa was the Piasta with guts, the girl who made the team by trying just a little harder, by playing smart.

When Theresa made team Thunder, her parents saw her confidence soar. And then she broke her wrist, and had to fight to catch up. She got lots of playing time, but that wasn't easy either. Emiria's offensive bent sent the top players up front. Theresa had to play a new position, fullback. Speed counts at fullback, and Theresa couldn't hide her slowness. Or her occasional blunders near the goal.

Joe and Kathy watched their daughter struggle, and worried. But they knew it was more complex than a player in a slump. Theresa was going through changes. She'd shot up like a Kansas cornstalk in the last few months, to nearly five feet seven inches. The growth spurt had left her awkward and weak.

T Rex wasn't her old fiery self.

Joe and Kathy thought Emiria gracious to meet them right away despite her own continuing graduate school studies. Joe took a couple of hours off from work and they met at a coffee shop near her apartment. Emiria seemed sick as a dog, under the weather with a cold she'd been fighting for weeks.

They talked and talked and talked. "Oh my God, she's grown that much," Emiria said, surprised. "I didn't pick up on that."

They talked about the upsetting practice, and Kathy thought it started to sink in. Why Theresa had been hurt by her coach's comment. "Ohh," Emiria said, as if a lightbulb had just gone off. "I know how she took that."

The young coach seemed to grasp what Theresa was going through, flash back on that stage in her own life. She told the Piastas that she herself was just learning how different the girls were. How some might brush off a harsh comment, while others were more sensitive.

Emiria phoned that evening, and Theresa just let her talk. She had learned a long time ago that her coach didn't like to be interrupted. But all in all she felt a lot better. Encouraged. Emiria explained she had been trying to lighten up the scrimmage, and hadn't meant to hurt her feelings.

Theresa considered herself a sensitive girl, someone who could sympathize with her teammates. She felt for Jessica, for instance, who she believed had an extra hard time with Emiria's rough language and harshness. But as low as Theresa had fallen the last few months, she'd never felt this was only about proving something to her coach.

Theresa was one of the few who chose to play no school sports that fall, diligently attending nearly all the Thunder practices because she needed every possible edge. She simply didn't have the benefit of excessive talent. Indeed, when a couple of the dads filled out a team questionnaire, they noted one or two Thunder girls weren't the best athletes—a pointed reference to Theresa.

But that didn't stop her from having dreams. Theresa believed she was going to play varsity soccer at the Catholic girls' high school, Ursuline, one of the city's top teams. She knew it was a long shot, and that few freshmen made the squad. Survive Emiria a few more months, and maybe, just maybe, she'd have a fighting chance.

Kevin Brown, director of coaching for the Santa Rosa United's twenty-three youth teams, surveyed the coaching evaluations that would help him decide whether the club should renew Emiria's contract. The young coach's marks were impressive. Many parents gave Emiria high ratings on teaching skills, making the girls better players, running organized practices, being fair about playing time, and responding well to questions and discussions.

There were only a few written comments, among them a hand-scrawled suggestion that parents were the biggest problem. "We need to keep the parents on the sidelines and allow the coaches to coach," recommended one dad. "We need to provide positive support of the coach and team, and be good role models for our kids to follow as team players and sportsmen."

But the two letters that accompanied the coaching

evaluations couldn't have been more different. In a strange way, the letters were proof of the most basic fact of coaching, how impossible it was to get sixteen sets of parents to agree on where a team was headed. One viewed Emiria as a threat, the other saw her as a strong role model, the team on the cusp of something beautiful.

Phil Molling's letter made no bones about its purpose, noting up front that it would outline the young coach's faults. He conceded that many players and parents disagreed with his opinion, but felt his points were valid nonetheless. Bemoaning what he called a lack of mentoring from Luke Oberkirch and another celebrated Santa Rosa coach, Phil questioned whether a young adult was equal to the challenge of coaching a top-flight girls' soccer team:

Dear Kevin:

. . . The bottom line was that Emiria was on her own since August 15th. A 22 year-old coaching for the first time at this level. Her training and fitness were very good, the best that these girls had ever received. Each girl raised their skill level quite a bit. But the results of tournaments and league play mirrored the lack of coaching experience. In fact, I solicited opinions from two other coaches. The three of us agreed that the biggest problem with the team was the lack of experimentation in terms of playing positions (e.g., defense was not in place) and the lack of creativity, desire (i.e., the girls were scared to make mistakes) on the field. Emiria, Luke and Brian excused the poor performance on the fact that this was a "transition" year: new coach, 6 new girls, etc. What was not said was that with better training and fitness and better personnel, Thunder had worse results than the year before . . .

Typical of a young coach's impatience, inconsistency (playing time and subbing) and little team spirit began to take its toll . . . To Emiria's credit she has dramatically improved her patience and inconsistency over the course of the season. But she still singles out certain players as "reliable" (her favorites). It appears that her "reliability" is based [on] her perception of hustle or natural ability. This intangible quality she says is a "coaching decision." Suffice [it] to say my opinion is that her "favoritism" has yielded a low trust and low teamwork . . . Reinforcement of teamwork is demanded, not created on the Thunder team . . .

The lesson to learn from this coaching experiment is that a young trainer needs to learn coaching by watching a seasoned coach. I have no doubt that Emiria will be a great coach given 1 or 2 years (transition years). The question is, is it fair to subject kids and paying parents to the maturing process necessary to creating good coaches from young inexperienced talented soccer players? . . .

Thanks for your consideration,
Phil Molling

One of the most significant differences between the letters was something a casual reader might have missed. Phil sent his letter on behalf of "my daughter," never mentioning Erin's mother or including her signature. Perhaps he felt more qualified than his wife to critique Emiria on a technical level. (His letter included a paragraph on his college career and coaching experience.) But wasn't the coaching and mentoring of a daughter something that should matter at least as much to a mother? Indeed, the second letter Brown received was written jointly by a mother and father, who spoke of "our daughter" and signed both their names:

Dear Mr. Brown,

Emiria is a great role model for our 14 year old girls. She has tremendous energy and enthusiasm. Her story whereby she advanced from humble beginnings as the fifth of eight children to be Piner's best soccer player, and then an All American at Sonoma State is (and should be) an inspiration for our young ladies. She knows what level of dedication it takes to reach the pinnacle of success, and she insists that the young women strive for this kind of perfection. Hard and frustrating work is part of the diet . . . Sacrifice of many of the fun things that their peers are doing is a necessity to play at this level. The young ladies are faced with the adult decision to make tough choices.

On a technical level, our daughter and her teammates have all advanced substantially in their soccer abilities this year. Emiria has drilled them in how soccer is to be played at a college level. This has been a difficult process, and undoubtably, had she simply turned loose our better athletes at times we may have won several more games. But they would not be as good now. The team is definitely coming together at this vital time with State Cup looming.

Emiria has grown as a coach this year. She would be the first to acknowledge that she has a lot to learn about dealing with 14 year old girls—with all the competing events going on in their lives. She has also learned that she has to watch how she communicates with the team, and with individual girls. They are very sensitive and anyone can unintentionally hurt them, and prevent their further growth as both a soccer player and person . . .

What might be helpful for Emiria next year is to have a committee of parents to talk with periodically about both soccer and life in general. Periodic dialogue as to what's going on in the teenagers' lives in general, or individually, could be helpful to her coaching endeavors.

In summary, we strongly recommend that Emiria be retained.

SIXTEEN

El Niño

"Why are you going bowling with your soccer team?" Kristin's friend asked.

"It's something our coach wants us to do."

"Is your coach crazy?"

"No."

Emiria laid it out in simple terms. To take the next leap forward as a team, they had to become better friends. And to become better friends, they had to start doing things together, apart from soccer. So they breakfasted together at the International House of Pancakes, exchanged gifts at a Christmas dinner at the Piastas', took in *Grease*, *Titanic*, and *Doctor Doolittle*, played rounds of miniature golf, and ice-skated up a storm. And bowled.

But team bonding went down about as easily as cod liver oil for some of the girls. Erin skipped the Christmas dinner, and thus one girl didn't get a present. Angela flaked on *Titanic* because she had plans and had already seen it. Emiria knew the girls wouldn't grow closer if half the team showed. But by making it clear that she expected everyone to attend, Emiria ticked off the more independent or social-minded girls. Catherine, Trinity, Shannon, Erin, Angela, Kristin, and others could think of plenty of better things they could do with their free time.

But the shy girls loved these team evenings out. Jenny got a kick out of crashing into the walls at the ice-skating rink, even if her normally fearless friend Arlene declined to venture on the ice. Jessica thought the evenings brought out the girls' personalities, let them see each other more clearly, peel away the layers. And nothing matched bowling for injecting a little humility. Kristin, so cool and fashionable until the ball slipped behind her. Theresa bowling like a grandma, dropping the ball three feet in the air.

"Sit down and roll it, Theresa!" the girls howled.

But it was smooth Shannon who managed to bring the team together, who sent captain Shauna cackling to the floor in an uncontrollable fit of laughter. Shannon did it by showing that she was human, anything but the seemingly impenetrable, reliable glue that held together the team. Shannon fired an absolute stinker, a gutter ball that refused to die, hopping out like a fish and mowing down every last pin for a strike.

It wasn't just bowling and movies that brought the girls together. Something else happened that winter. The rains came and the fields closed and the girls had to find a place to play.

By early November, Belluzzo was shut for the winter. Thunder quickly migrated to the scruffy fields behind Slater Middle School, but it wasn't long before the girls sliced open dark wounds in the grass. When Emiria moved the girls to the blacktop one afternoon during a torrential downpour, the principal came out and told her

it wasn't safe to play on the slick surface. They'd have
to leave.

El Niño had struck, and no one seemed willing to let
the girls run their fields into mud. They were nomads, a
team without a place to practice, and in January, when
Thunder regrouped after the holiday break, there were
plenty of reasons to think that they should cool their
heels.

Santa Rosa was Northern, not Southern California.
Half a day's drive from Oregon. From November through
March it rained in Santa Rosa. Average annual precipita-
tion in San Francisco was twenty inches; Santa Rosa usually got thirty.

But the winter of 1997/1998 was not average. Fierce
storms washed away Northern Pacific tracks and flooded
the banks of the Russian River. A wall of mud threatened
Rio Nido, a small hillside community just twenty miles
from Santa Rosa. Vice President Gore himself came to
view the wreckage. February was particularly brutal, the
region battered by twice its normal rain. In all, 54.6 inches
would fall in Santa Rosa, one nearby town topping a phenomenal 101 inches.

But El Niño or not, Thunder had goals. Less than five
weeks remained before the President's Cup in Arizona.
And State Cup was only about two and a half months off.

Joe Walsh scheduled them regular time in Slater's basketball gym, a classic middle school facility built in the
early fifties with hardwood floors, faded penants on the
wall, and a gaping stage. When Slater wasn't free they'd
occasionally trot up and down the aisle in Jessica's dad's
church, waiting for a turn in the tiny, adjoining basketball
gym, complete with stained-glass windows. Finally they
found a school willing to let them turn its remaining
patches of grass to mud. Rincon Middle School wasn't
exactly a beautiful facility, but as the rains steadily poured
down, the girls grew to love it.

The dirt and rock track that circled the field grew so wet and muddy that the girls had to loop wide when they did laps, adding distance to their miles. Emiria could tell when a girl was exhausted. The last few laps, she'd brave the mud and water, slogging through on the inside, finishing up splattered and sopping.

The field lacked goals, but Thunder had a solution. The three-foot corner flags. A rule that a goal had to be even or below the flags. You might call it a handicap, having to practice for months without goals, but the girls learned a new discipline. Shots that once boomed high like field goals suddenly had to be low and precise. No one complained. If Pelé learned the Beautiful Game in the streets, what was the big deal about not having goals?

But still there were afternoons when Emiria thought she might be a little nuts. She'd been suffering from walking pneumonia since December. Standing in rain or hail without an umbrella or even rain gear, she often wondered what she was doing out there.

But then there were the girls. They practiced in nothing more than T-shirts and shorts. Showed up rain or shine. How could you deny them? Even the parents had to adapt. After picking up the girls a few times after practice, Steve Marshall realized he had to be prepared or Jessica and her teammates would ruin his car. He'd bring a big stack of towels for the girls to sit on, and blankets to wrap them up so they wouldn't start shivering. Fruit drinks to slake their thirst, and apples and oranges to munch on. Other parents took more extreme measures. Some demanded the girls bring a change of clothes, and tossed the muddy T-shirts, shorts, socks, and cleats into garbage bags before letting them in the car.

Jessica Marshall loved the mud, loved to get dirty. When it rained steady for a few days, Emiria would exploit the dark troughs that spotted the field. What a wonderful opportunity to practice slide tackling. Line up the girls. Sprint ten yards and then let fly. Hips down, legs out to sweep away the imaginary ball. Shake off the mud and try it again. Jessica loved the drill and didn't even mind the little hidden rocks that hurt a little. Cuts and scratches were battle scars. Proof of accomplishment.

But there were times when practice seemed impossible and the coach crazed. Take the day it hailed at school, covering the parking lot with a white carpet. There was thunder and lightning that afternoon, and Jessica worried about the obvious. Electrocution and certain death. As she left school, a hail ball clipped her ear like a rock. There can't be practice today, she thought. Emiria couldn't. But she did. And every minute Jessica dreamed of summer. Even the hills at Sonoma State began to seem appealing.

Or there was the day that winter when a flu kept Jessica hovering over her toilet. She threw up for two days straight and lost nearly ten pounds. Sank to under a hundred pounds. She wasn't anywhere near fully recovered, but Jessica made it to the next practice.

"If you really need to sit out, you can," Emiria said in a dull monotone, her shrug and her impassive expression saying what the words didn't. This wasn't like elementary school. Mom didn't call up and get you a pink slip. You couldn't stay home and watch the soaps.

Why did Emiria always have to make it so hard? Why was it always their choice? Jessica secretly railed against the guilt trip. The way Emiria always turned questions back onto them, never giving them a crutch. But Jessica had her own issues too. Her teammates already considered her dramatic. She cried more than almost anybody. She didn't want to be considered a wuss.

Jessica ran.

Deer Trail was on that day's agenda. Weaving in and out of sidewalks, streets, and muddy paths. Trotting up the monstrous hill, and then fording a street swollen with water. They looked like a team of horses splashing across, the current tugging near their knees.

On a sane team that would have been a good day's work. But after the two-and-a-half-mile cross-country jaunt, Emiria put them through quarter-mile repeats at the track. Two and a half miles worth. Then ten hundred-yard sprints. The track so muddy Jessica felt her feet slide and stick. The field was unplayable, but that didn't stop Emiria. So what if there was no grass? Or dirt? They scrimmaged on the tennis courts for nearly an hour.

Jessica cried nearly the whole time, but she wasn't the only one suffering. Shannon was in tears, and Angela was wheezing through a full-on asthma attack. At times Jessica thought she was dying, but through the pain something else was happening. Her will not to finish last. Her love of the challenge. And so it was that the day Jessica had wanted her coach to give her an out didn't turn out quite the way she had expected. When they started on Deer Trail, Jessica worried about finishing last. But that day she challenged the leaders, and finished an incredible fourth.

Nobody could call Jessica Marshall a wuss.

The Rincon tennis courts defined the new Thunder. Rain, hail, mud. Nothing could stop this team. As the middle school's field became increasingly unplayable, they commandeered the three tennis courts lined up side by side.

They warmed up drumming against the three brick practice walls at one end of the courts. Piano players doing scales. Ten minutes with only the inside of the left foot. Then the right. Switch to the outside. Left, right. Sixteen balls slapping the bricks like fighters slugging the bag. On to volleying, quick jabs, then heading, moving in tighter, competing to see who could keep the ball in the air the longest.

The wall was a dance partner, a perfect companion to

practice moves. They did the step-over. Swinging your foot inches over the ball, selling the defender that you were going one way, then planting your foot on the side of the ball and pushing it in the opposite direction. And once they'd worked through their set routines, Emiria would just let them go free-form. Invent their own moves, take a touch, a fake, and then crank on the wall.

Thoroughly warmed up, they turned half of the three side-by-side courts into a field. One sideline the net, the other the brick walls. They played eight against eight. No dribbling. Just two-touch, the ball unpredictable, sometimes stopping dead in a puddle or hydroplaning. The girls loved it. Passes had to be smooth, traps subtle. Any roughness about your game and you might as well be playing on ice. But the strange thing was that soon the girls forgot about their hardships. Cassie started it really, diving wildly on the tennis courts in shorts as if she were leaping on cushy gym mats. Once the keeper sacrificed her body, how could the rest of the team resist? Shannon shocked herself by going down for the ball, drawing a little blood. Sliding tackles on the tennis courts? No problem.

The uninitiated ventured onto a Thunder tennis court scrimmage at their own risk. Brian occasionally was drafted to even out the teams, and one afternoon it nearly turned disastrous. He took the pass right by the tennis net, shielding the ball well.

BOOM!

Brian was teetering facedown on the net, on the verge of flipping. The girls laughed wildly as he swayed back and forth on his belly. And when Brian finally touched ground again and turned around, there was Arlene, her eyes half hidden behind those stray red locks.

"I didn't mean to hit you." She smiled mischievously. "I thought it was all ball."

When the end of practice rolled around at five-thirty,

Emiria was generally soaked to the bone. She wanted to leave, go home, get dry. She knew the girls probably thought she was mean. But that wasn't why the practices ran over like the rains that wouldn't stop. She cared enough about them to do that. Thunder came first. The team was on fire. How could she stop now?

Erin usually left promptly at five-thirty, but the other girls stood firm. The car-pool vans and cars lined up, the engines humming, promising the warmth of car heaters. "It's six o'clock now!" Greg, Cassie's dad, hollered toward the courts. "It's time for me to take Cassie home."

Cassie would reluctantly leave, but no one else. Not until six-fifteen, sometimes even six-thirty, would Emiria call it a practice. By then even the white ball was disappearing in the dark.

SEVENTEEN

Catherine's Commitment

*i*t was just another rainy January afternoon at Rincon. Another five-on-five scrimmage like any other. But Catherine looked like she was treading water. Jogging in smaller and smaller circles like a wobbly top running out of steam.

In fifteen minutes the girl with the shoulders of a rower had barely touched the ball. Years of relying on strength and instinct had left their mark. Break the sport down to a small pickup game like this, and Catherine's weaknesses blared like neon lights. You couldn't hide in a five-on-five. Catherine may have been a natural sweeper, but she struggled with possession soccer. Her touch was rusty, and she wasn't sure where to move. The reason was simple. She'd missed practices, hadn't worked through the dozens of hours of drills like her teammates.

Kim had told her dad a few weeks before that she

thought her old friend wasn't long for the game. Brian asked Catherine himself in December, and she confessed she'd made up her mind. She'd finish out the season, but this would be her final year of serious club soccer.

Brian had a talk with Emiria about Catherine's spotty commitment. The prospect of losing one player was bad enough, but two could be catastrophic. Catherine always warmed up with Trinity before games, and when Catherine was unfocused, so was her giggly friend. Thunder's youngest player, Trinity had the most to learn about the fine line between friendship and sport. "Your friendship is separate from soccer," Emiria and Brian warned Trinity after practice one day. "You may need to choose somebody new to warm up with. You've got to prepare yourself."

Brian considered Catherine a friend, but he knew her soccer days were numbered. He'd tried every motivational method he could imagine. Last year on the Fury, when Catherine kept skipping practice, he took away her starting position for a few games. That made Catherine angry enough to try a little harder, but practice still rated a distant fourth behind friends, school sports, and the mall. He considered confronting Catherine, but he knew she'd just quit, and the truth was, he couldn't bear the thought of losing such a critical player—halfhearted or not. When Brian finally confided in Catherine's parents about their daughter's fading interest, it was as if he were talking about another child. That couldn't be *our* Catherine. She starred in games. How could she not care about practice?

"Stop!"

The girls froze, the ball rolled to a stop. Nobody dared say a word.

Emiria looked straight at Catherine. "I'm absolutely disgusted with you! You have not touched the ball. You don't want it. A core player on this team, and you're scared to get the ball in a five-on-five."

Catherine's jaw dropped slightly, her eyes straying toward the clouded sky, her thoughts transparent. *You can pick on me, but you can't reach me.*

Catherine's defiance only fed Emiria's fury. The girls stood gaping as she hammered Catherine.

"Are you tired?"

"Yes," Catherine admitted, shifting her weight almost imperceptibly, one hand on her hip.

"That's because you're not fit! The whole team is working so hard to be fit and you've let them down!"

Shauna took in the scene. Catherine obviously didn't want to be out there slogging about in the rain and cold. This wasn't fun for any of the girls—the tension, the conflict. Shauna knew the yelling and confrontation wouldn't have happened on the old Eclipse or, for that matter, most other girls' teams. Dads never dared say the things Emiria did. But standing there, looking at the shocked expression on her friend's face, Shauna wasn't so much feeling sorry for her teammate as trying to send her a simple message. *Pick it up, Catherine. You can do it.*

The yelling continued for two solid minutes. The worst thrashing Emiria had delivered to date. She could see Catherine was furious that she'd singled her out in front of the whole team. But how else could she make her point? Making nicey-nice with Catherine wasn't going to get her anywhere.

To Emiria, Catherine was Thunder's social butterfly. The girl with her fingers in a lot of candy dishes, wanting to taste them all, a metaphor that fit her to a T. For quite literally, Catherine was the team's closet sugar junkie. She didn't dare eat the stuff in front of Emiria, but the coach had heard the stories. The stashes she'd secreted away on some of their tournaments.

But this was about a lot more than Catherine's love

of sugar. Catherine had told Emiria straight out that her
social life was important to her. Catherine sailed through
almost everything she put her mind to. Why come to practice to get her ego smashed to bits when she could be
somewhere else, giving half the effort and having a good
time? Why would any teenager find that an easy choice?

"It's your decision!" Emiria shouted, ending her outburst with an ultimatum. "You either step up on this team
or you sit down!"

That evening when the car-pool lights flashed on the
muddy field and the girls tossed their soggy shorts and
shirts into the trash bags, Brian turned to Emiria, waiting
until the girls were out of earshot. He grimaced.

"We won't see her for a couple of weeks."

Confrontation?

The modern coaching handbooks confirmed that it
didn't work. Girls just closed down and tuned out, their
self-esteem too brittle to handle the challenge. But Brian
knew from his years of coaching that there was another
way a girl might respond. Sometimes a girl might get so
angry that she'd fight. Decide to earn back her position.
Work her way out of her slump.

Emiria had taken a huge gamble with Catherine. You
couldn't retreat after cracking down. And sure enough,
the first practices after the confrontation seemed to prove
that Emiria had indeed miscalculated. The tough woman
coach had crossed a line that men believed couldn't be
broken. Catherine continued to emotionally withdraw
from the team. The battle of the wills appeared doomed
to stall in a standoff. Brian worried, and not only for Catherine's sense of self. Naomi had put her heart into playing
sweeper, but she just wasn't meant to play the position.
If Catherine kept fading, Thunder would be like a car
without a steering wheel.

*   *   *

Just lifting her head off the pillow in the morning was a struggle.

"I really can't go to school," Catherine despaired to her mother, the usual lilt in her voice turned to gravel. She felt drained. But skipping school and practice for a couple of days made no difference.

Catherine didn't appear to have a cold or a flu. Could it be some weird virus?

"You really need to get your blood checked," Leslie Sigler suggested on the third day. Leslie was anemic and wondered if her daughter might be too. Or it could be something else.

"Maybe you have mono. It doesn't hurt to go to the doctor and check this out."

But the doctor found no evidence of mononucleosis or any mystery virus. Exercise-induced asthma was the simple diagnosis. Catherine's lungs were so tight that she was having trouble breathing. He prescribed allergy medications and an inhaler, but there was no miracle cure. And there was nothing he could prescribe for her other problem.

Catherine really didn't feel she had her place on the team.

Catherine's father lacked the same day-by-day sense of where his daughter stood. He never fretted about whether Catherine started, seldom heard the play-by-play of tough practices, never thought too deeply about whether her soccer "career" was petering out. In an age when dads often hoist their Walter Mitty dreams on their children, Chris Sigler was oddly mellow. Sport wasn't anything new to the broad-shouldered man. An all-American swimmer at Springfield College in Massachusetts, Chris had won New England titles in the fifty- and hundred-meter freestyle.

Before beginning a successful career as a sales executive at Fireman's Fund Insurance, Chris had worked as a sports information officer on campus and as a coach. Come Thunder game time, the all-American was uncannily cool. He'd amble up the sideline half an hour before kickoff, prop up his lounge chair, and read the paper, maybe two. He watched the game as attentively as any parent; he just didn't say much. Maybe it was because as an executive, he knew how tricky it was to motivate people. Or perhaps it was because he'd been to so many soccer games and sporting events with his three older children. Chris simply didn't believe there was a place for parents to be vocal on the sidelines.

When the parents amped up, even his own wife, he'd just tune them out. He'd seen too many kids yelled at by their fathers at high school games, too many kids who'd eventually told their dads to just "shut up." Chris wisely used the car pool to talk to the girls, let the conversations naturally bubble up.

To Chris's mind, his daughter's struggle was simple. Catherine was the most balanced of his children. When Chris would sometimes find himself squabbling with his older daughter, Catherine would be the one to cut to the chase. "Why are you guys arguing about something so stupid?" She had a directness with adults rare for a fourteen-year-old. There was no filter or hesitation with Catherine. The girl spoke her mind.

If something interfered with Catherine's social life, she didn't want to do it. She adored her friends and other sports, and juggled more activities than her parents thought possible. Though the Siglers were the only Thunder parents who both had competed collegiately, there was no careful grooming of the future college star. Indeed, Chris and Leslie told Catherine that they didn't want her to specialize, that if she wanted to try and do it all, they'd fully support her.

Chris understood his daughter was struggling with

more than asthma and her own maturing body. Soccer under Brian had been about fun and family, and though Catherine had tested her old coach, the Hallorans had loved and accepted her as if she were one of their own. Catherine couldn't help but mourn the passing of that comfortable world, the bracing realization that her future was likely to hold its share of Emirias.

More than perhaps any other Thunder parent, Chris Sigler understood why his daughter was burnt out. With three extremely athletic siblings, if Catherine wasn't playing soccer one weekend, the family was usually on the road to watch another sibling in a tournament. There were plenty of times when Chris himself just said no. Saturdays he just didn't want to bake in the sun or stand in the rain and watch soccer. Saturdays he couldn't drag himself into the car and log another body-cramping 150 miles. He figured Catherine felt just what he felt: I'm pooped. I want to sleep in until noon, stay up until two on a Friday night. Dad had been there and he didn't even play. You reach a point when it's just too much.

"This is how I see you."

They sat on the concrete curb lining the muddy track at Rincon, Catherine clasping the note card Emiria had given her listing her skills and weaknesses. That month each girl got an evaluation. Ten minutes one-on-one with the coach during practice.

"You are an exceptional player. You have the ability to be great."

Catherine nodded her head nervously as Emiria praised her vision, her sense of the field. Just as a smile nearly crept onto the eighth grader's cautious face, Emiria changed direction. "Whether or not you want to be great is your own decision."

Making the team the next year wouldn't be easy. "I'd

rather have a player that has heart. You've got to commit to the team and yourself."

That night Catherine came home and told her parents about her talk with Emiria and her own new feelings about her teammates and herself. Her change of heart wasn't simple. It had meant a lot to her to hear from her coach that she had talent. But something else had been happening to Catherine. She had started to really like and respect her teammates, and she couldn't imagine letting them down.

On off days, between practices, Catherine started running for half an hour to build her fitness. Met with Kim occasionally to sneak in a workout. Worked on her ball skills. This in a girl who had been lucky if she made two out of three practices, and never dreamed of training on her own. At team meetings, Catherine, never one to hold back her feelings, told her teammates about her changed attitude. "I'm gonna be committed."

Trinity figured she was just trying to kiss up to Emiria. She rolled her eyes and shot her friend a questioning glance. "Look, I am," protested Catherine. "I'm gonna try."

She did. At Rincon, Brian could see the glow on Catherine's face, the spring in her step. He couldn't believe the magnitude of Catherine's accomplishment. To be willing to go out and run on her own. To be willing to give up other sports to play soccer. To go hard in practice to the point that she looked to be dying. Catherine had broken out of her comfort zone, and leapt forward to a degree Brian could never have imagined.

The proof of the new Catherine was in the tough practice, a day not that different from the one in which Emiria had chewed her out a few weeks before. Two miles of quarter-mile repeats were on the agenda that afternoon, and midway through the first lap, Catherine looked ready to throw up. Her body just wasn't cooperating that day.

It happened to all the girls at one time or another. Sometimes it just wasn't there.

But her teammates encouraged her. Emiria too. Catherine was struggling with her asthma, gasping for breath. She had The Out. She could have easily stepped off onto the curb and taken a breather. But she kept running, the girls and Emiria cheering her on, her endurance returning. Catherine didn't just finish the two miles of intervals that day. She paced her teammates through the practice-ending sprints, winning or taking second in most of the short dashes.

That's when it catches, thought Brian. That's when they see they can overcome adversity and build self-esteem. This whole mind-set that says you have to tell girls, "It's OK. You tried. It wasn't that bad." That doesn't make 'em feel better. What makes 'em feel better is when they fix it themselves.

Catherine was fixing it. She phoned up Emiria, the first of a flurry of calls to her coach. Catherine being Catherine, she just had to talk about it. Her new attitude. Even Emiria couldn't get a word in edgewise. Catherine sometimes talked nearly as fast as she ran.

"I just want to thank you for everything you've done for me," she said breathlessly. "Before, I wasn't enjoying it. Now I go out there and I love being there. I love the team, and I love what you're teaching me.

"I didn't know that before. But I see it now. I just want you to know that I'm fully committed to this team."

EIGHTEEN

Bug Eyes

*t*he clattering racket slowed imperceptibly with each step, the girls struggling up and down the creaky wooden bleachers of Slater Middle School gym.

It had been a long practice. The usual twenty laps, sprints, and an hour or so of five-on-fives. Brian had watched from the gym's stage and was impressed by what he saw. Catherine and Theresa had been talking up a storm, everything from strategy to old-fashioned motivation. The team on the sideline looked eager to get in and knock off the winner.

But now the girls were trudging through the second set of bleachers, the pace slowing with each step. When the clock finally ran, Emiria called out, "Jog in quickly!"

Out of breath, wiping the sweat off their faces with their jerseys, the girls huddled around. "You don't want to feel that pain, right?" she asked. "It's just a natural human emotion. You wouldn't want to put your hand in the flame."

She paused a bit to let it sink in. She'd been where they were headed. Believed it was the only way to become a true champion. "This pain is what you want. Be proud you're doing it. Pay attention to it. Know that if you endure this pain, nobody else is doing it. Break through it here and you'll be a great player."

Brian shook his head. Nobody could get inside the girls' heads like Emiria. Another coach might have told the girls to knock off early, but instead Emiria was telling them to embrace the pain, to view it as proof of their heart and dedication. Knute Rockne couldn't have said it better.

The girls lined up before the bleachers, Emiria leaving them with one last thought. "When you're running, think this is just one minute of your entire life."

Fifteen seconds into the final set, Emiria didn't have to watch anymore. The proof could be heard, a thunderous clatter that rocked the gym. Brian forgot for an instant that he was fifty pounds overweight. I'm ready to do step-ups, he thought. *Hey, Emiria, let's go!*

Arizona was a dads' trip, scheduled over the mid-February weekend, one of the few tournaments where dads greatly outnumbered the moms. The first game of the President's Day Tournament pitted Thunder against a highly regarded Nike-sponsored squad, the Colorado Swoosh. It was the first time most of the girls had ever played a team from another state.

Joe Piasta couldn't believe his eyes. The way he saw it, the girls came out and no one knew who they were and nobody cared and the whistle blew and the girls attacked Colorado as if they were mad dogs. What a fury! Colorado thrown back on its heels, Thunder just attacking, and it was all the incredible passes, what Emiria had been working on. The kids knew something Joe and the rest of the parents hadn't seen in months.

Brian was incredulous. The last time he'd seen Thunder play, he'd considered them an average team trying to get better. Suddenly, in the space of a few months, the girls had leaped up a few levels. And even though he'd witnessed the gradual improvement in practice, he'd had no idea they could translate what worked on tennis-court practices and a middle school's gym to the big screen of a real field.

The first goal was a thing of beauty. Three quick touches—in, out, and back inside, Natalie stepping over a ball she looked ready to shoot, freezing the goalie, leaving it for Kim to slam a twenty-yarder into the back of the net.

The Swoosh equalized early in the second half, but Shannon niftily assisted Kim in close. It was a total team victory, down to the last girl, but it was Jenny Drady who amazed Emiria, Brian, the parents—and her teammates. The shy distance runner, the girl who at times had been a black hole, missing traps and shanking crosses, was all over the field. Slide-tackling right and left. Taking the ball to the end line and whipping off crosses. Jenny Drady, the girl whose dad had talked about skipping Arizona because she seemed destined to sit on the sideline, had suddenly turned into an impact player.

Emiria had planned everything for Arizona. The week before at a team meeting, she'd surprised the girls with the news that they'd have to go to their rooms and do two hours of homework each day during the trip. Then there was the strict, healthy diet she expected them to adhere to. Lots of water, fruits and vegetables, even tofu.

But there was one thing Emiria hadn't planned on in the dry Southwest. During the night after Thunder's first game, Brian awoke to the familiar patter of rain. What a godsend, he thought. Nobody knew more about slick fields than Thunder. Rain would be a tremendous advantage.

But when they arrived at the fields the next morning, the parking lot was crammed with kids. An inch of rain in Arizona was nearly a flood. Some of the fields were underwater. Rumors flew that the day's games might be canceled, even the whole tournament. Then word circulated that they might do shoot-outs instead of games, a twist on penalty kicks. As they waited for the final decision, a couple of dads started getting antsy.

"Why don't we go do something?" they grumbled. They'd come a long way and spent a lot of money just to watch their daughters take some penalty kicks. "Why don't we go to the Grand Canyon?"

Emiria's face clouded. "We came here to do this tournament," she gruffly declared, squashing the mutinous talk. "We're staying and we're going to do whatever they tell us to do. If we have to do shoot-outs to be in this tournament, we're going to do that and not walk out."

And shoot-outs it would be. Eleven players. Each starting out on the thirty-five-yard line with five seconds to score. One-on-one with the goalie. Emiria gave a demonstration of the arcane art, sprinting toward goal, faking Cassie, and slotting the ball on the near side.

It looked so simple when Emiria did it, but the girls had never really practiced shoot-outs before. They didn't have much time, and there was all that grass to cover before they were in shooting range. Shannon hit her first dribble so hard trying to eat up the distance to the goal that the keeper grabbed the ball before she could get another foot on it. One after another, the girls fired wide or banged it straight to the keeper. And one after another, they jogged back in tears, devastated.

"What the hell is this?" Luke exclaimed, trying to put

it in perspective. "Shoot-outs don't have anything to do with soccer!"

It wasn't meant to be. Cassie may have been great at blocking penalty kicks, but this was another game. Afraid to come off her line, she watched in frustration as one opponent after another dashed in and popped shots into the back of the net. When the ordeal was finally over, the girls ran up and showered Cassie with hugs, as tears streamed down her face.

Luke could say it didn't mean anything, but Cassie and the girls knew the facts. That afternoon they'd face a powerhouse, the Michigan State Olympic development team. Tank another shoot-out and they'd be on the next flight out of town. One game and a few shots on goal and they'd be back to the mud and the tennis courts for a couple more months.

At the pizza parlor, Kim could feel the pressure mounting, and Luke offered some advice. He suggested a few arcade games to take their minds off the field, and gave Cassie a big hug and told her to have fun.

Before the second shoot-out, Emiria advised Cassie to sprint out and cut down the angle. She blocked two in a row, and then they chipped it over her. But Cassie didn't panic. Instead, she bolted forward and readied herself, making it tougher to chip.

The funny thing was, Thunder blew its first three chances. But somehow the misses had the strange effect of relaxing the next shooters. Thunder knocked in a couple of balls and the pressure swung to the other goalie.

They were improving with each girl's shot. Finally it came down to the last four. Make them all and they'd win. Kim knocked in hers and watched Trinity and Catherine score in succession. When Natalie's ball smacked the back of the net, they piled on top of each other in jubilant celebration.

Maybe it wasn't soccer and maybe they'd flown a long

way just to take a few shots. But it's a funny game. Kim knew something big had happened out there on the slippery field. They'd come back from defeat, crawled their way back in.

They could handle pressure too.

The dads cut loose after their daughters' success, and were having a good old time. They'd been to the horse races and were tossing Frisbees in the parking lot with a boys' team from Missouri. The motel room where they congregated looked like a frat house on a Friday night. Junk food, clothes, chips, and beer bottles strewn about. The windows open with the screen tossed aside to make it easy to climb in. Trinity's dad dropped beers down from his second-floor room to outstretched hands below.

Phil Molling walked into the chaos, a bemused look on his face.

"Hey, Joe, don't worry about it, but Angela is out driving the Cadillac."

They poked their heads out the window, and sure enough, Angela was driving her dad's beautiful rented white Cadillac, with Kristin, Natalie, Erin, and Jenny along for the ride. No adults in sight. And no driver's licenses either.

But the dads didn't get too worked up. They told them to make sure everybody got a turn. And don't hit anybody.

Something was happening out there in the desert, and it wasn't just the dads letting loose. Maybe it was the way the girls had played, the way they'd risen to a challenge. Or maybe it was just the closeness that comes naturally from spending time on the road together. On the plane ride out, Jenny had sat with several girls in seats that faced one another, and had a great time. Cassie, too, found it thrilling to be away from her parents for the long weekend.

Emiria had made team bonding an assignment, but now they were soaking in the real thing. Everybody ate breakfast, lunch, and dinner together, caravanning everywhere and miraculously reuniting like a flock of migrating birds at each destination. Sharing rooms in a dingy motel that ran out of sheets and towels, the girls learned things about one another and their coach they'd never find out at practice or going to movies. Once they'd finished the mandatory two hours of homework, they migrated to Emiria's room, sprawling on the beds, the chairs, and the floor, laughing and cracking jokes. Emiria let slip that she could braid.

"You've been holding out on us!" Kim exclaimed, incredulous, lining up to be first.

Jessica's mother, Maggie, had been against the trip to Arizona, part of the vocal minority who wondered why they should pay all that money if they couldn't beat the competition at home. Out of respect and support, she and her husband had gone along with the majority. But she, too, was sitting in the room with Emiria and the girls that day. And what she saw delighted her.

"So, Jenny, tell me what time you wake up," Emiria probed as she separated the strands of her fine strawberry blond hair in her fingers. "What do you eat for breakfast? Who do you hang out with at school?"

To hear Jenny Drady, the team mouse, chatter on in front of the girls was a wonderful thing. Maggie thought it quite a change from Emiria, the old drill sergeant. She seemed genuinely interested in the girls in a fun, lighthearted way, like a big sister who'd been away and had finally returned home for a nice long catch-up.

Sandy Cavalieri couldn't believe her ears. The rain from two nights ago had been largely soaked up by the desert heat, and the fields seemed dry as a bone.

Surely they're gonna open the field. They're not going to send us home without playing another game.

"You mean today?" they asked the field marshal.

"No. At all."

"You mean today. We're going to have a game tomorrow!"

"No!" snapped the field marshal. "All the games from this point on have been canceled."

Emiria stepped in as if she were sliding in for a tackle. The girls needed to perform. They were playing without fear. Emiria had to let that energy flow.

"This is really strange." She pressed closer to the irritated official. "I mean I'm looking at the field and you're telling us the field is closed," she said skeptically, shaking her head, her tone beginning to threaten. "I don't understand it. When are we going to be called and told we're going to play a game?"

The field marshal was a squat woman with large, bulgy eyes. "You can't play on the field," she declared, seeming to spit out the words, adding, as if it made perfect sense, "The horses have to run on the field."

Horses, Emiria thought, incredulous. They're saving the soccer fields for polo players! What about girls!

Sandy couldn't believe this was happening to them. After months of training in rain and mud and hail, they'd spent thousands of dollars to fly to the desert for a few dry games and now were being told a little rain and soccer didn't mix. A team out from Massachusetts had been playing in snow. Thunder practiced in mud. What was wrong with these people?

Sandy pressed, and more than a few Thunder parents were amazed. This was a woman who wore a country frock to church, who looked as sweet and even-tempered as her daughter, Naomi. "You had people coming from all over the nation and you don't have a backup plan?"

"It rained," the official deadpanned, as if that explained everything. "What do you expect us to do?"

"You could have let us know ahead of time," Sandy fumed. "We could have saved ourselves a lot of money!"

"Well, that wouldn't have made you very happy."

Sandy was stumped. "Are we happy now?"

"Well, if you're that unhappy about it, don't come back, because we have a lot of people on waiting lists," snapped the official. "We don't need you."

Word slipped out that something fishy was going on. All the games were canceled except a match between two Arizona teams. It just so happened one of the field marshals had a daughter on one of those teams. And he was the coach.

This isn't right, thought Jeff Young and Joe Piasta. They cancel the tournament and then let two Arizona teams play. So the insurance man and the attorney started making their case, and found a mother of one of the girls on one of the Arizona teams sympathetic to Thunder's predicament. She said they'd played the other team half a dozen times, and wouldn't mind at all if Thunder took their place.

Joe Piasta and Jeff Young decided to put on the screws. Strode on over to the field monitor's table. Joe did most of the talking.

"Did I just hear another Arizona team is coming to play on this field against your team?" the lieutenant colonel in the army reserve began. "Well, I'll tell you how you can solve the problem. You let us play that team, because we're from Northern California."

When this didn't get much of a response, Joe pushed a couple more buttons. "Why didn't you call and tell us you were going to shut down the fields? We spent thousands of dollars to come down here."

"We don't want to have any trouble here—"

That was the wrong thing to say to a trial attorney, and Sandy listened as Joe went on the offensive, tossing out phrases like *terms of default* and *misrepresentation*. But it wasn't all legalese. Joe talked about the games they'd played in Northern California in rain and mud. Single moms who'd saved up for the trip. Kids who'd sold candy and Beanie Babies door to door as fund-raisers. "And you're telling me that your team is going to play a game?"

The full-court press worked, and soon the girls found themselves on the field playing a top-ranked Arizona squad. But they were a player short. Brian had taken Kim to watch Brian Junior play, thinking the situation hopeless. The girls would have to win without their star striker, the player who'd scored both goals in the opener.

But Thunder could have fielded ten girls and won that day. Nothing fazed them, not even the Arizona squad scoring first. The girls stuck to their quick-passing game, winning easily by 4–2, downing one of the tournament's top teams.

A few months before, an early goal might have sunk Thunder. But the talk in the back was inspired. Having finally won the coveted sweeper spot, Catherine wasn't about to let anything stop her now. She directed the defense, alerting fellow defenders when they were drifting from their marks, letting Cassie know when she needed to come out of the box. "This is *you*, Cassie!"

But the keeper and the sweeper didn't just direct one another, they deflated the pressure. "Take a deep breath," Cassie would say, calming Catherine before her goal kicks. Pretty soon Catherine and Cassie found themselves chattering away the whole game. They made up their own little private jokes, expressions of confidence, a lyrical method of easing the tension of being the two girls most responsible for keeping the ball out of the net. What they said didn't have to make much sense, it was the banter that counted, the connection.

"How'd ya like them apples?" Catherine would quip after she turned back an opposing forward.

The refrain always brought a smile to Cassie's face. "Those are sweet apples!"

Emiria stretched her eyes wide with her hands. "You can't play on the field because the horses have to run on it," she droned, mimicking the poor woman they now referred to as the frog lady, cracking up the girls. "Bug Eyes" was what they called the routine, and soon nearly the whole team was doing it.

With several hours left before their flight home, the girls and their parents weighed their options. People began to make plans. Some wanted to go to the mall, others wanted to drive out to see the beautiful cathedral rocks of Sedona. Theresa could see by the expressions on her friends' faces that most of them were ambivalent about a bunch of red rocks, no matter how spiritual a lot of visitors might find them. Sedona was a long drive, the mall nearby, a known quantity.

But Emiria insisted the team stay together. Now that they were just hours from going home, she wasn't going to let them go separate ways. They'd vote. Girls, moms, dads. There was a lot of grumbling, but finally the hands rose. It was close, and plenty of girls weren't happy that the rocks had won.

But when they reached the glorious rich red plateaus, the girls looked out in wonder. Jenny and Theresa had wanted to go to Sedona because they were in Arizona and you could go to the mall at home. They got out and snapped photos, the girls perching on the fenders and climbing up on the car roofs, taking in the natural beauty.

Everything about the Arizona trip had been a surprise, from the rain to the shoot-outs to the now infamous Bug

Eyes. And then just a short jog up the road was something else they'd never expected to find out in the Southwest. Glorious white snow.

The girls had played magnificently, and now that the soccer was behind them, they let fly. Emiria started it, firing from behind the van upon the unwary occupants of the shiny white Cadillac. Then Jenny, Angela, and Theresa staged a vehicular counterattack, running beside the Cadillac as Joe Walsh drove, leaping out at the last second and blasting Emiria with a barrage of snowballs.

But sneaky Shannon wouldn't let her fellow van-mates be beaten. While the girls were caught in cross fire, she found a giant, crusty chunk of snow and, with some help, heaved it in the backseat of the brand-new Cadillac. That pretty much settled it. Shannon, Cassie, Emiria, and the rest of the van team won. But the moms and dads knew the true winners. The girls had overcome so much in such a short time. It was more than the mastery and heart they'd shown on the field. The joyful, wild snowball fight was proof that the bonds were growing even stronger. Out in the desert, far from home, they'd come together as a team.

Driving back from Sedona, on the way to the airport, they stopped at the Nike outlet and a food court. At Burger King, Cassie spied a bunch of golden Burger King crowns.

"Hey, Jessica, I want one of those crowns."

So Jessica went and got her one, and Cassie tried on the paper crown for size and scribbled her name on it. "Cassie 'The Keeper' Kays."

Cassie had a feeling this was going to be a lucky crown.

NINETEEN

Growing Pains

"**a**m I going to get a meeting?" Heather nervously asked Emiria after practice at Rincon.

"Oh, I forgot about you."

Day by day the other fifteen girls had gotten their meetings, a chance to find out where they stood and anxiously pore over the three-by-five index cards listing their strengths and weaknesses. And then Emiria had continued on with practice as if Heather didn't exist. Heather tried to be optimistic. Maybe it had just slipped her mind. But Heather hadn't felt she was doing well. She wasn't getting a lot of playing time.

Emiria did like her moves and thought her an intelligent, attacking player, but that didn't change what she viewed as the immutable fact. Heather weighed ninety-five pounds, and her frailty and defensive weaknesses made her a liability. At times she seemed all uniform and bones, giving up balls so easily, shying away from tackles. "You need to be more aggressive and defensive," Emiria said.

"OK," Heather cheerily replied, nodding her head and then pursing her lips as she often did when she contemplated a tough challenge. Heather could read between the lines. She knew the odds were long against her making next year's squad.

Time and the competition seemed to be catching up with Heather. As a child, she'd been a natural, making her first traveling under-ten team when she was just eight. In little Rohnert Park she was a star, and learned early on to be comfortable with the ball, dribbling and controlling play. But the year before, the Eclipse coach had cut Heather. It wasn't just that she had the out-of-towner knock, and seemed at times to hold the ball too long, the common result of playing too many years on weak teams. Even the date of her birthday, August 23, seemed stacked against her. January 1 was the cutoff date for the Olympic development teams, the regional squads that serve as the talent pools for statewide, and ultimately national, teams. The district ODP team covered the territory from the Golden Gate Bridge to the Oregon border. Making the squad wasn't just an ego boost, it was a great way to pick up new skills. But with a late August birthday, Heather was often competing against older girls born in the winter and early spring, and she was always cut on the last round.

Not making the regional Olympic development team was one thing. That was a dream; Thunder was Heather's life. And her predicament was only tougher because of all the time she spent with her coach. Emiria lived around the block from Heather, and often gave her a ride to and from practice. They seldom talked about soccer. Jeans, shoes, music—making fun of your sister—were the main topics. But one day, after chatting for a few minutes, Heather took a chance.

"Emiria," she ventured in her bouncy voice. "I would like to learn how to slide-tackle."

Emiria had assumed Heather was just afraid. On a team where Arlene was held up as a paragon of virtue, it was hard to imagine a girl who didn't understand the importance of being physical. But there was something wonderfully brave and sincere about Heather admitting her shortcoming.

If she wanted to try, help was as close as a teammate. "Why don't you talk to Kim or Natalie or Trinity."

Heather asked Kim at practice, mainly because for some reason she felt more comfortable asking the Thunder star. They were an odd pair, the short, muscular fighter and the tall, willowy blond. Kim played the role of dance instructor, teaching her friend the mud tango. After practice, when everybody else readied to leave, Kim tossed a ball into the mud and let Heather take a crack at it. She lunged at it a couple of times but got all tangled up.

"OK, we need to work on getting that foot out," Kim patiently suggested. "Don't worry about being perfect."

A few girls circled round, cheering her on, Natalie's vibrant voice the loudest. The encouragement boosted Heather more than she could have imagined. But still her first two lessons were a bust. Heather fell clumsily to her knee, a leg tucked under her rear, afraid to lean back into the tackle.

Brian stood back and watched the scene, waiting to give Kim a ride home. He was impressed by Heather's effort, but he wasn't a believer. Heather hadn't caught on during the season like most of the other girls. Could it be her frailty? Or something to do with her being the new girl on the team? Heather was the only field player who hadn't been on Eclipse or Fury.

But before her third practice, the impish girl had a conversation with herself. *Heather, you're going to slide-tackle today.*

Fifteen minutes later, splattered with mud from head to

toe, chunks of it in her cornsilk hair, Heather Stenmark made her run. She eased back and suddenly felt completely natural, her leg sweeping out, the ball and mud flying.

Maybe, thought Brian, watching Heather shake off the mud. Maybe she really wants to be on this team.

Angela's room was a pantheon to her independence, hardly the stuff of the average American teenage soccer player. While her teammates plastered their walls with Mia Hamm, Angela's ceiling featured a giant poster of her idol, Courtney Love, who made numerous appearances in smaller posters throughout the room. Fiona Apple was pinned up too, along with the Rolling Stones, Kurt Cobain, and the Doors. Skateboarding posters blocked out the last remaining stretches of ceiling and walls.

Her teammates tended to display their trophies front and center, but Angela's were hidden away in her closet, next to her large collection of rainbow-colored candles. Still there were ample signs she was fourteen years old: the stuffed animals and, not to be forgotten, the piggy corner, a crowded shelf of little porcelain and stuffed pigs. But it was the Barbies that proved Angela didn't fit any stereotype. Because "nothing in creation is perfect," Angela had disfigured her Barbies. They had tasteless clothes, bad hair, awful makeup. They were almost human.

Angela left her stamp on life. When her grandma gave her a diary for her fourteenth birthday, she started filling every page with miniature writing that only she could read. She wrote about the sorts of things that consume a fourteen-year-old girl. But that winter, soccer was a recurrent theme. And her ambivalence toward her coach:

> *"Scrimmage was so muddy, I've never been muddier in my life. We all look like we were at Woodstock. It was so fun, I was a big slide tackle mess."*

"Soccer went pretty well. I scored and did some sweet moves and then Emiria started being herself."

"I got really muddy at soccer. It was O.K. I guess and Emiria actually had a few nice things to say to me for a change."

"Emiria is full of B.S., lecturing the team on crap. When she asked who didn't go to the movie, [another player] was the first to yell out my name. She was pissing me off. I'm really sick of soccer."

As her diary proved, Angela had an up-and-down relationship with her coach. The same instinct that caused Angela to disfigure her Barbies made her resist Emiria. Team bonding drove her nuts. She already spent two and a half hours several times a week with her teammates, and she fought the fact that the social gatherings were required. These weren't fun for Angela. She always seemed to be the girl on the outside, the awkward one, the girl no one talked to. She knew that her stubborn loyalty hadn't helped, that her teammates were faced with difficult choices. But Angela wasn't about to abandon her friend Erin.

The Christmas break had been good for Erin. She'd played indoor at Sports City like the rest of the Thunder girls, and reveled in the break from Emiria. The girls had coached themselves, and loved competing without pressure. In January Erin returned refreshed and in better shape. The often rainy and muddy practices were tough, but even she had to admit that Emiria was encouraging.

But Erin's newfound confidence and love for soccer were fragile. The old Fury players didn't seem to want her there anymore, and even the Eclipse girls she'd once considered friends shied away. Shannon liked Erin but stopped practicing with her because she knew if she did, she wouldn't concentrate on soccer. No one said it out loud, but everyone knew it wasn't a good idea to hang out with Erin. Pretty soon the only girl who would warm up with Erin was Angela.

Isolated from her teammates and her coach, Erin struggled. Practice, games, every act became an act of defiance. Erin and Angela talked about school, friends, the ballroom dancing class they went to each week. Anything but soccer.

"Stop talking!" Emiria shouted. "There's time for that after practice."

Erin never stood with the other girls, and she began to let them know what she was thinking. "Arlene, don't you think that was inappropriate?" she snapped after one of her tough hits. "That was definitely a foul."

Erin and Kim clashed too. When Kim asked Erin to pass in a scrimmage or a game, she'd ignore her or tell her to do it herself. As time went on and Erin's protest began to be abundantly clear to the whole team, Emiria didn't feel like she could ignore it.

"Is that a sprint, Erin?" Emiria asked with disbelief, as Erin jogged through a drill her teammates were running full bore.

"Yes," Erin defiantly replied, refusing to step up her pace.

"That's a pretty sorry sprint."

Even Erin's old Eclipse teammates were losing their patience, wondering when the coach would step in. Kristin Young spent her share of time on the sidelines and understood how hard it was whiling away the game minutes. You couldn't have found a fairer, more sympathetic girl on the team. But Kristin, too, tired of Erin complaining under her breath about running or drills.

And there was the afternoon at Rincon when they readied to start the nearly three-mile Deer Trail run. Erin and Jenny didn't feel well, but only Erin went home. To Kristin that showed Jenny was truly committed to the team and Erin wasn't. To Jenny, who had earned every minute of playing time with grit, Erin was the one separating herself from the team. Jenny was probably Erin's closest friend on the team next to Angela, but she, too, wondered. Why should the girls support Erin when she boycotted the bonding events? When she didn't even give her teammate a present at the secret Santa party?

Erin knew she didn't always give her all. Didn't give 100 percent at practice. Wasn't always totally committed. But by then she'd abandoned hope. She believed Emiria would never give her a chance. And once Erin got down on herself, she found it hard to pull herself back up. She couldn't see anything good coming out of it.

"It's not worth it," she complained to Angela. "Emiria doesn't like me. Why should I be worried about making mistakes all the time just to get playing time?"

When Erin told her dad she wanted to quit, he told her to stick it out. She'd made a commitment. "You need to go out there and prove to her that you're a good player and that she's wrong."

But the pep talk failed, and Lou Ann watched sadly as her daughter's effort slumped. Her dad had a solution. Erin could try out for another team for the upcoming season. Suddenly Erin brightened. She shared her secret with Angela at practice. It would be so much fun. Did she want to switch too?

February 24, 1998

Dear Emiria:

Erin, Lou Ann and I have decided that Erin will try out for the Santa Rosa United Avalanche U-16 Girls Soccer team for the upcoming 1998–1999 [season]. This is contingent on the SRU Board approving Erin's play-up request. [The Avalanche coach] has asked us to notify you of Erin's decision.

Let us assure you that Erin is committed to finishing

the season with Thunder and is looking forward to the State Cup competition.

Many reasons have led us to this decision. Primarily, she feels more comfortable on her high school team. There are 4 to 5 girls from her high school team that play for Avalanche. As you know, success at the top levels of soccer (or any sport) is 90% mental (Luke Oberkirch, 1997, pers. comm.). With this in mind, Erin's progress in soccer requires she take this chance.

[The Avalanche coach] has no problem with Erin trying out and assures us she will be evaluated based on her merits with all the other candidates. Her high school coach, Debra La Prath, has also endorsed her decision.

> *Sincerely,*
> *Phil Molling*

"Erin, I want you to stay after practice."

It was a couple of days after Phil had silently handed Emiria the envelope. Emiria waited until she got home from practice to read it, and when it sunk in she felt a sense of overwhelming relief. But the more she thought about it, the more she realized this wasn't something that could be resolved in a father's letter.

When the girls left that afternoon, Emiria walked to the side and spoke privately with Erin. She wanted her to know that she realized she didn't want to play for the team the following season, and she thought that was fine. "I want you to know that that's not going to affect how you play on Thunder."

But a part of Emiria thought it was sad that it had come to this. Maybe she wasn't the coach for everybody. An athlete or a parent might clash with her confrontational style. But why did it have to descend to letter writing? Why couldn't it be about Erin?

"I think you have potential," Emiria told Erin. "I think I could have helped you, made you a better player."

"What's wrong?" Erin pressed. "Why aren't I getting more playing time?"

"You've missed a bunch of practices and you've regressed. You're not the player you were at the beginning of the year."

Erin disagreed. Her heart just wasn't in it anymore. "I still have the skills. It's just the desire is not there."

"I'm sorry." Emiria shrugged. "I can't help you with that."

"Well, it's not like I've gotten any support from you. You haven't been encouraging, and you obviously have a problem with me."

"No," Emiria stonily replied. "I don't have a problem with you. You seem to separate yourself from the rest of the team. You're the first one to leave from practice and the last one to arrive."

"What do you expect from me when I don't want to be here!" Erin cried. "You exclude me and treat me like I'm not part of the team, and that's rubbed off on a lot of the players."

So it had finally come down to this, the classic player-coach struggle. Emiria saw a prima donna demanding special treatment, while Erin saw a heartless coach who had withdrawn her encouragement, making it impossible for her to give her all. Neither could see how the other might be at least partly right, and this wasn't something they were likely to resolve in ten minutes, standing in the rain after practice. Emiria suggested they try to make the best of these last weeks. Erin agreed. She at least felt better about getting things out in the open.

But as Emiria turned, she noticed that Lou Ann had inched within ten yards of them, close enough to eavesdrop. First the letter, now this.

How could she possibly coach Erin if her parents wouldn't let go?

TWENTY

Round One

*t*he girls stuffed a couple of practice jerseys into the gaping hole, but they'd need more. The hole was a good foot and a half deep, nearly the width of a manhole. Step in it and you'd be lucky if you just twisted your ankle.

The Bay Oaks tournament held near San Francisco on the Alameda Naval Station was supposed to be a perfect tune-up for Thunder before the State Cup. But it wasn't just the potholes. The fields were narrow and short, the weedy grass heavy as a buffalo's coat. Thunder knocked off its first opponent two to nothing, but then physics caught up with them. They should have called it the "All Amazon" tournament. The teams all seemed to have four or five amazingly tall and strong girls in the back. The tiny pitch made it a boom-ball festival, the big girls heading or booting every ball upfield like a punt. Thunder's short passes skidded dead on a clump of grass or bounced awry.

Thunder's second match was against Bay Oaks, a team with a towering back line that might have played high school basketball. When the rains came, it grew desperate. Trinity went to clear a ball in the penalty box, and the ball spun backward off her foot into Thunder's goal. Luke lost his temper at the ref, and the next morning Thunder seemed to have the fields and the refs against them. When the weekend was done, Thunder had two wins and two losses, not exactly the performance of a budding champion.

But out there on the soggy field, Thunder lost something more precious than a little confidence and a couple of games. Before the start of the second match, Luke could see Shauna's hamstring was paining her and he huddled with Emiria. Shauna had been silently suffering for months. Thunder's thoroughbred stretched diligently, but the knotty hamstring she'd tweaked at the beginning of the season was still as temperamental as an old clutch.

Brian always knew when it was hurting Shauna. "I stunk today," Shauna would say, her self-deprecating way of saying that she'd been trying to play on one leg. More than once Emiria had ordered Shauna to sit down in practice when it was clear her leg was acting up.

But this was worse. They weren't going to let her play anymore. She had to get help for her leg, take a break from the team. The timing couldn't have been worse. Though Shauna's family seldom watched her play, by coincidence they'd driven down for the weekend tournament. They saw her, all right, standing on the sideline injured, watching her teammates lose.

Shauna began her physical therapy early the following week. Technicians stuck patches to her leg, stimulating it with ultrasound and electrical current. The doctor ordered regular massage, and a physical therapist started her on a complex stretching and exercise regime.

Shauna religiously attended practice as if nothing had changed. She couldn't run or play, but she was captain, part of a team she'd grown to love. Brian gave her a quick tutorial in shagging balls, but there were plenty of times when all she could do was sit and watch, longing to get out there and play.

"How's it going?" "When are you going to come back?" the girls asked cheerily every day, showing their support, including her in conversation. But Shauna had torn her hamstring, and the first month she couldn't even jog. Rehab began painfully and slowly. She brought a stopwatch to practice. First she'd jog, then stretch, everything timed and ordered.

Brian's respect for Shauna grew daily. He'd seen how she'd shake off compliments, and now that she was a regular member of his car pool, he saw she was always upbeat, never once complaining about her leg. Brian doubted anyone else on the team had the discipline and heart to endure what she was going through. Even Arlene might have cracked.

Emiria thought part of Shauna's patience and strength came from years of caring for her severely retarded brother. But Shauna was a quiet, hard-to-read girl. She had first imagined she might be sidelined a month at most. When five weeks came and went, it became harder to bear the frustration. Now her teammates started asking what game she'd play in. Shauna had no idea how badly she'd injured herself, no idea how long her rehabilitation might take. State Cup wasn't that far away. Her leg had to get better soon.

The teasing began once the girls of Thunder started doing things socially together. Other friends didn't understand why they couldn't go to the mall anymore. Or the movies.

"Why are you going out with your soccer team?" Natalie's puzzled pal asked.

"Because it's so much fun."

"Oh God!"

Arizona only widened the communication gap. Natalie's friends mocked her for having to study during the tournament.

"Let's have study hall with soccer players!" they joked.

"At least we're friends!" Natalie shot back.

But it didn't seem to make any difference if Natalie stuck up for herself and her team. Just asking if she could use a friend's phone to call a teammate could spark trouble. "I don't want you calling your soccer people from my house!"

Natalie chalked it up to jealousy. Most of her friends were on Class III teams, and they assumed her Class I team was full of rich snobs. They tried to make her feel like she was missing out by spending so much time with her team, but Natalie hardly even noticed the change. She still found plenty of time for homework, and even to dress nicely and wear a little makeup when she felt in the mood. Soccer didn't turn her into a social cripple. Her guy friends were athletes, too, and they thought it was cool she was a soccer player. They often inquired about her team.

Natalie had always been a girl to speak her mind, so perhaps it wasn't surprising that she ultimately decided upon an amazingly grown-up tack. She wasn't the type to succumb to peer pressure. When it was clear their teasing wasn't going to disappear, she decided to do something about it.

Natalie signed up for a conflict-management session at school with her friends. They met with a counselor in a big room. Natalie laid it out on the table. What they'd been saying about her and her team angered her. She didn't make fun of their lives, and she hadn't thought they'd make fun of hers.

Her friends listened and said they were sorry. They admitted, just as Natalie suspected, that they had indeed been jealous of her blossoming friendships. And just like that the teasing stopped.

Emiria dropped her hands in frustration. Nobody checking back for the ball. No passing. Would somebody please foul Arlene?

She yelled for them to bring it in. "Practice is ending," she said, glowering. "I'm leaving you guys to sit here and decide what kind of team you are."

Just two weeks remained before State Cup. Emiria was done with it. Finished with telling them things over and over again. But somebody else appeared to be finished too. As the girls gathered it in and began talking it up, Emiria watched incredulously as Erin walked off. Emiria looked at Brian and shook her head. Could it be any more blatant? It was one thing to fight your coach, another thing not to stand with your teammates.

Emiria's outburst might have bludgeoned the confidence of a lesser group of girls. But fifteen out of sixteen girls wanted to fix it. So what if their coach and a disillusioned player had walked out on them? They'd stunk in practice before. They vowed to make it right the next day. And they were true to their word. The next Thunder practice was inspired.

On the eve of the first round of State Cup in early April, the girls met at Natalie's house for a pasta feed. The spread was bountiful: lasagna, ravioli, pizza, barbecued wings, with ice cream and pie for dessert. The girls were signing a thank-you card to Emiria for the simple reason that that weekend might well spell the end of their season. But the girls were not talking as if they were going to lose. After dinner everyone howled at a screening of Joe Walsh's highlight video of Arizona (appropriately short on soccer and long on snowball-fight sequences). Emiria briefly spoke to the girls and their parents about how far the team had come and then handed out the trophies for winning the league championship over Sebastopol. And then the parents were asked to leave the room.

The girls were initiating a new Thunder ritual. At practice Emiria had asked them to come up with an individual and team goal for the first round of State Cup. And so around the room the girls went, reading from their scraps of paper. Many had written entire paragraphs, neatly ordered sentences about switching the ball and playing one-touch.

When all sixteen had shared their individual and team goals, Natalie stood up. Thunder's spitfire had something more to say. For the first time she felt they were really one team. "We're not just Eclipse or Fury anymore," she declared, her face flush with emotion. "We're Thunder."

Emiria beamed proudly, and Brian nodded to himself. Yeah, that's it. They're getting it.

Catherine, too, had to talk. "We've worked so hard. We've been through so much together. Now is the time we just need to work even harder."

She might still be an eighth grader, she might still connect her phrases with "like" and "you know," but Catherine had an uncanny ability to talk to her teammates, to connect the emotional and the technical in a way they could all understand. "You know how we used to never be able to pass the ball. Like how we didn't trust each other, and now it's total trust. Like you know with me as sweeper, you know that I'll be back there, or that when I go forward, I know that Shannon will be back there for me. We just need to keep up our hard work."

Cassie, too, had something to say, but it wasn't really about soccer. She spoke of how Thunder had become her second family, and Arlene, of all people, was thinking how hard it must be for Cassie to only see her mom on the weekend in distant Sacramento. But Cassie wasn't afraid to be vulnerable, to let her teammates know the depth of her feeling.

"I like being with you guys a whole lot," she cried as a watery-eyed Kim leaned over, the first to give her a big hug.

The first round of the State Cup was played thirty miles south of the Alameda Bay Oaks tournament in the working-class East Bay town of Newark. The setting was typical for a youth soccer tournament: fields bordered by the basketball courts of an elementary school and a low-slung fence separating it from a cluster of modest suburban homes. As they had in the Bay Oaks tournament, Thunder would play two games on Saturday and one Sunday morning game. Lose the first match and Thunder would be another Eclipse, a first-round State Cup flop.

The first couple of minutes were shaky, Thunder giving up a corner kick. But Cassie leapt off her line and confidently punched the high cross, Shannon right there to clear the bouncing ball out of the box. Seconds later, Cassie barely had time to backpedal into position. She lunged for a long shot that curved to the far post, pinning it to the grass inches from the goal.

"Excellent, Cassie!" Emiria cried.

The near misses awakened Thunder. Arlene punished a girl with a midfield foul, making a statement. Kim punched a ball to Jenny on the wing, and only a desperation foul could stop the sprinter. Suddenly it was all Thunder: Trinity stealing a ball and driving hard toward the penalty box; Catherine whipping it up quick to Trinity, who headed it to Kim, who one-timed it to Arlene, outmuscling two defenders to get a shot on goal. The early panic replaced by calm, the girls slinging the ball easily around the field, testing for openings.

And then the blunder. Kristin miskicking what seemed an easy clear, the ball glancing backward toward Thunder's own goal. The parents gasped. But steady Cassie was right there on the near post, pulling down the rebound as if it were no more dangerous than a party balloon.

Thunder controlled the rest of the match. Two to nothing was the final score, though it wasn't that close. Jenny and Angela owned the wings, making runs down the line at will. One midfield tussle for possession summed up the Thunder effort. Natalie went down once, twice, finally wresting away the ball, the battle lasting long enough for several parents to cheer on the spunky little brunette. "Way to go, Natalie!"

The second game was when Thunder usually let down. But not today. In the second half the girls were electric. They won corners as if they were throw-ins, getting the best of nearly every confrontation.

"Pressure now, Thunder!" Emiria cried. "Every ball now blue."

Shannon snapped a one-touch pass to Kim's feet a good twenty yards out.

"Oh, take the shot, Kimee!" Chris Sigler cried, uncharacteristically losing his cool.

A quick trap and then a rocket to the upper left corner. The keeper didn't have a chance.

Kim was on, the girls' passing inspired. One of the Thunder parents counted the consecutive passes out loud: *One, two, three, four, five!* Minutes later, Trinity crossed inside to Arlene, who tucked it in close, readying herself for the inevitable blow. It was the kind of foul Arlene could take all day, the kind of strength and patience that made her indispensable. Kim lined up the twenty-five-

yard free kick calmly, bending at the waist as her fingertips loosely placed the ball on a tuft of grass. She stood
back a few paces, waiting patiently for the defenders to
form their wall. In the morning match, she'd been just a
couple hands wide, bouncing the ball off the side netting.
This time she trotted up and struck the ball easily, looking
as if she weren't even trying. The shot was a dazzler,
another bomb to the upper left triangle of the goal. "Oh
my gosh!" a stunned Thunder mom cried. "Can you believe that!"

But Heather Stenmark had a different perspective on
Thunder's quick dispatching of its first two State Cup opponents. She fixated on the depressing sound of Emiria
crying out her name. A couple of bad touches and
Heather was out. Not that she'd worked up much of a
sweat. About seven minutes was the extent of Heather's
playing time in game two. Mop-up work just like the
day before.

Standing next to Erin on the sidelines didn't make it
any easier. Heather gave everything she had at practice,
and Erin—well, everyone knew Erin's heart wasn't in it
anymore. So why then did Emiria give both of them
roughly the same lousy few minutes? Did Emiria think
she wasn't trying? It wasn't just Heather's vanishing playing time. When Emiria yanked her, she knew how to
make it hurt. She ignored Heather, just as she ignored
Erin, never telling her how she might make it right.

Heather's mother didn't know what to do. All season
long Stephanie had encouraged Heather to talk to Emiria,
to sort out her problems directly with her coach. Today
was a first. Heather was so furious she could barely speak.

Emiria's cool expression made clear that Stephanie
was treading on thin ground. This was State Cup after
all. Tomorrow they had to tie or win to advance. This
wasn't the place or time for mother-daughter theatrics.

But Stephanie pleaded. "Please, Emiria, if you would just talk to her. Heather doesn't know what she's doing wrong."

By now Heather feared it had gone beyond her defensive failings. She wanted to know if she was finished, and she had the courage to ask. "Heather, you're not at the same level as Erin," Emiria reassured her, standing alone with the girl on the edge of the parking lot. "Erin's practically quit the team."

Heather didn't believe her, unable to look directly at her coach, her eyes still swollen with tears. If that were really true, she'd be getting more playing time. "No," Emiria corrected her. "We're in State Cup. When the girls are playing well, I don't like to take them out."

The conversation didn't last more than a few minutes, and through it all Heather felt Emiria only spoke to her out of a sense of obligation. When she reached the car, Heather realized she couldn't face her teammates. Her mom drove her back to the hotel, and she cried all the way, overcome by a sense of hopelessness.

At the hotel, Natalie, Theresa, and Jenny gave her hugs. "It's OK, Heather," Natalie comforted her, trying to cheer her up. "You'll play tomorrow. You've just got to prove yourself."

Heather had spent the last nine years proving herself.

She was one of two or three Thunder girls who truly believed she was going to win a scholarship to play college soccer. The facts might have argued against that lofty ambition, but struggling substitute or not, Heather had at least one advantage over most of her teammates. Heather's mom had been a tough athlete. Stephanie Stenmark had swum collegiately and played on the University of Nevada's tennis team. By the time Heather hit the tender age of four and a half, it was already abundantly clear that she had inherited her mother's furious drive. "It's going to be fun, Dana," Heather encouraged her reluctant older sister when her mom said she'd signed them up for soccer. "We'll learn how to play."

That was before Heather got sick. Suddenly the once energetic preschooler was exhausted. Stephanie took her to the nearby Kaiser Hospital, and the friendly HMO doctors told her not to worry about it. She probably just had a flu or a virus.

One evening after washing Heather's snow white hair, Stephanie noticed something odd as she parted the strands. A mole, black as night. A mole that hadn't been there before. It looked jagged, and her dad, a surgeon, told her to watch it. One week later, a black hair sprouted out of the mole.

"We're going to have to remove it," the doctor told Stephanie.

Heather couldn't really see what was happening. They held a needle above her head and anesthetized her. Two surgeons and several nurses in the operating room, Stephanie holding her five-year-old's tiny hand.

"Can you feel this?" the doctor said as his scalpel sliced open the top of Heather's head.

"No," she said. "Feel what?"

The doctor motioned to the nurse. "I need the tongs."

Stephanie watched as he plucked what looked like a small carrot from her daughter's head.

"What's that?" she asked, fearing the look the doctors gave one another.

The doctor wouldn't say. He dropped the white root in a vial and sewed Heather's head back up.

It wasn't until the doctors called them back in to take out the stitches that they told Stephanie what they'd found. The inch-and-a-half root they'd pulled out of Heather's head was a malignant basal cell tumor. Generally only much older people had these tumors. But the doctors thought they'd got all of it.

Stephanie didn't say much to her daughter on the drive home, but she couldn't hold back the tears. "What's wrong, Mommy?" little Heather asked. "Don't cry."

Stephanie couldn't bring herself to tell her daughter. She ordered another set of tests and cried again when they confirmed the diagnosis. The doctors thought sun might have brought on the tumor. Heather would have to wear hats all the time, even in winter. Her odds of getting another tumor in the next five years were high, and she'd have to be checked every few months. But Heather hated wearing a hat. If she forgot her hat, she had to sit in the principal's office while the kids frolicked outside. She thought it punishment. The kids called her Heather Feather.

"This hat thing is really important," Stephanie told Heather. "What the doctors took out of your head was cancer. It kills people. The doctors want you to wear a hat all the time."

"I'm fine," Heather stubbornly insisted.

"You are fine," her mom agreed. "We just don't want you to get sicker."

Heather never cried or complained about getting cancer. She was sick and tired those first couple months after the surgery, and she often hid her hat from her teacher. But she took her chemotheraphy. In the fall, just a few months after the cancerous tumor was plucked from her head, Heather started playing soccer again.

If she made it to ten years old without a relapse, her odds were good.

As they strode out to the center line for the third and deciding match, Natalie rolled her sleeves up to her shoulders as she always did before games, looking like she was ready to box. Within minutes Thunder was peppering the opposing goal, passing even better than in its previous two games. Naomi gathered up a quick through ball in

Thunder's defensive half, galloped downfield, and dished it off to Trinity, who knocked it to Shannon. The fake inside, and then the perfect switch to the opposite side. Kim ripped a shot, but the blocked ball sprung up as if buoyed by a fountain. Who got a foot on the falling ball was hard to tell. But Jessica swung it back to Shannon, who fed Trinity on the wing.

Trinity's cross was dead on her teammate's foot. Arlene trapped it with her back to the goal and spun around, eye to eye with the keeper. She jabbed with the outside of her foot, the ball arching just beyond the keeper's arms. It was a once-in-a-season goal, an amazingly long sequence in which seven girls played a role.

The clincher was launched by Angela, a symbol of her will. She won a battle on the right wing, lost the ball and chased it for twenty-five yards, finally winning it back again, and dashed back up the line. Angela's speed caught the defense off guard. She crossed to Jessica, who drove to the end line, turning her defender, cutting right and left, waiting for the opening. Trinity raced toward her teammate as if drawn by a magnet, and knocked Jessica's perfectly timed pass into the box. Arlene banged the crossing ball into the back of the net.

Three games, three strong victories. Thunder had taken a big step. Swept the first round of the State Cup. Made it to the quarterfinal. But on a team of sixteen girls, it was not easy to please everyone. Heather felt better about getting a little more time, but she couldn't help but wonder if she'd only played because of her mom's intervention. Erin, meanwhile, had given up all hope. By her count she'd gotten just twelve minutes in the three games. The Mollings were steaming, standing apart from the other Thunder parents, thoroughly convinced that Emiria had played Erin sparingly to publicly humiliate her.

As the girls bounded together off the field after the

final victory, Theresa lifted her arms in jubilant victory, crying out to the cheering parents. Only Erin separated from her joyous teammates, a planet breaking from orbit, her shoulders slumped, one hand cupped over her mouth.

TWENTY-ONE

Cassie's Choice

The late afternoon scrimmage between Thunder and Santa Rosa's older girls' team, Avalanche, wound to a close.

How the conversation began wasn't clear, but Phil Molling felt good about what he was doing. He thought Cassie was a tremendous kid, and knew she wasn't getting the best goalie training on Thunder.

Santa Rosa United had rules about recruiting players from one team to another. Coaches had to stay out of it. Players or parents were required to make the initial contact. Otherwise, the opportunities for poaching might tear the club apart.

Greg Kays, of course, knew nothing about the rules. He was just listening to the man, and Molling wasn't a coach anyway. Just someone offering to help. As a single dad, Kays hadn't been to many of the team meetings, had no idea that there was a rift between Phil and Thunder. Kays was just trying to look out for his daughter. The Avalanche coach was a former goalie. Wouldn't Cassie be better off making the switch? "I'll mention it to her and see if she wants to," Kays told Phil Molling.

The Avalanche coach gave Cassie a call at home. "Would you be interested in playing on Avalanche?"

The position was hers for the asking. He promised great goalie training and told her she had a lot of potential. Cassie was surprised and a bit overwhelmed by all the attention. She thought it would be neat to have a coach who played her position, but then there were other things she wasn't so sure about. The Avalanche girls were all older and . . .

"Give me a call when you make up your mind," the coach said. "Whatever you decide is best for you is what's going to happen."

Cassie immediately phoned up Emiria to give her the news. By chance Emiria had just walked in the door, fresh from talking to the Avalanche coach an hour earlier at the scrimmage. "Oh, really, that's interesting," Emiria said, sounding surprised. She'd just talked to him about possibly moving people up to his under-fifteen team. He wanted Heather, but Cassie's name wasn't even mentioned.

"Am I going to make Thunder?" Cassie asked.

"Absolutely," Emiria replied, surprised at the question.

"Are you going to take the other girl?"

These didn't sound like idle questions. Someone apparently had been putting fears about playing time in Cassie's mind. But Emiria wasn't going to change the way she coached because of one player. The truth was, she hadn't decided on whether to keep the backup keeper trying out for Thunder. Sure, Cassie would probably get the majority of time, but she couldn't give her a guarantee.

They talked about how far Thunder had come as a team, and how much they'd accomplished in the past few months. How close they'd become. But Emiria acknowledged there might be advantages to the move.

"Cassie, if you think you'll get better training there, then you really should go. As a player, it's the best decision for you. I can find another goalkeeper."

Cassie weighed her options. Maybe she'd get more training and experience on Avalanche. But then what about all her great friends on Thunder? How far they'd struggled together? And her coach? Cassie felt she could bond more with a woman. Not that men were horrible coaches, it was just that she felt more comfortable with a woman.

"I want to stay with Thunder," Cassie told her coach. "I love the team."

But Emiria wasn't about to make it easy for her. "If you feel like you'll get better training with Avalanche, then that's where you need to go," she said. "I don't ever want to feel like I'm holding you back."

After Cassie got off the phone, she asked her dad what she should do.

"It's your choice, Cassie."

"I'm really sorry, Emiria, but I have to ask you these questions."

It was Kevin Brown, Santa Rosa United's coaching director, on the phone. Phil Molling, it seemed, had fired off a couple of charged E-mails. Molling believed Emiria was punishing Erin for quitting the team by taking away her rightful playing time. He asked to be reimbursed for his travel and hotel costs for the first round of the Cup. And demanded a written apology. If Emiria did not apologize, the Mollings promised to make a presentation about Emiria at the next Santa Rosa United board meeting.

Emiria refused to apologize to Phil or his daughter. But she was ready to answer the coaching director's questions.

"Is she not playing because of her decision to play for Avalanche?"

"Absolutely not."

Emiria informed Brown about Erin's loss of interest, her early departures from practice, her open rift with her teammates.

"I'll give you their phone numbers," Emiria offered. "You can call any of the parents, the girls. They'll tell you what I've told you."

"Are you going to play her?" Brown asked. Phil Molling had demanded that Emiria promise she play Erin in the next round of the State Cup.

"I don't know." She paused. "I'm only going to play her if she performs." Emiria had never promised to play anyone. She saw no reason to start now. "Kevin, it's a miracle she's gotten the time she has with the way she's been acting."

It was odd how parental involvement worked on a team, how it warped the experience for the daughter. Phil Molling's flurry of demands forced Emiria's hand. And Erin appeared to be the one who suffered. Her father's protests only put her in a more precarious situation.

Under the threat of Phil's heated demands, Emiria felt she had no choice but to phone Erin and tell her she wouldn't be getting any playing time in the second round. She had fifteen other girls to think about, and she wasn't going to let one angry father spoil the team's chances. They had a game to get ready for. Emiria requested that Erin and her father not come to the team meeting and pasta feed at the Youngs.

Erin felt she was being pushed into an impossible situation. She couldn't quit—her father had told her she should never quit. But how could she go to the game if she knew in advance that she wouldn't play? How could she endure another game of her teammates judging her as a failure?

Erin pleaded with her coach. "What do you expect me to do?"

"Erin, I don't blame this on you," Emiria told her. "This is your parents' fault."

"My parents have nothing to do with this, Emiria," Erin argued. "It's between you and me. You told me at the beginning of the season that if we had problems or questions, we should confront you. So why are you saying now that my parents had anything to do with it?"

Emiria's answer was short. "They haven't supported me as a coach."

Erin thought she simply meant that they'd encouraged her to play high school varsity instead of on Thunder. She couldn't see the campaign her father had waged against Emiria. Erin was the girl in the middle. On one side was her father, a man she greatly admired. On the other, a new coach and team. How could she choose?

Kristin's mother, Karen, wondered who could be calling. The Thunder pasta feed was set to start in about half an hour. Could it be her husband? One of the parents bringing food?

Phil Molling was on the line, warning that he and Erin would be coming to the pasta feed after all. Phil insisted he had some "treasury" issues he needed to talk about. He was calling as a courtesy. "I wanted you to know that it's probably going to be very uncomfortable for Emiria and myself."

Karen rang her husband at his office and told him he'd better get home fast. "I don't know what's on Phil's mind, but I don't like the way I'm feeling about all this."

The party began innocently enough. The Mollings were the first to arrive, Phil pleasant and chatting away like old times. Jeff Young wondered for a moment if his wife had overreacted. Phil didn't appear to have any hidden agendas. But a few minutes later, Emiria and Brian arrived, and Jeff Young couldn't miss the bad vibes. Phil staked out one end of the spacious house, and Emiria the other.

Angela noticed that Phil was dressed well for the pasta feed. Slacks, nice shoes, and a tie. She skipped upstairs and found Erin in Kristin's room, wearing a pretty dress, curled up alone by the window.

Erin told her friend the news. Angela expected her to say, "Oh, I hate Emiria," but she didn't say anything like that. The anger she'd shown at practice had emptied out of her like a spent party balloon. Erin looked crushed.

Angela knew where things had been leading for a long time, but she never thought Emiria would kick Erin off the team. "I'm sorry," she sympathized, giving her friend a big hug.

Erin glanced around the room to make sure no Fury girls were about. She didn't trust them. They wouldn't understand. When she saw that only old Eclipse players were there—Theresa, Kristin, and Jenny—she told them she wouldn't be staying for the party.

"Why?" a dumbfounded Theresa asked.

"Emiria asked me not to come to State Cup with you guys, so I feel it's best that I'm not on the team anymore because it would be awkward for all of us."

Theresa felt like crying. She'd played with Erin since she was a little kid. She couldn't imagine being on a team without her. How could Emiria be so mean?

"Gosh Erin, are you OK?" Theresa asked.

"Yeah, I just want to say 'bye to you guys," Erin cried. "This is really hard for me."

But this was just the first in what was shaping up to be a night full of disclosures. When Erin was out of earshot, Angela had a confession to make to her teammates.

Erin and her father had been trying to talk her into something. She couldn't explain why she was tempted, she was
just glad she'd had the strength to say no.

"I need to apologize to you guys because I was consid-
ering leaving the team to go play for Avalanche."

The girls and parents gathered in the Young family
room. Jeff Young wasn't going to take any chances. He
stood by Phil's side. If things got out of hand, he wanted
to be close by, ready to jump in if need be.

The treasury matters took just a couple of minutes.
Phil's trying to have the last word, Angela thought as she
listened. Emiria told him not to come, and here he shows
up anyway, making some excuse about the accounting.

"Erin's been asked not to appear tonight for the dinner," Phil said, "because she's not going to be getting any
playing time in the next round."

The room went deadly quiet. "We thought that it
would be best if we just part company with the team at
this point." The Mollings wouldn't be traveling with the
team for the next game. "We wish Thunder lots of luck
and congratulations. We hope that you guys move on. It's
been a lot of fun."

Jeff Young looked out over the crowd, and the reaction
floored him. The girls were staring at Phil with disbelief.
Their chins had dropped, their eyes wide. They had no
idea what was going on. They had no idea how to handle this.

"With that, we're not going to be staying," Phil said
abruptly. "Good-bye."

Jeff Young searched for words as he shook the man's
hand at his front door. "Sorry it's come to this."

Angela felt every girl was staring at her. Giving her
weird looks, looking to gauge her reaction. What was

going to happen now that Angela's friend was gone? Would she be the next girl "kicked" off Thunder?

But nobody said anything for a long while. At dinner, the tension in the room still thick, Emiria felt she had to tell her side of the story. "There have been a lot of issues that Erin and I have been trying to deal with over the year," she began slowly, clearly pained. "I've been trying to support her and get her playing time. I've also been trying to teach her to be respectful and willing to play the way we need her to play on Thunder."

When it didn't work out, Emiria felt Erin's father turned against her—and the team. She recounted Phil's efforts to take his grievances to the board of Santa Rosa United. His angry threats of formal complaints. And something else many of the girls in the room knew nothing about. Phil had been trying to recruit two Thunder players.

Emiria didn't mention any names, but once again Angela felt the girls' eyes on her. "I don't think that it's fair that Phil's acting this way," Emiria said, getting emotional. "I've tried to make it work for Erin, and unfortunately, it's not working."

The parents quickly gave Emiria a vote of confidence. They understood. She didn't have to say any more. "You're doing a good job with the kids," piped up one mom. "Let's not let this upset us. Let's just move forward."

Jeff Young felt a wave of relief sweep over the room. Everyone knew the brooding conflict had been hanging over the team. Was it the right decision? Hopefully it was for Erin. After all, wasn't this about the kids? If she wasn't getting anything out of it, maybe it was time for her to move on to something else.

By the luck of the draw, Thunder's quarterfinal opponent was Sebastopol, its season-long nemesis. Emiria wanted everyone to be involved. "OK now, you're going to be on the sidelines, parents," Emiria said. "We want you to know the strategy."

The girls put three cardboard poster boards up. One for the fullbacks, another for the midfielders, and one for the forwards. The girls stood up and talked about what they were going to do. They drew the lineup, how they'd play Sebastopol. What they'd do when pressed. Emiria made sure it was a two-way process.

"Challenge them!" she demanded of the parents. "Ask her why she'd make that outlet pass!"

Catherine got up and started drawing little Xs and Os, slinging lingo around like a coach. "Here's how we switch the ball. This is how we step up to put them offsides. And when I make a run, Shannon drops back for me. Right, Shanno?"

Chris Sigler was usually bored stiff at team meetings. But here was Catherine, standing up in front of her peers and twenty-odd parents, articulating her surprisingly intricate knowledge of the game. Oh, sure, she was a bit spacey and funny, and cracked a few jokes, especially about the big Sebastopol girl for whom they had special plans. But this was what was different about Thunder. Emiria had put Catherine in a leadership position without saying, "You're a leader." Catherine could talk and here she was, an eighth grader, telling parents what they were going to do in the game of their lives. But it wasn't only Catherine. Even the quiet, subdued Naomi stood up and described what she had to do.

But the strongest, most mature girl might have been the one who knew what didn't need to be said that tumultuous night. Cassie Kays had made up her mind that she was going to stick with her friends and her coach. Nobody told her what to do, but she knew it was the right course. Her teammates didn't need any more distractions. So on the eve of Thunder's biggest game, she didn't tell anyone that they'd nearly lost their goalkeeper.

That would be Cassie's little secret.

*   *   *

Later that night, Emiria opened the letter Angela had handed her before the pasta feed. Moved by what she read, Emiria dialed Angela's number and told her no one had ever written her such a beautiful letter. Emiria had shared it with her mother, and she, too, had cried at the sensitivity and insight of the fourteen-year-old girl.

Angela had held nothing back, pouring out her struggle to remain loyal to her friend and committed to her teammates. She was frank with her coach, thought she had her faults. But even though they had their differences, Angela didn't regret the experience. Emiria had pushed her as no one had ever pushed her before. Helped her mature as a young woman as well as an athlete. On her own.

Angela had taken the initiative. She'd written the letter. Not her mom or her dad. And now as she listened to her coach still smarting from the experience of Phil's parting speech, she was the one trying to shed light on the situation. When Emiria asked Angela if she had any idea why Erin "did this to her," it was Angela who had the wisdom to suggest that more might be involved. That she shouldn't look at this as strictly an Erin-versus-Emiria situation. That the events of the past few months revealed more about a father than a daughter.

For Angela, too, had learned something that emotional night. She'd been shocked to hear Erin's father had taken to writing letters. She thought Erin had told her everything, and she'd never once mentioned that telling fact, saying instead that whenever Emiria bothered her, she phoned her and confronted her. Angela thought that was the stronger approach.

Angela could only wonder. If Erin had only stood up for herself, maybe her father would have stayed out of it, and the whole thing wouldn't have blown up.

Maybe her friend would still be on the team.

TWENTY-TWO

Miracles

"I want you to go first, Cath," Emiria said.

That morning they'd driven toward the edge of what seemed endless rows of crops, and stopped where the road ended at the unlikely patch of green. There wasn't a building or tree in sight, just green and fallow fields, some distant power lines, and a horizon that might have been Kansas. There was something lonely and fatalistic about a couple of soccer fields in farming country, just west of the state capital. The idea that soccer was about spoiled suburban kids seemed remote.

Rivalries are part of what make team sports great, and so there was a certain irony in playing Sebastopol for the right to make it to the final four. Thunder's battles against Sebastopol had defined the team's promise and flaws. Sebastopol wasn't merely a strong team, it was a team that had beaten them soundly twice, a team that could make the girls doubt themselves.

Brian had arrived early at the fields and was excited. Long and broad with golf-course-like close-cropped grass, the fields would suit Thunder's possession style. But by the late morning kickoff of the quarterfinal against Sebastopol, the wind was gusting over thirty miles an hour, carrying the last bite of winter. The girls' uniforms rustled; the Sebastopol and Thunder team flags snapped like bullwhips. Games got called for rain or hail or snow, but never wind. It wasn't pretty out there. The ball got stuck on the right, hemmed in by the wind. Throw-ins down the line were blown out—by seven yards. At times it resembled a rugby scrum, a mass of girls shoving the ball forward, the ball seldom moving more than a few yards. When the Thunder girls tried to talk, their voices were swept away. Jenny was beating defenders down the end line with her speed, but nobody was there to capitalize on her crosses. Naomi watched the gusts lift up what seemed like perfect Thunder shots right over the goal. They weren't adjusting fast enough to the conditions. Naomi knew who would win. The team that was tougher, the one willing to stick it out till the end.

Kim was bored, not getting the regular touches she needed to stay connected. Her head sunk down a few times and she looked out of her game. At times like this the parents wondered if Emiria should substitute the star. But midway through the second half, Thunder won a free kick. "Look at me!" Emiria shouted at Catherine. "Move the girls to the far post!" The girls trotted into position and Kim fired away, a bullet to the upper right corner just a couple of feet high.

Suddenly Thunder was controlling play. Natalie to Theresa to Arlene inside, then out to Kim on the right flank. The defender dove in and missed, and Kim saw the goalie come off her line. Kim was at least eighteen yards out when she lofted a rainbow, the ball hitting the net as if it fell out of the sky.

Sebastopol went on the offense, substituting for its goalie so the fine athlete could play on the field. Sebastopol's star, McKenzie Blechel, had been challenging Thunder with her speed all day, and Brian watched as Naomi once again stuck with her first and second move. But on the third cut, McKenzie got a step on Naomi, and cranked a hard shot. Cassie brushed it with her fingertips, and the ball hit the post and bounced in.

"Come on, Thunder!" the parents cheered. "Come on, Thunder—you've got to want it."

Tied up in regulation, they went into overtime. Double overtime.

Catherine was a natural at penalty kicks. Used to take them all the time on Brian's team. But Catherine usually took them last. This going-first stuff made her a little nervous, and she let Emiria know about her fear.

"If you make it, it will inspire people," Emiria said.

With the game tied at one all, the quarterfinal would be decided by five penalty kicks by each team. Twelve yards out from the goal, the referee would place the ball on the chalk-marked central spot, the teams alternating shots. The goalie had to stand on the goal line, her body looking insignificant in front of the twenty-four-by-eight-foot target. In theory, once the ref blew the whistle, the goalie had to wait for the shot before she could move.* But the best goalies often anticipated which corner the player was aiming for, reading the player's body language, already diving before the ball was struck.

Both teams sat clumped at midfield, gulping water. Parents and sisters and brothers toed the sideline. The

*Current FIFA (Federation Internationale de Football Association) rules permit the goalie to move whenever she wants as long as she stays on the goal line.

quarterfinal on the adjoining field had ended and the crowd had moved over to watch, more than 150 people lining the field. Brian kept his thoughts to himself, but he figured the season was over. He'd watched Sebastopol's goalie in a shoot-out recently and never seen a youth goalie so good. And while he knew Heather to be an excellent penalty kicker, it was hard to forget that she might not make next year's squad. Nor were the girls who'd played on Eclipse overly confident. Theresa, Jessica, and a few other girls were praying. They were going to need every possible edge. Several tournaments the previous year had been decided by shoot-outs. And the Eclipse hadn't won a single one.

But as Catherine strode up to the ball, she just kept thinking, *it's simple. Shoot to the same corner I always do. On the right.*

"Go low!" her brother, CJ, shouted. *Yeah, yeah,* Catherine was thinking. *I always go low.*

As she approached the ball, Catherine couldn't resist a little humor, a little statement that this was, after all, only a game. She glanced back at her teammates and wiped the sweat off her brow, as if to say, *Whew.*

Catherine had learned a long time ago never to rush a penalty kick. When the whistle blew she felt under no pressure to hurry. It was the goalie who had to worry. The crowd hushed for a moment, and Catherine leisurely trotted up and drove the ball in the lower right corner.

Shannon had been taking her leadership role seriously. That is, as seriously as Shannon could get about such things. She paced in front of her teammates doing her best Bug Eye imitation, webbing her fingers and stretching her eyes wide. Getting plenty of laughs. It seemed to work. Heather banked her shot off the inside of the left post like a cool pool player.

But as Shannon lined up the ball on the spot, she

couldn't help but be nervous. In the final seconds before her kick, the last year of soccer flashed before her mind's eye. The scruffy hill at Sonoma State, her pink bottle of Pepto-Bismol, the days they played in the rain on the tennis courts. Even the bright blood on her knee from a tumble.

I have to make this, Shannon thought. This is the game we've been working toward all year. Don't let anyone down. Don't let this all go to waste.

Shannon always went left. She wasn't like Catherine. She didn't wait more than a second after the whistle. The ball smacked the net in the left corner. She'd done it.

Cassie didn't feel nervous at all. She was just concentrating on the ball. She'd already saved one penalty kick. Her Burger King crown was in the bag. She knew they could do it.

But Catherine sensed it wasn't going to be easy. Penalty kicks were so final. You felt the weight of the whole team on your shoulders. Kim was up, and Kim had a little history with penalty kicks. Three years before in the state semifinals, the Fury had matched kick for kick against the Carmel Acorns. The ninth shot had been Kim's. The winner. *Just relax,* Catherine had told her. But Kim's nearly perfect shot had rebounded off the bar. She didn't forget such failures easily, and Catherine knew the miss still haunted her.

So as they gathered by midfield, Catherine tried to calm her teammate. "Just take your time. Breathe in, breathe out. There's no pressure. If you miss it, there's no big deal. Nobody's gonna hold it against you. You make some, you miss some."

Kim struck the ball well to the left and felt it going in. But luck wasn't with her that day. Sebastopol's tremendous goalie guessed right, blocking the high ball just before it crossed the line.

The funny thing was, Kim didn't get that discouraged. Natalie gave her a big hug, and Catherine too. "You know, Kim, this one isn't going to affect our team at all," Catherine comforted her friend. "Let's give the other girls kicking support."

But the tension built like a boiler about to blow. Thunder and Sebastopol traded misses, all tied after the first five players. Double 0, Angela, the sixth player, fired hard, but the talented keeper knocked it down. Yet Cassie rose to the challenge, digging out the next low Sebastopol shot.

Fate had a strange way of picking the girl upon whose shoulders Thunder's future would rest. Natalie had kicked the deciding shoot-out in Arizona, but today she was only the seventh kicker for Thunder, hardly a selection that showed she was one of the team's best.

But Natalie walked confidently to the line. When the whistle blew she struck it hard and low. Natalie wasn't the type to keep her emotions inside. She leaped high before the ball even reached the goal line, firing her arms out in a joyous one-two karate punch. The girls went wild, celebrating. The shoot-out score was four to three Thunder, but it wasn't over. Sebastopol had one more chance. By now the kicks had become a test of team depth. Thunder's seventh girl had hit the ball as solidly as its first. But Sebastopol's final girl knew Cassie had just saved a tough shot. She crumpled under the pressure, bouncing it wide.

"We won! We won!" the Thunder girls screamed, hugging one another and leaping about.

The referee was oblivious to the celebration. He didn't blow his whistle or make the game-over motion. Instead, he gathered up the ball and motioned Sebastopol to take another kick. This was just the seventh round. The girls had to kick three more each before the game was decided. Thunder had jumped the gun.

"It's sudden death!" Catherine's brother and sister yelled from the sidelines. "It's sudden death!"

Anxious minutes passed. The girls weren't cheering anymore, standing there puzzled in the wind. Did they really have to take three more shots? How could they go on after already thinking they'd won?

But finally the referee acknowledged he didn't know the rules. The game was indeed over. Natalie, Thunder's seventh shooter, had delivered the final karate punch. After the cheers and hugs died down, Emiria gathered the team in at midfield. "What a great game! You hung on through two overtimes. To everyone who took those kicks, I understand the pressure. You stepped up. To do this in our first year. Against Sebastopol. I'm very, very proud of you."

The girls came together for a cheer. Fists clasped in the huddle like a human flower ready to bloom. Arms flying up to the sky, fifteen voices screaming into the wind.

"Thunders kicks ass!"

That night at the Governor's Inn in Sacramento, the girls readied themselves for another morning match. Trinity was lying on the hotel bed reading from her father's favorite book, *A Course in Miracles*. Lately her dad's life had been a bit of a miracle. A former plumber, he'd invented some simple but tremendously useful plumbing widgets. Half a dozen patents came through, and now he had a company and major contracts. In the morning in the shower, Trinity made a promise to herself. If they could win the semifinal, she'd read more of *A Course in Miracles*.

Trinity's first four games in State Cup had proved beyond a doubt just how critical she was to Thunder's success. The hard scrabble forward with wings never seemed to give up. Game by game, Trinity had improved, proving not only her own resolve, but the astonishing synergy of friendship. Catherine's newfound commitment had clearly helped hoist her friend up a notch.

But since late February Trinity had been keeping a secret from her coach and most of her teammates. It didn't seem to matter if she practiced or not. Three or four times a day her stomach twisted into an excruciating knot. The pain worsened. Sometimes she gasped for breath. Finally, in early April just before State Cup, her mother found a doctor who uncovered the root of the problem. Trinity had never considered telling Emiria about her pains; she knew how Emiria viewed most signs of weakness, and wasn't about to be considered a wimp. But the sonogram changed all that. Trinity suffered from ovarian cysts. Running could worsen the problem, causing the cysts to contract. Trinity's mother finally decided to talk to Emiria. She wanted her to know the facts, but she was careful not to be overly emotional as she shared her daughter's condition. Emiria sounded sympathetic and concerned, but Trinity's mother wasn't certain she fully understood. Emiria was an athlete, and unless you'd suffered through the kind of pain Trinity faced daily, it was hard to imagine her challenge. The doctor thought a couple of weeks rest might help clear up the problem. But resting now would mean abandoning her team. Trinity didn't have the time.

"Heather!"

She was stunned to hear her name so early. They were, after all, only ten minutes into the semifinal against Elk Grove.

"Get warmed up. You're going in at the next throw-in."

"For whom?" she asked meekly.

"Arlene!" Emiria shouted.

Heather was shocked. Arlene was Thunder's rock.

She'd played masterfully virtually every minute of the first four State Cup games, scoring three goals, her physical prowess intimidating opponents. But today she trapped as if her legs were wooden, holding the ball far too long, her shooting foot seeming to be glued to the grass.

Arlene didn't touch hands with Heather as she trotted off. It just wasn't Arlene's way. On the sideline, Emiria ignored Arlene, giving her a taste of life as a sub. Emiria had screamed at her in her few minutes of action, "Trap it! Trap it!" and Arlene began to understand what it must be like to be Heather or Angela or Jessica or even, a few months ago, her good friend Jenny. Emiria's support fuse was dangerously short for subs. Standing there on the sidelines in the biggest game of her life, Arlene didn't know how anyone could stand it. The girls might think her tough, but she doubted she had that kind of inner strength. How could they have the patience to play just a few minutes, ever fearful that Emiria might yank them after a single blunder?

Out on the field, something started to happen. One of the ponytails bobbing up and down the center of the field belonged not to an athlete but the first female center referee Thunder had played under during the whole State Cup. It was funny how things tended to work in reverse of expectations. Many people expected women refs would be overly protective of girls, but it often seemed just the opposite. As the game progressed, the ref waved many minor fouls on, letting the game flow.

Arlene watched Heather take charge. First she slide-tackled, knocking the ball away from an opponent. Next she perfectly trapped a long pass and sent a quick ball down the line to Jenny, who won a corner. Heather's cut move was sending girls spinning, her sharp elbows keeping pursuers at bay. To Arlene it was simple. Heather wasn't going to take crap from anyone. Her intelligent play only complemented her sudden physicality. She got rid of the ball as if it were hot: firing sweet diagonal balls for Jenny and Angela to run on to. And the longer she played, the more her confidence grew. It meant a lot to Heather that she'd replaced Arlene, one of Emiria's favorites. This wasn't mop-up time. Heather had been handed a golden chance to help Thunder reach the State Cup final.

Less than thirty seconds were left in the first half of the still scoreless match. Heather cut sharply back, sending the girl marking her to the turf. She stepped politely over the fallen player, calmly dribbled once, and then knocked a pretty pass that caught Jenny midstride on the wing. The speedster banged it inside. Kim was fifteen yards out, but it might as well have been a free throw, her shot smacking into the upper right corner as if she'd done it a thousand times.

Urgency underlined the goal's simple elegance. Just seconds after Elk Grove kicked off, the ref blew the half-time whistle.

But Heather wasn't the only Thunder girl possessed that day. Trinity was a terrier, scrambling all over the field, tackling, dribbling, punching through balls, and cranking shots. The girl the doctor said needed a couple weeks' bed rest was Thunder's workhorse around the penalty box, outsprinting and outhustling Elk Grove, nearly scoring a couple of goals. Trinity couldn't explain it, except as a feeling. She was on.

Arlene only played the last five minutes of the second half, and wasn't happy about not contributing, but she couldn't argue with Emiria's decision. Heather was inspired, slide-tackling, trapping as if giving a clinic, freezing defenders, and smartly switching play, once even smacking into the goalie. Arlene watched with pride as her frail school pal Jenny burned a path down the wing, beating defenders time and time again with her speed and phenomenal endurance, herself toppling the goalie. I've played so much, Arlene thought. This is their moment of glory. They're on fire.

Emiria stood over the girls on the sideline and beamed. They'd played a nearly perfect game. It wasn't just the magical trio of Heather, Jenny, and Trinity. Catherine had been solid at sweeper, Angela strong on the wing. Theresa, too, had risen up to play one of her best games all season, showing her increasing awareness, her ability to make the smart pass under pressure.

Though the score had been 2–1, it could have easily been 2–0 were it not for one goof. In the final minutes, Cassie left the box to clear a ball and shanked it straight to an opposing forward, who chipped the ball deftly over her head. But that lapse stayed only in the mind of Cassie. The girls of Thunder were all smiles, sitting in a circle, yanking off their cleats, showing off their trophies.

"I got blood!" Catherine bragged, holding up a leg with a good scrape.

"Me too," Heather quickly seconded, pointing to her bloody knee.

Emiria just shook her head. "Who would have thought a year ago we'd be here?"

"I did," Kim said proudly, Kim who'd scored both of Thunder's goals.

"Heather," Emiria began, pausing as she grinned at the wispy girl's bloody knee. "What a great game, Heather!"

Emiria turned to Jenny, her face glowing with admiration. "Jenny Drady, taking on three people down the sideline."

"She was baaad!" Shannon joked as she tugged off a soiled sock.

Luke stood there grinning in his broad-brimmed hat and sandals, taking in the girls' easy confidence. After

Emiria finished her impromptu congratulations, he asked if he could say a few words. He told the girls their performance was inspired. "I'm not around you guys enough," he said proudly. "You care about each other."

Luke reminded them of how far they'd come, the sweltering days last summer at Sonoma State. "You've got tremendous team spirit. You battle adversity. Some of you were not very good soccer players eight months ago," he said, his emotions taking hold. "But you want to be good."

Luke was struggling, his sun-creased face streaked with tears. He wiped one away and smiled. "I'm just thankful to get a chance to see you play. Look at Natalie, all dirty. And Jenny's leg, all dirty.

"Catherine with all that crap on the back of her shirt. How did that get there? Your parents are going to have to wash that jersey twice."

Luke paused. The girls knew there was something magical about high praise from a coach who'd led a women's college team to the NCAA's final four. But Luke was a friend too. The softer side of Emiria, the coach who inspired with praise and calm direction. "Every time you had the ball you were playing smart soccer. Building the ball out of the penalty box under intense pressure—"

Luke lost it then, his voice cracking. "Be proud of yourself. Regardless of what happens next week."

TWENTY-THREE

Last Rites

Shannon smacked Catherine. An arm, an elbow, no one could be sure precisely how it happened. But as Catherine lined up for the one-on-one drill, the blood was clearly flowing from her nose. Jogging back to the line, she sopped up the mess with her shirt like a dishrag.

"Cath, why don't you sit down?" Natalie asked, incredulous her teammate wasn't stopping.

Crimson red soaked the top half of her jersey, crumpled from all the wiping.

Cath didn't even pause. Snapped right back with her own question. "I wouldn't sit down in the game, so why would I sit down in practice?"

Even Emiria was concerned. Shannon had cracked her a good one. She suggested Cath take a breather, but the player brushed her off as well. Half an hour later the coach tried again to make her stop, but Cath wouldn't hear of it. Repeated her mantra about not stopping in a game.

"No, I'm fine, I'm fine."

This was Tuesday's practice. Four days before the State Cup final. Catherine wasn't going to let there be any doubt. Thunder was ready.

Fifteen girls, three coaches, and half a dozen parents squeezed into the hotel room bordering the busy freeway. Friday night about twelve hours before kickoff. The pasta and salad and bread heaped high in tins, the stench of garlic filtering out into the narrow hallway. Girls in sweats and jeans everywhere. Sprawled on the beds, cross-legged on the floor, leaning against the walls.

Emiria called the evening to order, propped up on the bed, her head resting easily against the wall. A few words for the parents before the last game of the season. She wanted to let everybody know how Thunder's run had been received in the community. Being written up in the Santa Rosa *Press Democrat*, for one thing. And all the calls and compliments she'd gotten from coaches. Players too. The other day when Thunder was practicing, a boys' team walked by and started clapping for the girls, shouting congratulations.

"Without the parents, none of this would ever have happened. I think it's nice to know that it's appreciated and what a huge part of it you are. And how proud it makes people."

Emiria had written no notes. She spoke best from her heart. "And I can't thank you enough for allowing me to coach and for allowing these girls to experience something that can be very painful at times and a real learning process."

Catherine nodded knowingly at her coach's words.

"And for trusting me enough to allow them to experience that," Emiria continued. "It's not easy. If athletics were easy, you wouldn't have champions. You wouldn't be all the things I tell the girls I want them to be.

"I just want to thank you and tell you how proud I am. How grateful I am. How grateful I'm sure the girls are without telling you.

"No one expected Thunder to be in the State Cup championship," she said, spirited shouts momentarily drowning out her words.

"I want you to realize what a special time in life this is. You don't get this on every team. I could go to another team and it would not work at all," she said, shaking her head. "But something on this team worked. Something clicked and something happened along the way.

"If I didn't have the parents, the support wouldn't be there. Our success is your success. I think we should all feel a little bit proud of that. I think the girls maybe should show their appreciation."

After the clapping and cheers had died down, Emiria talked about what they had scheduled that night. As was the team's custom before big games, the girls would discuss their individual and team goals for the match. But first Emiria thought it might be nice if the parents wanted to add a comment or a goal they might have for the team.

The room was oddly quiet.

"I'll say something," piped up Joe Walsh. He was standing by the TV, wearing a T-shirt, running shorts, and running shoes, clasping a beer.

"There are few opportunities you get in life to create memories that will last you the rest of your life," he began. "Really the days go by so quickly. I've watched some of these kids since they were seven years old, and now they're fourteen. And that's going to go by quickly and they're going to be off to college.

"You guys are on the edge of an opportunity to create

a memory that will last the rest of your lives." He paused. "And that's tomorrow."

A few girls and parents wiped away tears. It was a tough act to follow, but Trinity's dad, Scott, the plumber turned successful inventor, had something to say. He thought this was a good time for the girls to know what went on in those meetings when the girls weren't present.

"The parents sat around and asked why should we go to Phoenix. We're not beating the competition around here. Some of the parents were unsure.

"But we all came to the conclusion that we'd seen you walk out of tournaments where you were the best team and you were going home," said the dad who believed anything was possible. "And we all agreed right then that we were going to stick with you and stay behind Emiria. See where this whole thing goes.

"Miracles happen for a reason. It really is a shift in perception. You guys have real dedication. It's not just hard work that gets you here. Miracles happen out of a love for each other, and that's what happened on this team. You guys fell in love with each other."

The girls laughed nervously, but Emiria encouraged the sentiment. "Natalie said it best in our meeting," she said. "You guys are not Eclipse, you're not Fury, you're just Thunder."

Tucked over in the far corner by the pasta tin, Kristin's gracious mother, Karen, told the girls how proud they'd made all the parents. "And, Emiria, you've brought them all this way by yourself. They've done a lot, but you've done a majority of the work, and we want to applaud you for what you've done."

Cheers and clapping broke out, and then an awkward silence hung over the crowded room. Just the sort of silence one girl knew how to pop. Shannon cocked her head and asked gently, "Are those tears, Emiria?"

"Not yet," answered the coach, barely holding back. "I've been known to cry now and then, though."

Brian let out a big sigh and jumped in. He'd had a feeling the last week. He didn't know if it would matter whether Thunder was in the State Cup finals, regional finals, National Championship, or a practice. The team had achieved such a unity and respect for the game that it now played at the same level regardless of the competition.

"The pressure isn't there to be State Cup champ," he said. "It's just getting on that field again and doing what you do."

Brian's square face beamed his pride. "You guys practice as a unit. You achieve a consistency in practice that now carries over into play. I've seen some amazing things over the last year. I mean amazing things."

Brian applauded Jenny Drady for her standout performance in Arizona, and Arlene, of course, for showing this team what physical play was all about. But his was a tribute to the whole team. He recounted a lyrical day at Slater when the girls wanted to challenge the school's cross-country team to a run.

"I just want to say I'm honored to be able to watch it," he said, raising his chin. "It really is an honor. What I really like about this team is it's a personality team. We have fifteen personality players on this team, and that's very rare. Every one of you is a personality player."

Emiria thought Brian had hit on a larger truth. "You believe in yourselves and you believe what you have to offer the team is valuable," she said, every girl's eyes upon her. "That's why you're so successful. Because no team can look at our team and say this is how we play. Because the minute they throw that at us, that's the minute we take over. All of a sudden Naomi's going to come out of the back. Or we play the sweeper back. They almost have to defend us as individuals."

Emiria paused, smiling proudly. "You really play beautiful soccer."

But it was more than soccer that impressed Karen Young. "Emiria, the relationship you have with the girls. It's just incredible. You work them hard, and yet they respect you. I think that's a hard balance in life."

"I have a question," Shannon said, cutting through the awkward silence, pausing to make sure the whole room would hear. "Emiria, do you know how scary you are?"

That one nearly brought down the room.

Joe chuckled, "I guess she got your attention quick, huh?"

After the laughs, Pops, Emiria's father, stood up and said his piece. How fortunate they were that they liked each other. How they wanted to make the good pass because nobody wanted all the glory.

"I think you're so lucky," he said in his thick Dutch accent. "The team's spirit. It's like love. It binds you. Later on when you work, you'll be looking for that spirit. You want to work like that because that's food for your soul."

Spunky Natalie liked what Pops had to say. How it's rare that teams bond. "My friends," she said, sitting cross-legged on one of the beds, as if she were chatting with girlfriends at a slumber party. "I tell them I'm going bowling with my soccer team, and they're like, 'Natalie, why are you doing that? Why are you going out with your soccer team?'

"They don't get it!" she exclaimed, arching her dark eyebrows. "They don't get the commitment you have when you're on a soccer team. I don't know what to say, so I just don't say anything. I know what we do is good even if people don't understand it. We all understand it. We all know why we work so hard."

Shannon sure did. " 'Cause we're cool," she joked, cracking up the room.

" 'Cause we're in love with each other!" Natalie shouted wildly.

But before the parents were asked to leave the room, Emiria wanted them to know that this love stuff was no joke. You could always tell a team by how it treats its injured players. "Shauna has not missed the team at all just because she hasn't been on the field. That is amazing. Practicing three, four times a week. Going to the games. Going to State Cup. And she is still the cocaptain of the team."

The girls cheered Shauna, and she didn't look away, pride written all over her.

"Same thing with Naomi. Naomi was getting tired. Now the girls say, 'Naomi, did you bring your food?' It becomes a topic of fun for the team. Naomi, I mean, everyone's packing her lunch."

Through the team's chuckles, Naomi's eyes stayed wide, drinking in her coach's every word.

"Naomi and Shauna are still the captains," Emiria continued. "They have not missed a beat for anything. And the team respects that. They rally behind that.

"You can tell this team wants everybody to be there. You can see it in how they treat the girls having self-confidence problems. Several people on this team, you can see in their faces in a couple of practices that they are gone.

"And you can see it in the line. 'Come on! Pick it up! Take her on!'

"When someone's down, there's always someone to pick them up."

"Tomorrow when you face the parents in your lineup," Emiria began brightly, "I want you to cheer and let go of that emotion for the parents. Take a bow."

The parents had been sent to their rooms. It was just the girls and the coaches. A few pregame instructions.

"Because it's the parents' chance to cheer for you. Show the energy. Let them feel proud of you. They want you to go out there. Pick your head up."

Emiria's face suddenly grew serious. "Second. If anyone goes down tomorrow, I want the team to be around that person. If you see someone go down for a long time and the ref stops play, I want the team to be there, immediately around your player."

Emiria hadn't planned what to say next, but it made sense for two reasons. The girls naturally rallied around the team's feisty chipmunk. And she had been hurt before. Emiria turned toward the girl sitting next to her on the bed. "Like Natalie twists an ankle or something. Everyone sprint over to Natalie as soon as the game stops. You can hold hands around her, but form a circle because that's your teammate. When someone goes down, don't just watch them. Protect your players."

It was time for the girls to share their individual goals. Words they'd scribbled on a card, a piece of paper, or in Shannon's case, a scrap of cloth. Dreams for tomorrow. Captain Naomi started. A simple goal. Something she'd done nearly a year before, ironically in a game against tomorrow's opponent. To make a run all the way up the field and score.

"Arlene, what are Arlene's goals?" Emiria asked.

"*Score!*" Arlene exclaimed, holding her arms over her head.

Emiria smiled. "I like that."

Earnest Theresa had three goals. To slide-tackle. Go 100 percent on every fifty-fifty ball and breakaway. And score.

"Can I say something?" Shannon cut in. "I think you're putting too much pressure on yourself about slide-tackling. Because I notice at the beginning of the game, you'll say, 'Tell me if I need to slide-tackle,' and then you're so worried about slide-tackling that it takes you out of your game for the first couple of minutes. If you need to slide-tackle, it will just happen."

"That's true." Emiria nodded. "That's good advice. Natalie?"

"My personal goal is to look for the switch, be aggressive on my players, keep my head up and play the simple pass, kick some ass, and be composed."

But she wasn't done.

"And I want to be the hero."

Emiria smiled. "I love that. Kim?"

"My personal goal," she deadpanned, wearing her sour game face, "is to get the ball off my foot and shoot."

This cracked up the room.

"Cassie?"

"My goal is to be ready all the time," she said sincerely. "Be ready to go for anything. Not to get game anxiety and get all nervous because that's why I don't like coming out. And to talk. And let people know that I'm back there," she said, pausing.

"And if I do get the ball, not to screw up."

They laughed at that one.

"Brian?"

He'd memorized his goals. "To be confident. To assist when needed. To show my support for the team and be a positive force."

Shannon couldn't resist adding with a mischievous grin, "And to shag the balls."

"No, Shannon," Brian cracked back. "When I'm as good at shagging as I am, I don't need that as a goal."

"OK, let's move on to the team goals. Arlene?"

"Mine is to play simple," she said softly. "And kick their ass."

"I like your style AR!" Emiria smiled. "Cath?"

She'd been braiding Shannon's hair earlier, cracking jokes in her easy way, but now she was serious. "My team goal is to talk and play simple. And not get nervous as a team. Because I get nervous. You know, like the last defender, I don't know, we get nervous because we get thinking if we make a mistake, there's nobody behind you.

"So I'm thinking there is someone. There's Cassie. I have a lot of trust in Cassie. I know if I make a mistake, Cassie is there. So I don't have to be so nervous."

That quieted down the room.

"Heather?"

"My team goal is to have fun. Winning is your reward for having fun—and," she added gently, "I want to kick some ass. And I want to score in the first ten minutes."

"Heather, I like that!" Emiria beamed. "Heather stepped up. Luke?"

"I would like to see the team play thoughtful, intelligent soccer just like every time I've seen you play. And put on a show, win or lose."

"That's true," agreed Emiria. "Another thing, you guys. Whether we win or lose, you want to show people what we are about. Don't hang your head. Walk off that field proud."

Angela tried to put it in perspective. "I think what you're saying about don't hang your head is so true. Because even if we lose, it's still a great season. We've trained hard, and no one deserves to feel bad at all."

"Kim?"

"Lately I've been getting down on myself," whispered the girl slumped in a chair. " 'Cause I just get caught up in the game. If I start doing that tomorrow, I want you guys to help me."

"I think you guys pretty much covered it," concluded Emiria. "I think you're ready to go. Tomorrow is a game everybody's just gotta go out and perform. You've gotta play for the team. Find what makes you a better player. Whether we win or lose tomorrow, the real winning team is the one that comes off and says I gave everything for the team."

Jessica, a girl who'd spent her share of anxious minutes on the sideline, agreed. "You've also gotta remember that everything you do is helping the team," she said, her braces only hardening her expression. "Even if you don't feel like you are, you are."

"Just movement helps the team," added Emiria. "So that's it," she concluded comfortably. "We don't need to talk about it anymore. We just need to do it. And we have for the last five games. Sixty-four teams and there are two left.

"Don't think about Placer tommorrow. Think about you."

TWENTY-FOUR

The Second Stringer

*t*he referee led them out for the pregame introduc-
tions, the Placer girls' hands hanging stiffly at their
sides, their faces distant, the picture of cool detachment.
Two teams couldn't have appeared more different. The
Thunder girls were joyous, holding one another's
hands, seeming to skip along. Lined up facing the fans,
Natalie swung her hands up, whipsawing her teammates' arms in unison. The girls hollered, leaped, and
bowed for the parents. On the sideline, Maggie and Michelle and Carol gave each other big hugs. They looked
at it as good luck. The more you hugged, the better the
girls would play.

The Placer Sharks let their balloons make their statement, dozens and dozens of yellow and blue orbs released
up into the sky like colorful doves. Some of the Thunder
parents fretted. They only had ten balloons. No giant

blow-up shark. And not nearly as many fans as the Sharks.

The pristine Robertson Park Stadium in Livermore east of San Francisco only heightened the anticipation. This was a true soccer complex, with long, broad, immaculate fields and towering lights for night games. No one could blame a bad pass on this carpet-smooth grass.

Placer framed Thunder's season. The teams had met the first time nine months before at the July California Cup, Thunder's first Beautiful Game against a worthy opponent, the first time the girls had beaten a team with passing and artistry. But in a rematch it was often better to be the underdog. Placer knew what to expect and, from the opening whistle, wasted no time. With two girls faster than anyone on Thunder, why bother with midfield play? Placer's fullbacks and midfielders drove long diagonal balls toward the corners, and after a minute or so of cool passing, Thunder quickly found itself chasing.

It didn't take long. A Placer girl drove to the end line, slipping the ball across the goal mouth. Theresa, perfectly positioned on the goal line, managed to block the volley. But the ball flew right to the foot of another Placer forward. And Cassie couldn't touch the rebound.

One-zip with just seven minutes gone, an ominous start in a championship game. But Thunder steadied itself. Catching on to Placer's kick-and-run, the fullbacks quickly stepped up and won an offsides call. Shannon headed the long free kick to Arlene's feet, and Arlene knocked it out to Jenny on the wing. Shannon swept in on the ensuing corner kick, cracking a volley just blocked by a defender.

The jitters were far from gone, but at least they were starting to play. Arlene was called for her first foul in Placer's penalty box, and then the ever-tenacious Natalie rose to the occasion. This was what her game was all about, controlling the midfield with scrappiness. Off balance, Natalie lunged back for a loose ball with the foot she'd broken the year before. But the Placer girl had a full head of steam and ran over Natalie like a locomotive.

She couldn't have been down for more than a couple of seconds before her teammates flowered around her, grasping hands.

"It's OK, Natalie! you're going to be OK!" Shannon cheered on her friend. Sprinting sixty yards from her goal, Cassie joined the huddle. The girls kneeled around their fallen teammate, a chorus of encouragement.

It was uncanny, exactly as Emiria had prophesied the night before, right down to the player she innocently used as an example. Twenty seconds later, Natalie wobbled up under her own power, trotted over to the sideline with the ref to make sure she was fine, and then returned to play with a round of applause.

The felling of Natalie jolted Thunder to life. Just a couple of minutes later, Trinity swung the ball to Jenny, who took it wide and won a corner. Placer headed Catherine's near-post corner out, but the second corner curved farther out. Somehow Natalie got her head on it, spinning it back toward goal.

But Jenny couldn't quite get a foot on it.

The big Placer girl sunk to the field like a deer that had been shot. Hands clasped over her head, wailing. Her teammates shrank from her, appearing to walk away. Not one girl put a hand on her shoulder or tried to calm her.

"Can I give her her inhaler?" the girl's mother cried frantically from the sideline.

Two chunky male trainers ran out, helping the whimpering girl off the field. Only a few minutes had separated the two incidents, which, to Thunder parents, underlined what was unique about their daughters. The girls might be losing, but they were demonstrating a respect and love for each other that transcended the game. No moms had offered them asthma inhalers. No dads had carried them sobbing off the field.

The Placer tears seemed to embolden Thunder. Angela sliced a through ball to Kim, who spun and snapped off a cross just cleared by defenders. Kim was a touch player. The more she touched the ball, the better she played. She possessed a ball on the right flank, zigzagging through a couple of defenders, sucking up the field toward goal. But as luck would have it, the dribble fell to her left foot, and her shot spun wide. It was Kim's best chance of the game, and she knew it, tossing her head down in frustration. But she wasn't down for long. A minute later, Shannon, dominating in the air, headed it down the right flank. Kim turned hard on the ball, threaded two girls, and cranked a line drive narrowly deflected by a defender.

But momentum is a strange beast. The near misses had the curious effect of draining the heart out of Thunder's play. Catherine nervously fumbled three goal kicks in succession, the strength seeming to abandon her leg, handing the ball over to Placer. Thunder was on the ropes. Giving up a second goal before half would put them out of the game. But it was just as Catherine had said the night before. There was someone behind her. Cassie. And the goalie stood firm, confidently stopping a couple of shots.

You could always tell when it was coming. Emiria wasn't very good at hiding her emotions, and Brian feared the long, brooding silence, wishing Luke would step in. But Emiria gripped her clipboard tighter, glancing disdainfully at what she'd written, then tossing it on the ground.

"There's absolutely nothing I can tell you to improve. We are playing the most horrendous soccer we have ever played. There's nothing to fix. There's no adjustments to be made. We're just giving the game away.

"Has anybody in the midfield made a foul?" she demanded to know. "Raise your hand!"

The girls were silent. Not a hand moved.

"Nobody has even fouled anybody! An entire half of soccer in a championship game. If we're not going to play, there's just nothing we can do."

To Brian there were two halftime talks a coach might give to a team that comes out nervous for a big match. The gentle method, getting in their heads and pulling them out a little bit. Or the Emiria method, a full-scale thrashing.

Even Arlene, Thunder's toughest girl, preferred Luke's lighter halftime talks. He'd point out the bad too, but he didn't dwell on it, wasn't angry.

"You guys are afraid to win," Emiria pressed on. "You're flat-out afraid to win. You've got to get over it."

The girls were on the verge of tears.

"What's the point of coming here and training harder than any other team?" Emiria demanded. "What's the point of having better skills if you're not going to try?"

Emiria let that sink in a bit. She'd passed the fury point. Now it was time to slowly build them back up. Her voice was calm. "Who wants to win?"

The arms shot up.

"Shannon, Catherine. You've got to step up." Emiria's eyes bored into those of Thunder's striker. "Keep your head up, Kim."

There wasn't much more to say. She wasn't going to tell them everything was going to be fine. Only effort and results would matter now. "You need to score in the first minutes to get yourself back in this game."

Three minutes into the second half, Jessica curled toward Placer's goal kick, pulling the ball away from the defender and dishing it back. Shannon coolly first-touched a high return lob into the corner. Blanketed, Jessica punched a line drive cross for Arlene, who swung and missed.

"Awww!" a Thunder dad cried. Arlene heard the criticism and quickly put it out of her mind. After she'd missed, the defender had blocked out the cross. Get the next one, Arlene thought.

Catherine trotted up to take the corner. Catherine, who had just flubbed three goal kicks before the half. Catherine, who had sliced two other corners harmlessly out of bounds. The girls readied themselves for a set play, but Emiria had another idea.

"Just get in the box!" she yelled.

Natalie and Arlene trotted toward the near post. Out at the top of the penalty box, Shannon took a moment to tug up her socks just before Catherine struck a high curling ball toward the near post. Shannon swept easily toward the ball, and then abruptly slowed. Arlene was tracking the ball, the keeper on her heels. The angle's too tough, Arlene thought. I'll just flick it in the air, hope somebody knocks it in. The physics were against her, but Shannon watched her friend jab her head back, flicking the ball high toward the net.

Carol leaped up on the sideline, hugging and shouting, a thought penetrating her happiness. That's Arlene's new skill. Something Emiria had worked on with the girls.

To head those corners in.

Placer immediately went on the offense, but Shannon stood firm, sweeping in for a tough sliding tackle, clearing a dangerous ball, and booming a pretty header up to Heather. Three big plays in the space of ten seconds. Arlene, too, was on. Catherine headed the ball up to her on the wing. Two girls had Arlene boxed in, but somehow she deftly drew the ball back on the sideline, riding the edge of the chalk, sneaking a pass into Jenny, who drew a foul.

Thunder began to play its game. Shannon turned and switched to Natalie, who crossed it to Kim, who batted it back to Natalie, who sent it wide to Heather. Five sharp linked passes, controlling the game, splitting defenders, Placer only able to kick the ball out in desperation.

Then, just when Thunder seemed in control, a breakdown. Placer's star broke free on the left and fired a high shot that bounced off the crossbar, the rebound headed for the net. But somehow Cassie got a glove on it, the ball seeming to bounce on the line forever before Catherine raced in to clear it off.

Cassie's inspired save turned the momentum. The girls answered Placer's big kicks with precise diagonal passes and quick counterattacks. Thunder was holding the ball, making Placer chase, the girls' superior fitness starting to show. The burly Placer coach did all he could to slow the momentum, subbing his flagging girls, throwing fresh legs at Thunder.

"Owwww!" Natalie hollered, clutching her leg as she went down fifteen feet from the parents on the sideline. Shannon was the first girl there, Natalie crying as her teammates pressed in. "You're OK, Natalie, you're OK." Natalie didn't stay down long, Shannon helping her to her feet.

"All right, Natalie!" her dad yelled. "Go kick some butt!"

"Come on, Blue!" another hollered.

Less than a minute later, the referee blew his whistle.

"Ladies and gentlemen, we have regulation ending in a tie in the girls Under-fourteen Championship," the voice boomed over the loudspeakers. "We will go to two ten-minute overtimes. Once we start the overtimes, we must finish both overtime periods regardless of whether somebody scores or not. If there is no score and it ends up in a tie, we will go to penalty kicks."

Except for cocaptain Shauna, who, of course, couldn't sprint with her strained hamstring, no one had played less than Kristin. She'd only been in for fifteen minutes of the first half and hadn't touched a ball in more than an hour. But on the drive from the hotel to the game that morning, her father had told her it didn't matter how little she played. She had to be mentally ready. Even if it was just for a few minutes.

"Kristin, I want you to go in for Jessica," Emiria said.

The funny thing was, Kristin didn't feel nervous at all. She just wanted to prove herself. Show the coach and her teammates what she could do. Over on the other sideline, Carol thought it was a good idea to give Kristin a chance. Something different. Kristin looked so strong to Carol. Maybe it was all that tennis she'd played.

Thunder showed its cool in overtime. The girls controlled the game, working the ball around the field, pressing for openings. Cassie had to go down to save a skidding ball in front of the goal, but nothing fazed her: She came out and cut off a crossing ball easily. And then Arlene put on a show. Arlene rode the defender's back, waiting patiently, stripping the ball, turning and passing it neatly to Kim, who fired a bullet the goalie barely saved.

The passing minutes made two things abundantly clear. Thunder lived to pass, and Placer lived to boot and sprint. Thunder's legs were stronger, its passes crisper. Exhaustion only heightened Thunder's teamwork. Catherine was inspired. She dashed to midfield, tapping the ball forward with her head and then knocking it over to Theresa. The switch to Natalie, driving it wide to the onrushing Naomi, snaking through a couple of defenders to win a throw-in. They did it again, putting on a passing clinic. Working the right side this time—Catherine to Theresa to Kristin to Theresa to Heather to Natalie.

Angela snapped the throw-in, Arlene spinning with a defender on, punching it to Kim, who dashed toward her. On the opposite side, Kristin Young, playing left midfield, launched a forty-yard sprint. Kim fired to the near post, and for a moment it looked as if Thunder's perfection-seeking star had just blown another shot. But her teammate struck the bounding ball. A defender blocked it, the goalie reached, grasping at the ball. And then the girl slammed it into the net.

Rising from the beaten heap of the goalkeeper, Kristin raced upfield, the smile on her face ear to ear.

"Thank you! Thank you!" Theresa cried, hugging her friend.

"I'm so proud of you!" Angela shouted.

Catherine hugged Kristin once, started running back, changed her mind, and returned for another hug. Seconds later, the ref blew his whistle. Ten more minutes and the State Championship would be Thunder's.

Shauna stood on the sidelines in her sweats, thinking how awesome it was that Kristin, a midfielder, had scored. She couldn't remember Kristin scoring all season.

"Shauna, get ready to go," Emiria barked.

Shauna couldn't believe her ears. Didn't move at first.

"Shauna, get ready to go!"

It had all been Brian's idea. Before the game, he'd suggested to Emiria that it would be a great honor for Shauna to let her play for a minute, a tribute to all the dedication she'd shown in religiously coming to practice. Maybe they could let the parents know. Give her a standing ovation. But Brian was thinking a 3–0 blowout with a couple of minutes on the clock. Not a 2–1 nail biter in overtime with six anxious minutes remaining on the clock.

Shauna jogged a bit on the sideline. How could she possibly play? She hadn't really touched the ball in two and a half months. She walked up to Brian, a puzzled expression on her earnest face. "Shauna," Brian said, painfully slowly. "You go on the field. You don't touch the ball. Just jog around a little."

The players on the field received the same admonition. "Don't play with Shauna at all. She's just out there to get a minute in."

Before Shauna knew it, she was touching Heather's hand, trotting onto the field.

"Arlene, don't pass me the ball," Shauna cried. "I'm going to fall down."

Arlene, being Arlene, didn't just pass her the ball, but gave her a give-and-go. Shauna not only touched it but won a throw-in.

"Don't play with Shauna!" Brian shouted. "She's only in to get a minute."

It wasn't supposed to happen, but as the minutes ticked on, the game still in doubt, Emiria held firm, letting her crippled captain have her moment. Shauna found herself asking for the ball, passing, defending.

Shauna Tantarelli played.

TWENTY-FIVE

Overtime

School loudspeakers boomed their names, and friends shouted compliments in the hallways. All over Santa Rosa the girls of Thunder were heralded. The pastor at Santa Rosa Christian Church recognized Jessica, Shannon, and Naomi, though they didn't last the whole service, slipping out early for Thunder practice. Kristin was sitting with Angela at Montgomery High when her first-period teacher held up the jubilant team picture of Thunder at State Cup in the *Press Democrat* and read the story out loud to the class, including the line that made the neatly dressed blond blush proudly. "Kristin Young scored the game winner in the seventy-fifth minute on an assist from Kim Halloran."

Parents, too, were showered with praise at work, at church, even in the local coffee shop. The victory came shortly before graduation, and you could sense the optimism in Theresa Piasta's eighth-grade valedictorian address at St. Eugene's. "We are Santa Rosa's community leaders of tomorrow," she began confidently in her billowy white gown, humorously predicting the graduating class of 1998 would someday run the city. One by one Theresa praised her classmates in her lighthearted speech, shooting wry glances around the church, stepping back easily from the podium as she won laughs. Twenty years hence, she said, smiling, they'd be bankers, lawyers, computer engineers, journalists, restaurateurs, hotel owners, why, even luxury-car dealers. Theresa had the modesty to refrain from saying what she was going to do, but at least one part of her life wasn't going to change. Shortly before saying a heartfelt good-bye and striding off the stage, she joked that twenty years hence she'd be coaching her kid's indoor soccer team.

Before winning State Cup, Thunder's fund-raising had been the typical youth-soccer smorgasbord. The girls had run races, and walked door to door to sell everything from pizza to grocery scrips to candy. Shannon's mother, Michelle, had led the Christmas Beanie Baby charge, getting boxes of them from a dealer and raising over a thousand dollars herself. There had been car washes and garage sales, the girls serving up doughnuts and pretzels donated from Naomi's father's bakery. They even once held a goal-a-thon, in which the girls secured dollar pledges for how many goals they'd score in a shoot-out. But nothing compared to Jenny Drady's dad's effort. The building contractor led the campaign to print contributors' names on the back of a Thunder T-shirt, and Trinity's dad wrote a letter to the *Press-Democrat*, telling the story.

THUNDER SEEKS SUPPORT

You may have read the sports page about the incredible story of the Santa Rosa United under 14 girls soccer team known as 'Thunder.' Last weekend the girls won the California State Cup Championship.

Last year the under 14 girls were assigned a new coach, 22 year old Emiria Salzmann. A terrific soccer player in her years at Sonoma State, her sole objective was to draft the best players during tryouts. The transition was rough. There was tension and contempt for one another. A young determined coach and all new players! This team did not win a tournament all year and somehow managed on the last day of the season to win their league. With some renewed confidence, these girls started to click. Emiria, being 22, somehow expected these girls to work as hard and dedicated as college players and somehow they did. But more importantly, what was actually happening, is all the contempt was turning to love. These girls found that always missing element that makes a special team. Love for one another. You could see it and you could feel it. They loved each other.

Thunder consequently marched through all the rounds and found themselves in the championship game for State Cup and wound up winning 2–1 in overtime in typical Thunder fashion. Then a stunning realization came. As State Cup champs, Thunder would be going to regionals in Albuquerque, New Mexico on June 21st to represent the State of California.

When Emiria drafted this team she did not realize there were several single working parents. These parents have struggled all year to keep their daughters playing United soccer. The season is over and their daughters' team has won State Cup. Financially, some are drained already, and now regionals bring mixed emotions.

The parents have only 6 weeks to raise about $10,000 to send their daughters and their coach to New Mexico. Hotel, vans, flights and food.

We need your support. This isn't a sports story, it is a story about love in which we invite you to be a part. Mira-

cles can happen if you let them and I hope this story will touch your heart. These girls represent our whole community and they have worked very hard for you. What little you or your business can contribute will go a long way in sending these girls on a dream.

Rich Drady started calling on friends and business associates. Burgess Lumber generously pitched in $250, and Arrow Electric and Bay Alarm each ponied up a hundred. Every imaginable business in Sonoma County made a contribution. Clover Stornetta Farms pitched in, and the Cameron Vineyard, as well as Hank's Creekside Restaurant, Scorpio's Hair Salon, and La Tortilla Factory. Accountants, dentists, lawyers, pharmacists, insurance and title companies, the local newspaper, even mortgage brokers, gave generously. Success was contagious. The California Youth Soccer Association donated twenty-four hundred dollars and Santa Rosa United pitched in another thousand dollars. By mid-June, on the eve of the tournament, nearly a hundred businesses and individuals had contributed over twelve thousand dollars to the team's coffers. Thunder's thirteen-month season had just become a fifteen-month season.

Arriving in the late afternoon in the high-desert city of Albuquerque, Emiria wasted no time in beginning the acclimation to the five-thousand-foot elevation. The girls quickly changed and took off down the sidewalk of a busy four-lane boulevard for a two-mile run, cheered on by the honks of drivers. Practice was a celebration. The girls toyed for a half against an under-thirteen boys' team, exhausting them with quick passes that exposed the boys' dependence on dribbling and speed. It was shirts against skins, and more than once Arlene knocked a sweaty boy on his can. When one of the boys finally scored to even up the match, the coach abruptly waved the game to a halt. At least five minutes were left, but the coach said his boys needed breakfast. He couldn't have been more right. Any more ego bruising from these young Amazons and they'd be ruined for the rest of the tournament.

Emiria scanned the crowded practice fields for more victims, and after a couple of girls' teams wisely passed, she found a taker, an under-seventeen girls' team from Fresno, California. The friendly, bearish coach invited Emiria to stand in the middle of the field, as he planned to, coaching his girls during the scrimmage. Emiria smiled politely and declined the invitation. She'd stand on the sidelines as she always did. You could say it was only a practice, just a meaningless warm-up before the tournament. But the facts said differently. Thunder was playing one of the best under-seventeen girls' teams in the state of California. Sixteen- and seventeen-year-old girls who were bigger, stronger, faster. It wasn't even close. Thunder quickened its game, Catherine and Naomi making lightning runs from the back, Shannon dominating the midfield, and Kim pounding the Fresno keeper with shots. Thunder had never played better. Two to nothing in thirty minutes of play, and it could have easily been four-zip.

Thunder's first game of regionals was against the celebrated Los Angeles Stars, one of the nation's top teams and a past regional champion. Thunder had its hands full, and the fierce wind didn't help. Gusts ripped the coaches' small blue shade tents into the sky and sent them bounding down the field like giant tumbleweeds. Sand bit into eyes. The fields had been sliced out of sandy Indian desert for the tournament, and sloped to the east like an off-kilter pool table. More than a few parents saw shades of the Sebastopol State Cup quarterfinal, the wind and tilt pushing the ball to one side of the field.

But this was more like the Sebastopol league championship, the game in which Thunder had to beat a team—

and a man. Balls blown out careened fifty to a hundred feet down the hill, sending earnest Thunder players chugging down and back up again, often a fifteen-to-twenty-second energy-sapping jaunt. The well-trained Stars girls didn't budge when it was their throw-in. Nor did they have to. They were always tossed another game ball from a man who looked an awful lot like a Stars coach.

There was something wonderfully amateurish about the Thunder girls. They even sprinted down to retrieve a Stars ball once or twice, struggling back up just as play began without them—with the mysterious second ball. After just a few minutes, the Stars girls were gasping for breath at the high altitude, nowhere near as fit as Thunder. But the Stars substituted in waves, throwing a handful of fresh girls at Thunder every few minutes. With Jenny out with a bruised knee, Thunder only had three extra girls and couldn't substitute much even if that had been Emiria's bent. The girls played tentatively, the overwhelming confidence of Saturday's practice replaced by fear.

Yet remarkably, as time wound down, Thunder was within striking distance. The Stars usually pounded opponents by six or seven to nothing. But on this windy afternoon, they'd only managed to snake one shot past the inspired Cassie. Shauna, too, had kept them in the game. Her hamstring healed, she was the lone defender who could stay with the Stars' brilliant forwards. But Shauna couldn't cover everyone. In the last two minutes she was called for a foul outside the penalty box, and Cassie didn't have a prayer on the textbook-perfect free kick.

Emiria was stunned by the defeat. As the girls slowly tugged on their sweats, Luke quietly asked her if she wanted to say something to the team, and she shook her head and said no. That evening the girls and parents glumly ate together at a cavernous salad bar, and still there was no word from Emiria, the girls not daring to sit near their coach, her face blaring her disappointment. Back at the motel, the girls anxiously hung out in the parking lot, waiting. Every night so far they had adjourned to meetings in Emiria's room. They had a game the following morning. If they lost, they'd be on a plane headed home.

But then something unexpected happened. A group of rambunctious older boys from Oregon booted a ball down from the second floor. They'd lost their opening game too. Would the girls like to play? Makeshift goals in the parking lot. Cars as sidelines. Thunder parents standing outside their rooms on the sultry summer night in shorts and T-shirts, beers in hand, watching. Everybody knowing that Emiria would likely be furious if she knew about the rebellion afoot. The girls needed their rest and might get hurt. But there was something else going on.

Catherine waved off her mother's protests and kept playing. How could she resist street soccer, its roughness, how removed it was from the orderly game of girls' soccer? Catherine loved getting physical, and nobody pushed and shoved like the boys. The cars made it crazy, the ball careening off doors and bumpers. Catherine figured they were playing for pride, looking for inspiration out on the asphalt. Both teams had nothing to lose.

"Is everyone here?" Natalie shouted over the racket.

Fresh from shoving sixteen-year-old boys onto cars, all fifteen Thunder girls had crammed into the stuffy motel room. Street soccer had put smiles and sweat back on their faces, reawakened their love of the sport. So what if their coach had abandoned them on the eve of their next game? They were big girls. They'd called their own meeting. They were fixing it.

Captain Shauna cut through the noise. "Basically, you guys, it's time to play soccer."

"Keep the door open!" a voice cried, the heat still stifling even though it was after nine-thirty.

"Let's get on with it!"

First the basics, what color to wear for the morning's match. They settled on blue socks and gray shirts. Hats for the blazing sun.

"We totally lapsed today," Natalie began sourly, lying on her stomach on one of the beds. "And that was so unexpected because we did so good on Saturday and we had such a good warm-up."

"What about the intensity out there?" a plaintive voice cried.

"Did you check out our shots?" Kim snipped sarcastically.

"We had no shots on that goalie," Cassie complained. "I swear, you guys could have cranked on that goalie. We could have won!"

Shannon would have no part of it. "Forget about today, because it's the past," she declared somberly from her seat on the floor. "We've got a big game tomorrow."

But just as many of the girls needed to play street soccer, some of them seemed to need to verbally kick the loss out of their collective system: "What happened to our defense? Where was our communication?"

Jessica, slumped on the bureau in her sweats, summed it up in a deep monotone that underlined her point: "There was no energy on the field."

Kim shouted over the din, "No one was talking!"

The room cascaded into complaints. The wind. The difficulty of controlling the ball on the rock-hard surface.

"Guys!" Jessica sternly reminded them. "First of all, there's no excuses."

Captain Shauna couldn't agree more. "You can't blame it on the wind, 'cause they had it too."

And then Catherine shared her gift of candor, voicing what nobody else dared. "How did you feel coming off the field with Emiria not talking to us?" she asked from one of the beds, her face flush from street soccer. "I know you felt like shit, Kim. I felt like shit. Everybody felt like shit." She paused dramatically as the girls howled at her humor, her swearing. "We're in a lot of shit now, so we better get out there and kick some shit tomorrow!"

As the laughter died down, Kim volunteered her own quiet confession. She had none of Catherine's drama, but the room hushed as she spoke of what she saw as her own personal failing. "I was scared because I thought if we beat them, we'd have to win the whole regionals."

Fear churned through her every time she stepped on the field. Kim, the team's star scorer, was terrified of success because with it, she knew, would come more pressure. But that was then. "We can't be scared now," Kim continued. "We just need to step it up, and if we fail, we'll just go back to practice.

"You know what, you guys?" she sighed. "It's going to take a while before winning becomes a habit."

A knock came on the door. A dad. Emiria wanted to meet with them at ten. With only a few minutes left, the girls decided to take a team vow, repeating the words after Kim like a communal prayer. "I promise to work as hard as I can. And to play like I know how to play. And to not be scared and to step up to the challenge. And I will kick ass tomorrow!"

Shannon shouted over the din, "Guys, just say your personal goal! What you want to do tomorrow!"

And so they began, proudly sharing their personal goals, fourteen teammates repeating it like a cheer, the energy growing with each girl.

"To play simple and concentrate on the game."

"To get open for everyone and win all the balls in the air."

"To not be scared and front our man."

"To not get frantic when I don't see an option."

"To play the best defense that we've ever played."

They were down to the last few. The normally subdued Kristin wanted to play with heart and "just want it."

Cassie wanted to kick some A. "Wait, wait, I've got to say that again. To kick some FA!"

This was a tough act to follow, a little bit like going after Catherine, but from the corner, quiet, injured Jenny, who hadn't played a minute, ventured, "To play our game and talk it up on the field."

The last goals rang out like commandments. "Switch the ball! Win the air balls! Control the ball on the ground!" And finally, "To walk off the field with our heads up."

That about summed it up. The girls shouted in unison, "I solemnly swear to do all of the above!"

"Thunder kicks ass on three."

Emiria's body language and brevity said it all. Her shoulders as immobile as her face, sitting stiffly in her chair next to Brian, letting them know that the same woman who had braided their hair that morning had taken a giant step back. The Thunder coach famous for long-winded meetings was cruelly blunt. "I'm not going to tell you it's OK, because it wasn't OK. And I'm not going to tell you you played all right, because you didn't. And I'm not going to tell you you didn't get your asses kicked when you did."

The girls had disappointed and embarrassed her. All the confidence and maturity *she* had given them had not been returned. They'd disrespected her really. Not intentionally, but by failing emotionally, by choking in the big game. "What happened to the commitment and the discipline and the honor and the dignity that we talk about?" she asked the room full of glum faces. "All of a sudden you were just a team from Northern California."

It wasn't a question of ability or speed or skill. It wasn't even a question of winning. Even Emiria, who rarely acknowledged opponents, recognized the Stars were the better team. "They were quicker, they had better touches, they were smarter tactically," she said matter-of-factly. "But you guys are not far below them. You guys could have won that game if you had played the game you had this weekend. But something in you did not compete. There was no heart. There was no glimpse of the team that I know."

It was then that Emiria started talking about the changes that were going to have to happen. The emotional maturity the girls must find within themselves. "You have to decide tonight whether or not you're going to commit emotionally to this team, because I will not commit emotionally to this team if it's not going to return it."

Cassie kept waiting, wondering when Emiria would get around to saying it. On one level she agreed with her coach. During the game she'd exchanged plenty of nervous glances with Cath, wondering why everybody looked so scared. Emiria was right that the team hadn't played its best. But one girl had, and she knew it. Nearly the whole game had been spent in Thunder's half. Another goalie might have caved in and let in a handful of goals. Cassie didn't just save the close ones. Early on she punched a high ball over the crossbar, the kind of shot that weakens every fourteen-year-old keeper's knees. Next to the State Cup final, it was arguably Cassie's finest game as a goalkeeper. She knew she'd given it everything she had, and though she respected her coach, she knew Emiria was wrong. Cassie "the Keeper" Kays had not choked, and she wished Emiria could at least say "good job" to the one player who had left her heart on the field.

Catherine didn't buy Emiria's speech either. To her it was a question of experience: Emiria knew her ego got in the way of her coaching, but just hadn't learned how to deal with it. Ego was Emiria's Achilles' heel, a high ball she had trouble heading out. She was trapped by her years of being a success, fooled into thinking they were invincible. Regionals were teaching them all that it was a big country. Maybe that was harder for Emiria.

But this talk about how they had somehow embarrassed or disrespected her made Catherine mad. Whatever had happened today wasn't about Emiria. It was about the team. And Emiria had no right to say they had embarrassed her, because they were the ones out there playing.

Shauna could easily have been the other girl in the room wishing her coach would compliment her performance. Shauna's tenaciousness, like Cassie's, had kept the game from turning into a blowout. But giving up the free kick that led to the second goal weighed on Shauna. And Shauna was a captain, and when the team played poorly, she could find little reason to celebrate. But still Shauna was shocked at how quickly her coach had sapped the optimism of her teammates. Half an hour ago they had found the strength to call their own meeting, to cheer one another on, to make their own vows.

What Shauna heard from her coach was that she was hurt. That stunned her. She had had no idea that if the team flopped, it could be so personally hurtful to Emiria. But all of her talk about how they had to grow emotionally confused Shauna and most of the girls in the room. What in the world was Emiria talking about?

"I don't have anything else to say," Emiria snapped coldly after ordering them to report back to her room at 6:15 A.M. "Tomorrow we meet the other hard team in our bracket. We have to win the next two to advance."

The clock was running out on the season.

Thunder beat the Idaho State champions in its first game, but in game two Nevada was giving them trouble. The first half had been all Thunder, but Nevada, lacking Thunder's skill and fitness, worked the offsides trap like a machine. Time after time the Thunder girls threw down their arms in disgust as the linesman's flag rose with the regularity of a one-armed bandit. Mired in a scoreless tie, Thunder had to win to advance.

The warm rain was the first sign, and then the distant crash of thunder. The eerie desert storm invigorated the girls. Jenny could hear the talk, see the girls start to move, the passes string together. She'd started the second half, her bruised knee feeling better. Emiria was experimenting with a different lineup. Natalie was up at striker, and she'd been hounding the fullbacks all day, scraping for balls, taking hits, barely missing the net. Playing right midfield, Jenny watched a ball run out right by the coaches on the sideline. Two minutes were left in the game. She grabbed it quickly, and cool Luke looked into her eyes and calmly said, "Jenny, throw it to Kim."

Luke had a way of seeing things before they happened, of turning his vision into reality. Jenny arched her back and let the ball fly down the sideline. It was a long, perfect throw, right to Kim's foot. Two quick touches past the defender and the goalie could see it coming. Kim eating up the ground like a charging lion, every stride hinting of her strength. And then, just as the goalie dashed out to close the angle, the slight hestitation before she struck.

That night at the team meeting, the angry Emiria of a couple nights before was absent. She'd had to eat her words. "To come to these games and not play our style of soccer and still pull out the win shows a lot of character. I have to give credit where credit is due. I'm very proud of you. Whether or not we win tomorrow, we can go home saying we were in the quarterfinals. You're two games away from a championship, the biggest in the nation for your age group."

Emiria asked the girls to have fun the next day. She didn't expect them to win. She wanted them to laugh, to have fun, to rebound from mistakes. And she made a personal pledge to lighten up. "It's not in my nature, but it's something I have to learn. You're fourteen years old, you're not perfect, and you're going to make mistakes."

The odds were that this was the team's last meeting of the season. Thunder's chances of winning were slim. And so Emiria wanted them all to say good-bye—and hello. "I would like to go around the room and I'd like everybody to say one thing you like the most about Cath. Whether it be on the field or personally, and then tomorrow she's going to remember that comment. Maybe by someone she doesn't really know that well. 'Oh, wow, I didn't know she thought that about me.' And you're going to start gaining a little bit of confidence."

Catherine was first, but this was about the whole team, every girl finding something nice to say about every teammate. This definitely didn't happen on boys' teams. Luke, in all his years coaching men and women, had never seen such an outpouring of affection. There was laughter and tears, and if you were in the room, you couldn't miss the love.

"Nike Rush! Nike Rush! Nike Rush!" they chanted, trotting around the field in perfect military precision, shooting their arms and legs out like a drill team.

If Thunder was David, then its quarterfinal opponent in the Western Regional Championships was certainly Goliath. Wearing shining white jerseys with the Nike swoosh, the girls from Colorado chanted their sponsors' name for five minutes straight. To critics of elite youth soccer, this was the case study of parental excess. The Colorado Rush club was the result of the youth soccer equivalent of a corporate merger. The year before, on July 1, 1997, to be precise, two successful Denver area clubs had decided they needed to be a little more successful and merged, booting their old sponsor, Adidas, and signing on

with the ever-powerful Nike. The new club was so golden
with talent that it fielded two top teams, a Nike and, yes,
a Swoosh team. Thunder had beaten the Swoosh girls in
Phoenix, but those were the players not good enough for
the Nike squad. Nike Rush teams nearly always made it
to the Regional Championships and frequently won. Parents were said to move to the Denver suburbs just for the
chance to make the club. They understood the payoff. If
your daughter played for Nike, the odds were she'd pay
you back one day with a full ride to a Division I college.

Blessed by strikers who could have played on a wom-
en's college team, the Nike Rush bombarded the Thunder
goal with rocket shots. The Nike Rush were fit and blaz-
ingly fast, and the girls of Thunder appeared sluggish,
not having slept more than five hours or so after a long
night of team testimonials that ran till midnight and
began again shortly after dawn. But they could have slept
a week and they still would have been clobbered. At the
end, even the steady Cassie lost her cool and the goals
came in bunches. Disgusted, Emiria shouted angrily from
the sidelines, her promise to make it fun forgotten. When
the final whistle mercifully blew, Catherine, Jessica, and
a few others sobbed openly on their mothers' shoulders.
Against the Stars, at least they'd kept the score close. But
this was an old-fashioned blowout, a six-to-nothing mas-
sacre. And the coach who'd encouraged them twelve
hours before to make it fun, to just go out and enjoy the
game, was once again giving them the silent treatment.

Back at the motel, Thunder was rudderless. Eliminated
from the tournament, the girls had no idea what was next.
Would they fly home early? Stick around? No one was
even sure what they were doing for dinner. The moms
were fed up with Emiria's theatrics. If the girls could call
a meeting, so could they. Emiria and Luke arrived last,
standing by the door, just as Phil had months before when
he was blasted. When the harsh words flew, Luke cried,

speaking of the beautiful testimonials he'd heard that morning, one of his greatest moments as a coach. With tears in her eyes, Michelle rose to Emiria's defense, and Jessica's and Trinity's dads also struck a conciliatory tone. But a couple of moms who'd wiped away their daughters' tears gave Emiria a piece of their minds. Before the Stars game she'd ordered the girls not to talk to their parents about soccer, to ignore all their comments and loving words of encouragement, to listen only to their coach when it came to the game. Now she'd shunned them after their greatest defeat.

Didn't she realize they were only fourteen-year-old girls?

On another team the roller-coaster Albuquerque trip might have been the beginning of the end, the acrimonious parent meeting in the New Mexico motel room the first step in removing a strong-willed coach. But to a team that had survived the worst El Niño could throw at it, even the emotional crash of regionals wasn't much more than a speed bump in a long journey. The girls weren't happy with the silent treatment they'd received out in the desert, but several also made clear that they were equally uncomfortable with the criticisms that a few distraught parents had leveled at a coach they greatly admired.

The facts and the girls spoke for themselves. Fifteen of sixteen girls had found a way to survive and thrive under what the experts said no fourteen-year-old girl could withstand. Emiria had broken every cardinal rule of girls' athletics, yelling, swearing, tearing the girls down in practice and games. Popular thinking said that the girls should have been shattered by their coach and her unreasonable demands.

That summer I found out for myself where the girls stood, apart from their parents and the pressure of their teammates. I was lucky enough to meet with the girls of Thunder one by one, to hear what their season of soccer had meant to them in their young lives. As my tape recorder ran and my notebooks filled up, I realized that many of the girls wanted this chance to order their experience, to put the physical season in an emotional context. What had a year under the Bobby Knight of girls' soccer wrought? The girls I grew to respect were not timid or insecure, but strong and independent. They were not afraid to speak their minds about the strengths and failings of their inspirational coach. Virtually every girl longed for the encouragement and confidence Emiria gave so sparingly. They knew their coach was wrong to withhold that support, and they knew that until they found it, their talents would never fully blossom.

Emiria's genius or madness was that she never treated them as fourteen-year-old girls. They were athletes. Chugging up the weed-snarled hill at Sonoma State in the sweltering heat and skidding across the tennis courts in the freezing rain had taught the girls that nothing was impossible. Those were gifts they'd carry with them the rest of their lives. No coach had ever pushed them so hard, and though at times they'd hated Emiria, every last girl said she'd found something precious in that effort. This was confidence earned through their own will and the love of their teammates. That Emiria was a talented and flawed coach only added to their achievement. The girls knew that school, work, and life would present their share of Emirias, and along the way they'd learned a profound and simple lesson: You could hate your coach sometimes, know that she was wrong, and yet play through it. Every girl told me she wanted Emiria to cool it, to let the girls play, but for some reason the words of Arlene spoke even louder than those of Catherine, Theresa, Jessica, Heather, and other teammates. Arlene was one of Emiria's favorites from day one, and yet she, too, wanted her coach to recognize that she had to trust her players:

"She always says how she's frustrated. She goes, 'I'm losing my patience.' Well, I'm losing my patience with her.

"Basically, I feel that she has taught us everything that she can teach us, tactic-wise. When we're out there, she can't say, 'Just a little chip to Kim. Shoot and score.' We should know that by now—our set plays. And she taught us fitness, so now she's got to just sit back and hope it all clicks."

In Albuquerque Emiria had talked about how the team needed to grow emotionally, that there would be big changes. Though Emiria gave no further clue about what she'd been talking about, a funny thing happened. The girls did indeed grow emotionally. You could see it at the Santa Rosa Hall Memorial tournament in late August. Jessica and Heather, two girls Emiria had been shunting to the sidelines, rose up to dominate a game, between them accounting for four impressive goals. Then in the match Thunder had to tie to play for the championship, Shannon was all over the field, scoring a late goal that was pure heart, showing no signs of her fear. Like it or not, Shannon had finally learned to give the 110 percent Emiria had demanded all season long.

But it was Angela who may have had the most to prove. By the start of high school Angela needed a break from team Thunder. Her high school coach at Montgomery was a friendly man in his fifties who'd never played soccer. Angela played striker the first few games, impressing her coach with her speed and scoring. And then she fell into a nasty slump. Emiria would have benched her, but her high school coach had faith, telling Angela that she was going to lead the team.

Her ultimate test would be against Emiria. The Catholic girls' school, Ursuline, boasting several Thunder players, was now the toast of the city league. Kevin Brown, Santa Rosa United's director of coaching, was head coach, his assistant none other than Emiria Salzmann. Before the game, Angela tucked a note under the windshield of Emiria's car. Number 21, Angela Walsh, was going to score a goal and an assist.

When Joe Walsh heard about it, he thought that was a pretty cocky thing to do. But Angela didn't promise lightly. Twice she dashed downfield under long through balls and scored, beating Catherine's older sister—and the keeper. At halftime the score was tied at two all. Emiria was furious about Angela's goals, and she made it abundantly clear to the Ursuline girls that she expected them to "Stop that———number twenty-one!"

But Angela's breakaway season couldn't be halted. She won second-team all-league honors, leading Montgomery High in assists and tying for the most goals. Angela's teammates finally accepted her, and school was going fabulously. She rose before dawn to take Latin at 7:15 A.M., and was also studying honors English. And the fifteen-year-old had a boyfriend too, a guitar player who'd once played soccer.

High school soccer was the litmus test for the Emiria experiment. The tough coach who the textbooks said would destroy a girl's confidence appeared to have had the opposite effect. All sixteen of the original Thunder girls made their high school varsity teams, many of them also excelling in their studies.

Jessica and Naomi played together at Rincon Valley Christian High, the tiny school's first year of soccer for girls and boys after dropping its football program. Naomi captured first-team honors in the Coastal Mountain conference, racking up sixteen goals, and Jessica, who led the team in assists, was the league's only freshman to win second-team honors. Another Thunder freshman, Cassie, started in goal at Elsie Allen High School.

The girls blossomed, and Emiria proved she had the strength and humility to change with them. Earlier that summer when an overwrought Kim had been on the verge of quitting, it was Emiria who talked to her for hours, reminding her that the game wasn't worth playing if it wasn't fun. The heart-to-heart talk meant the world to Kim, who went on that fall to score twelve goals at Piner (Emiria's alma mater) and to win second-team all-league honors as a freshman. Emiria began to gradually heed the advice she'd given so often throughout the year, lightening up in practice, cooling her yelling. Earlier, many had thought Emiria picked on certain girls. "She doesn't do that anymore," said Heather. "I think she's learned to accept us. Learned to work with us."

By refusing to believe that they were second-class citizens, the substitutes taught the coach the importance of respecting every girl. Angela's stunning high school season earned her a starting role as striker on Thunder, one of several sideline girls challenging the established players. Jessica hadn't just impressed Emiria with her high school play. She and Theresa earned invitations to the spring tryouts for the state Olympic development team, placing them among the top seventy under-fifteen girls in Northern California. Then when Shannon missed a game, Jessica finally got her chance at defensive midfield. She impressed Emiria with her passing and fierce tackling, and just like that, the former sub was starting alongside Shannon.

Heather, too, was noticed. She played so strongly at tiny Rancho Cotati High School that Emiria recognized she might excel at a new position. She got her chance before a Thunder tournament in late fall. When Catherine missed a scrimmage, Emiria tried Heather as sweeper. You'd never guess that just months before, Heather had asked how to slide-tackle. She'd had to play virtually every position to find herself, but there was little doubt she'd found a home. Heather's deceptive speed and skills made her a marvelous starting sweeper. She switched the ball gracefully, commanding the team with her great vision and presence, her subtle feints making forwards look like they were running on banana peels. Thunder's former ninety-five-pound weakling had become a symbol of the value of hard work.

After spending nearly a year watching these sixteen girls mature into proud, strong young women, it was nearly impossible to point to a single game that marked a turning point. But for me the Thunder season ended in an early-season high school game. Maria Carillo High was a fitting place for girls to square off in battle. The gleaming new school, boasting a stadium that would be the envy of most junior colleges, had been named after a legendary pioneer woman. A century and a half ago, Maria Carillo had ruled over much of Santa Rosa. A widow who broke with convention, Maria Carillo escaped the kitchen and rode horseback over her vast hacienda, surveying her herds of thousands of horses, sheep, and cattle. Her daughters, not surprisingly, could ride bronco.

That afternoon as I readied to watch the latest daughters of Santa Rosa, I had a dilemma I hadn't faced in countless games. What side of the field to stand on? I opted for diplomacy, splitting my time between the two sets of Thunder parents. Standing on the Ursuline side, I shook hands with the proud Siglers, who incredibly had two girls starting. Freshman Catherine was a standout marking back and won her team's "rookie of the year" award; her older sister, Brittany, was the team's starting

sweeper. Shauna was the other starting Thunder freshman, and Thunder's newest and youngest player, Haley
Stein, stunned the league by scoring five goals in a single game.

But when Mary Piasta walked up and said hello, I
knew the full scope of the Thunder miracle. Mary had
driven down from the University of California at Davis
to witness the dream she'd helped make happen. Her little
sister Theresa, the girl who might have been a cheerleader
and teen model like Mary, had beaten the odds and won
a spot on Ursuline's varsity as just a freshman.

The Marillo Carillo Pumas may have lacked Ursuline's
enormous depth, but they had something else, the old
Central Magic. Arlene and Shannon dominated Maria
Carillo's midfield, their physical, intelligent play placing
them among the league's best. But on this day Arlene
would have to shore up the middle without her good
friend. Shannon was back east visiting the father she'd
never known, and freshman Trinity and sophomores Erin
and Jenny would have to fill the void left by her absence.
Starting freshman defender Natalie had the tough assignment of stopping Ursuline's speedy senior forwards.

By the second half, I'd said good-bye to Mary Piasta
and joined Carol and Natalie's dad, Jerry, in the Maria
Carillo stands. The ref blew his whistle after a hard foul on
a Maria Carillo girl. "That's another Thunder player!"
griped one bearded baseball-capped dad to another.
"They're all dirty."

I couldn't help but chuckle to myself. It wasn't just that
Theresa, the former crybaby, had hammered the Maria Carillo girl. This Maria Carillo dad seemed to be momentarily forgetting that six current and former Thunder girls
played for his daughter's team.

"Look at that hand on her, ref!" the man hollered, as
Catherine tightly marked her girl. "That's a foul!"

The 250 or so fans in the stands sounded and looked

a lot like a boys' football crowd. But the bright-eyed girls clustered before the bleachers shouted the new order. They wore sweats or team jerseys and shorts, passing balls back and forth on the track, watching their big sisters and idols play. Many of them weren't more than seven or eight years old.

The score was one to nothing Ursuline when I first noticed the horde of Maria Carillo football players stomping their way round the track. "Go, Pumas!" they shouted, waving their helmets like young warriors. "Go, ladies!"

I figured they'd pause briefly, then file right out of the stadium. But they walked right by the bleacher girls and sat down in the stands in orderly fashion, five rows deep. Fifty boys here to stay. First they did an impressive stand-up wave, then a boy ran up to orchestrate the cheers.

"Let's go, Pumas, let's go!"

Suddenly the boys began stamping the bleachers with their cleats, the deep metallic boom rumbling like thunder. The boys leaned forward, churning their legs, quickening the pace. The scene sent me back to that winter afternoon at Slater gym when I witnessed my first Thunder practice. But this was a hellish roar. Parents clapped their hands over their ears, the noise deafening, drowning out every Ursuline cheer.

Amazed, I stood by the girls on the track, wishing I weren't alone, wishing my four-year-old could stand with me and these eight-year-olds and see boys cheer for girls. They waved their helmets like macho pom-poms. Many of them looked heavy or clumsy, several scarred with acne. They wore oversized shorts of mixed colors, the only real sign that they were a team their helmets and cleats. I found myself wondering, Who are the real kids in America gaining brawn and confidence from sport? Could twenty-two of these boys beat the twenty-two girls on the field in a mile run?

The boys booed Ursuline's fouls and cheered lustily when they missed a shot. When Arlene sliced a gorgeous through ball to a teammate, the boys erupted, punching and kicking each other, breaking out into a controlled brawl. Everybody could see what was happening. The boys had thrown the momentum to Maria Carillo like a quarterback sack.

Arlene was dominating the midfield, controlling the flow of the game, stepping up the pace, even rushing to the sideline to make a quick throw-in. The shot was a high ball in the upper left corner, and the boys went nuts, leaping up and down, slapping each other high fives, yelling like madmen.

Maria Carillo had tied it up.

The game ended a couple of minutes later, the Maria Carillo girls jubilant at coming back against their archenemy. After nearly half an hour in the stands, the football players started filing out. But a lanky, blond, ponytailed senior on Maria Carillo named Beth turned and shouted, "Hey, it's not over!"

One girl soccer player asked fifty unruly boys to stick around for overtime, and one by one they dutifully filed back in the stands. As play began, the boys chanted Beth's name, cheering her dribbles and shots. Suddenly Catherine leaped for a dangerous cross and headed it long, a booming twenty-yard drive. A big, heavy-shouldered kid turned to another and scrunched up his face. "That's gotta hurt."

But the game lasted too long for the attention span of the average sixteen-year-old boy. To be fair, football practice had ended more than forty minutes ago. As the boys slowly filed out, they rattled their helmets fiercely. "Be tough, ladies! Be tough!"

Carol Tuttle wasn't the only mom on the Maria Carillo side who wished the boys would stay. The energy seemed to drain out of the Maria Carillo girls. After the last boy walked down the track, Ursuline scored.

A month later, the two teams faced off for the North Coast Sectional Championships, as far as girls' high school soccer goes in Northern California. Ten Thunder girls battled on the field that day, six of them freshmen. Once again Ursuline was victorious in a thrilling overtime game, and incredibly, Emiria Salzmann added a top high school championship to her State Cup title, all in her rookie year of coaching.

But winning isn't everything. Next fall Arlene and Shannon will be juniors at Maria Carillo, and the football team should have their cheers down pat. The competition between Thunder girls should make it even more exciting. At the Maria Carillo awards ceremony, talented freshman Trinity was introduced by her high school coach with the phrase, "Trinity Duncan, who's going to be our leading goal scorer next season."

Arlene Tuttle muttered under her breath at that heady prediction. She'd had a tremendous season at midfield, but decided that she'd never stand out playing next to Shannon, a second-team all-league selection. Arlene's coach preferred speed up front, but the redhead wasn't about to listen. Slow or not, Arlene was set on playing forward, and she, not Trinity, would be Maria Carillo's leading scorer. It should be quite a battle. Last November at the acclaimed San Diego Surf tournament against some of the best teams in the nation, Arlene scored three goals for Thunder, among them a diving header and an improbable backward heel shot.

Coach may just have to eat her words.

ACKNOWLEDGMENTS
_____

*i*n early 1997 I began thinking more about soccer, the game I played in college and continue to love. As the father of two young girls, I thought it would be intriguing to find an interesting team and chronicle a season of trials and tribulations. My problem was obvious. How could I find the right team?

By chance through the years I'd stayed in touch with an old high school teammate. Steven Scholl, a left winger with a mean cross, had gone on to coach youth soccer and our old high school team. Steven suggested I take a look at a new under-fourteen girls squad in Santa Rosa with its first woman coach. Team Thunder had yet to prove itself, but Emiria Salzmann was unique. More disciplined than any coach that I played under, Salzmann both intimidated and inspired. At the first practice I watched, I told my wife that this was better training than I'd ever had in college.

Now that the eventful season has come and gone, I realize just how fortunate I was to find such a sincere and talented group of individuals. I'd like to offer my heartfelt thanks to the girls, their parents, Emiria and assistant coaches Brian Halloran and Luke Oberkirch. Everyone understood that the season was about something larger than sport.

I was also aided by some seasoned professionals who believed in this story. My agent, Kris Dahl of ICM, helped shape my initial idea and secure a supportive publisher; Trish Grader of Avon Books provided cool and skilled editing; Susan Davis and Michele Glode Jin brought their journalistic and research skills to the project; Steven Scholl helped review the manuscript; and the "Flying Fingers" Nancy Giusti and Susan Dupuis meticulously typed up the countless hours of interviews. David Diamond, my talented office mate, was always there with a word of encouragement.

Confidence is the buzzword today for adolescent girls, and writing this book reminded me how we all—boys too—need support and confidence. I remembered Jack Hyde, a gifted coach at Cal Berkeley who gave me my first chance to start in a college game and stuck with me even after I whiffed at the first ball that happened my way.

Through the typical whirlwind of researching and writing a book, my wife, Sherry, has been an inspiration. When my publisher sent out the emergency call for a photo for the book's cover, I asked Sherry if she'd be willing to help. An architect by training, she hauled out her old manual Nikormat and we drove up together to Santa Rosa. I asked Emiria to have the girls dash by Sherry one by one, make a move, take a shot, whatever she thought might show their soccer skills.

But the second shooter (readers can guess who that might be) fired a blast that struck the camera dead on.

Fortunately, Sherry wasn't hurt, and the camera seemed to work, though the shock jammed a roll of film. The next challenge was one every mother can understand. Our two young girls wanted to be with mom. As the players sped toward Sherry, cranking shots, our three-and-a-half-year-old and baby draped around mom. Gripping the camera in one hand, Sherry clicked away, and snapped the photo that ultimately came to grace the cover of this book. Not even the girls noticed that she was performing this task while breast feeding our baby.

Finally, I'd like to thank team Thunder for an incredible, courageous season that promises to never end. After the fall of 1998, I had to write full time and sorely missed following the team's weekly exploits. But Thunder, of course, kept surprising the competition.

In February 1999, Thunder entered the President's Day Tournament in Phoenix just as it had the year before. The competition in the highly regarded national tournament promised to be fierce. Among the 340 teams entered were squads from twenty-eight states: Fifty-eight state champions, eight regional champions, three national finalists, sixteen Olympic development teams, as well as teams from three foreign countries.

Thunder's tournament opener began on an ominous note. The girls were down 2–0 at half-time, and Emiria's new defensive focus seemed to be backfiring. But Kim and team newcomer, Haley Stein popped in three goals between them to grab the victory. The second game was against a top Illinois team that boasted a national team youth player. It was the most physical game the girls had ever endured. Shannon picked up a red card and Angela's mark got booted, but Thunder won convincingly 3–0 on two goals by Haley and one by Natalie. The male coach of the Illinois squad, who reportedly had a daughter on the field, told Emiria "the only reason you won was your girls were dirty." Thunder's coach wasn't about to let that charge stand. "You're just pissed because we kicked your ass."

The semifinal against the state champion Arizona Golden Eagles was a near repeat of Thunder's Sebastopol quarterfinal match. Shannon scored on a corner to tie it up, sending the match to penalty kicks. Win or lose, Emiria wanted the girls to support one another. After each Thunder player took a shot, the whole team rushed down en masse to cheer the goal or ease the pain. Shannon, Haley and Cath made it, and Kim missed. Cassie, who excelled throughout the tournament, made an unbelievable save, and then one of the Arizona girls shot wide. If co-captain, Natalie, Thunder's fifth kicker, hit net, they'd be in the final. Just before she shot, Natalie turned and winked at her teammates. The goalie didn't have a chance.

The final was against another Illinois team, the Windy City Pride, last year's midwest regional champion. Six Thunder girls were battling the flu. But Kim knocked in a free kick in the 15th minute, and the defense went to work. Catherine, Heather, Trinity and Natalie were tenacious. Cassie punched what seemed a sure goal over the bar. With ten minutes left in the tightly fought battle, Emiria did something she'd seldom done before. Five starters came off—Arlene, Kim, Haley, Natalie and Jessica.

Emiria put the championship in the hands of five substitutes. Jenny and Kristin excelled, and the sixteen girls of team Thunder once again rose to the challenge.

Mill Valley, February 24, 1999
Jonathan Littman
jlittman@well.com